THE SLENDER TREE

Alice Meynell, drawing by J. S. Sargent

THE SLENDER TREE
A Life of Alice Meynell

June Badeni

'The thrust of life in her was like that of a
slender tree with flowers and fruit for all
seasons.'

G. K. Chesterton: *Autobiography*

TABB HOUSE
Padstow, Cornwall
1981

First published 1981
by Tabb House, 11 Church Street, Padstow, Cornwall

Copyright © June Badeni 1981

ISBN 0 907018 01 7

Printed in Great Britain
by T. J. Press (Padstow) Ltd.,
Padstow, Cornwall.
Binding by R. Hartnoll,
Bodmin, Cornwall.

TO MARY AND MICHAEL
This book is dedicated

ACKNOWLEDGEMENTS

I WISH to express my gratitude to those members of the Meynell family who have helped me in various ways with this book.

I first started on the project of writing a life of Alice Meynell in 1952, and at that time the late Mrs Dallyn (Viola Meynell) and the late Mrs Sowerby lent me material from the Greatham papers, and allowed me to spend some time working in the library there. The late Sir Francis Meynell also lent me some material. In consultation with these two sisters and their brother I came to realise that the time had not yet come for a book to supplement Viola Meynell's personal memoir of her mother, and I put the work aside. Rather more than twenty years later, at the suggestion of one of Mrs Meynell's grand-daughters, I dug out my notebooks and typescript, and began again.

On the death of Viola Meynell the curatorship of the papers had passed to Mrs Sowerby, and she, in turn, left it to her great-niece, Gabriel Bergonzi. In her I have had a most valuable ally. She has not only allowed me to range freely through the material at Greatham, but has also taken a lot of trouble to seek out possible sources of letters, etc. that might be of value. My very special thanks are due to her.

Mrs Hardie and Mrs Wall, daughters of Madeline Lucas, both made available to me the letters in their possession, as did Dr Mary Fisher, daughter of Monica Saleeby. Mrs Hawkins, who now lives at Humphrey's Homestead, has suffered invasions of the library with the utmost good humour, and has also told me of her childhood memories of Alice Meynell.

My thanks are also due to Mr Jacob Dallyn for permission to quote from Viola Meynell's *Alice Meynell: A Memoir*, to which, obviously, I am greatly indebted. Eileen, Lady Gormanston kindly allowed me to quote from the autobiography of her mother, Lady Butler; and Mrs Anne Kimball Tuell gave me permission to use a passage from a letter written to her by Mrs Meynell and now in Boston College Library. Mr McKitterick, of Cambridge University Library, had photostats made for me, and allowed me to quote from letters of Alice Meynell in the Library's possession. The University of Leeds, the Library of Congress and Boston College Library, have allowed me to quote from material in their possession; while the George Meredith estate, the Humanities Research Center of the University of Texas, at Austin, Texas and the Oxford University Press gave permission for me to quote from *The Letters of George Meredith* edited by C. L. Cline (three volumes, 1970).

I wish also to thank the late Raymond Mortimer and Times Newspapers Ltd., for allowing me to quote from a review by Raymond Mortimer in the *Sunday Times*, and the late Walter de la Mare and the Editor of *The Times Literary Supplement* for a quotation from a review printed in 1913. Father Arthur Kavanagh, S.J., gave me valuable information concerning Father Dignam, and Father Francis Edwards, S.J., has also helped me in this respect. Mr John Walsh has published Francis Thompson's letters in America; I am indebted to him for the text of certain quotations and also in many instances for the dating of these letters (which must often involve detective work). Mrs F. N. Chamberlain and Miss Evelyn Thompson have both helped me at various times with the work of note-taking and transcribing. Father Brocard Sewell, of the Carmelite Order, has given me helpful advice and background information for which I am most grateful.

I would like to thank the Earl of Lytton for permission to reproduce the pastel portrait by his father, Neville Lytton, of Francis Thompson; the National Portrait Gallery for permission to reproduce Sargent's drawing of Alice Meynell; and members of the Meynell family for all the other illustrations.

Finally, I must thank the Information Service of the British Library and Mr Kirkman, Librarian of the Malmesbury branch of the Wiltshire County Library, for help in seeking out information.

June Badeni
1980

CONTENTS

LIST OF PLATES

Frontispiece. Alice Meynell, drawing by J. S. Sargent. By kind permission of the National Portrait Gallery.

INTRODUCTION

WHILE I have been at work on this book I have been asked, not once but several times, of my subject: Did she have an interesting life? The answer, I think, to that question is that the interest of any human life lies not so much in the external pattern of events that gathers about it on its course from cradle to grave as in the qualities of heart and mind, the beliefs, the emotions, the loyalties, the doubts and fears and loves with which a man or woman confronts that pattern and, to some extent, shapes it. Ever since I have known and loved Mrs Meynell's work I have been intensely interested in her as a person, and the closer knowledge of her that I have gained in writing her biography has further intensified that feeling. I find her a fascinating character.

Raymond Mortimer once called her 'absolutely civilised, a character shaped by self-discipline into a work of art'.[1] Herein lies no small part of the fascination. In her work one perceives how closely packed is the thought, how she abjured diffuseness, how she rejected and abstained from the trite, the obvious, that which would merely labour her point or fatten her lean and graceful paragraphs; how she whittled and pared away the volume of thought so that only the core, the essential and unsuperfluous heart of the matter, reached the page. Every verse, every paragraph, every line, was subjected to a stern discipline. 'She never wrote a line, or even a word', Chesterton said, 'that does not stand like the rib of a strong intellectual structure; a thing with the bones of thought in it.'[2]

Few writers have worked to such a consistently high level; even in her journalism, articles written under great pressure of time and the tiresome necessity of producing a certain number of words before tomorrow, there is hardly anything which, after the passage of years, one could wish had not been written or had been written otherwise. The slovenly, the commonplace, the careless phrase, are not among her writings, and behind everything that she wrote is her profound and lucid thought.

As in her work, so in her life. There, too, was abstention, rejection, discipline; abstention from that which was unworthy, rejection of that which was cheap, discipline of the wild emotions, the wayward passions, the hasty, the uncontrolled. She saw, when she was scarcely grown up, the shape that she wished her spiritual life to take, and she perceived that without the bonds of a moral law she could never attain it, never be wholly free of the domination of heart and passions. 'Those who have nothing to control', she once wrote, 'are they who call for liberty.' She discerned a truer freedom, that of the stars that keep their appointed courses, the ship that rides at anchor, 'the rooted liberty of flowers in breeze'. So she committed herself to the following of a rule of life, and set her will to serve, before all else, that end.

Had it been easy, had it been natural, spontaneous, Mrs Meynell's life would have been less remarkable and less deserving of our admiration. She was not a mystic, led onward by an incommunicable ecstasy, but a woman of the world, surrounded by admiration, subject to the world's griefs and temptations, holding to the course that she had set herself, often, only by the strength of her will.

Sylvia Lynd, writing of her after her death, touched the core of the matter. 'Though she was a believer in the discipline of religion, though she denied her poetry every redundancy of thought or word, this was not due to any natural asceticism of soul. Her beliefs were perpetually at war with her natural ardours. "Liberty, liberty from this weight of will" she cries in her poem "To Sleep". . . . The weight of will and the wild heart ever in opposition – out of such conflict did her poems spring. Discipline imposed upon the weak produces no notable thing. These poems flashed from the meeting of iron and rock. Whatever gentleness and meekness she showed to the world, to herself Alice Meynell was ruthless and unflinching.'[3]

That she suffered deep spiritual sorrows we learn by implication, by a chance word here and there. She wrote once of 'the reluctance – the question – wherewith you perceive the interior grief of poetry or of a devout life'.[4] And the nun who was the friend of her last years spoke of her passing through 'the dark night of the soul'.[5] Those who met her – even casual acquaintances, and even those who had, themselves, little interest in religion – received an impression that here was a woman of great holiness. Her conscience was too tender for peace, her sensitivity too great, her remorse frequent and grievous. But her dedicated purpose remained to the end, and her life can only be understood if it be perceived that this was its foundation and this its triumph.

Let the reader not look, however, in these pages for a life given over to sadness, for hushed voices, languours and timidities. Humour was never very far from Mrs Meynell and she lived among the laughter of a large and happy family; she was witty, she could on occasions be caustic, she retained until her death a young girl's zest for living. She looked slender and frail, yet had an extraordinary physical toughness; she loved danger, she was beautiful and intensely feminine and had a mind of remarkable brilliance. She had her little vanities, but she was not conceited; she had her pride and, with it, a great humility; she cared passionately for her art, and served it faithfully all her life.

She engendered in people of widely different taste, age, class, character, a great devotion which, though *she* might pass out of their lives, remained with them. To her friends she was intensely loyal, unselfish, always ready, despite her busy life and her constant journalistic work, to find time to listen. Yet for all those who loved her, except perhaps her husband, there was an awareness that her inmost heart was never shown to them. She could always share their griefs, their problems, but she could not, or would not, share her own. It was the reason why Katherine Tynan, one of her closest friends, could write: 'But you are somehow far away and seem as if you can do without people even if you can't';[6] the reason why George Meredith called an iris after her, Alicia Coerulia, saying that after the outer petals opened the inmost ones remained closed. Even a beloved daughter, to whom she gave maternal love in fullest measure, with whom she shared all the warmth and gaiety and happiness of their family life, said that the sorrows of her mother's life could not be interfered with by those who loved her. 'She was so private, so unapproachable, so convinced.'[7]

It is now more than fifty years since Alice Meynell died. The mortal is gone, and we can learn only at second hand of her beauty, her melodious voice, her grace in movement, the charm that made so many people love her. The immortal, however, lives on, not only in the immortality of the spirit, but also in that won for her by her writing. There we can still meet this rare mind at first hand.

CHAPTER 1

ALICE MEYNELL was born on 11th October, 1847, the younger daughter of Thomas and Christiana Thompson. To see something of the heredity which helped to shape her character it is necessary to go back to about the middle of the eighteenth century, when Dr Thomas Pepper Thompson of Liverpool emigrated to Jamaica, and there acquired sugar plantations. He had a son, of whose mother nothing is known except that she was not Dr Thompson's wife. This son, James, never married, but took as his mistress a Creole girl, Mary Edwards, by whom he had a son and two daughters.[1] All that is known of the background of Mary Edwards is that she was related to Bryan Edwards who became Chief Justice of Jamaica in 1855, and who suspended the Governor, John Eyre, while a Royal Commission sent from England inquired into the extreme severity with which he had put down the native rising of 1865.[2] She must, therefore, have had English blood; but the tradition in the Meynell family is that she was coloured. The term Creole may mean a person of white descent born in Jamaica, or a person of mixed blood. The urgent need for labour in the sugar plantations had led to constant importations, first of Negro slaves, and later, after the abolition of slavery, of Indians and Chinese. There were Europeans brought in too, to work on the plantations: Scots, Irish, and Germans. Many of the plantation owners, who mostly became very rich, spent only a limited time on their Jamaican properties, residing, otherwise, in their English homes. This may have been the case with Dr Thompson, as he owned seaside property in Lancashire, and land in Liverpool and Wharf.

Many of the white planters took coloured women as their mistresses; probably Mary Edwards was the child of such a union, and could be termed either Creole or mulatto.

James Thompson died in Jamaica before his father, and the doctor accepted his son's illegitimate family, and brought Mary and her three children to live in England. When he died, in 1820, he named his grandson (called Thomas like himself, and still a child) as 'the son of Mary Edwards of Rio Bueno in the parish of Trelawny and Island of Jamaica, and the reputed son of James Thompson, some time since of Liverpool but lately of Maria Bueno Estate.'[3]

Thomas Thompson was educated privately and at Trinity College, Cambridge, and, after unsuccessfully contesting Parliamentary elections at Portsmouth and Lowestoft as a Liberal, had given up the idea of pursuing any career, from which necessity he was freed by the inheritance from his grandfather. He married, had a son and a daughter, and was already a widower when, in 1844, he went with his friend Charles Dickens to the opening of a new Mechanics' Institute in Liverpool. Dickens was the speaker on this occasion, and a piano recital was given by Christiana, the twenty-year-old daughter of Mr and Mrs Thomas Weller. Dickens was amused by the coincidence of the name of Weller, and was much charmed by Christiana. Although a married man, and not free to pay her court, he allowed himself to seek the pleasure of her company by calling on the Wellers next day, and taking Thomas Thompson with him. He followed up his call with a piece of doggerel for Miss Weller's album, and a present of two volumes of Tennyson which he sent from London accompanied by a letter to her father. 'Will you tell her', he wrote, 'that I have marked with a pencil, in the index to each, those pieces which I would like her to read first – as being calculated to give her a good impression of the Poet's genius? And will you say that I have sent her a copy which is not quite new, in preference to a new one, hoping that she might like it none the worse for having been my companion often, and for having been given to me by Tennyson himself?'[4]

It had not occurred to Dickens that Miss Weller's charm, which had made so great an impact on him, might have made an even greater impression on Thompson. The latter, having remained in Liverpool when Dickens returned to London, was in a position to continue and to improve the acquaintance; and shortly afterwards he wrote to tell Dickens that he loved Miss Weller and desired to marry her.

Thompson's advances were not, at first, looked upon favourably by Christiana's parents. Her musical talent had led them to hope that she might have a great career as a professional pianist, and this hope would be dashed by an early marriage. Perhaps, also, the fifteen years' difference in age, his illegitimacy, and the fact that Thompson was a widower with children, influenced them to some extent against him; but the attachment between the two young people grew rapidly.

Dickens, from afar, encouraged his friend. 'I would not hesitate', he wrote, 'or do slight to the resolution of my own heart which hesitation would imply, but would win her if I could, by God.'[5]

For a time all hung in the balance. Thompson wrote despondently about the parental opposition, to which Dickens replied: 'At the father I snap my fingers. I would leap over the head of the tallest father in Europe if his daughter's heart lay on the other side and were worth having.'[6]

The father, by no means the tallest in Europe, but still a formidable opponent, was described as 'a man of taste and refinement, passionately fond of music, an amateur architect and devoted to arts and letters'.[7] Mrs Weller had, before her marriage, studied the piano under Pio

Cianchettini,[8] and, of her five daughters, it was Christiana to whom she looked, perhaps, for the vicarious fulfilment of her own musical ambitions.

Thompson wrote to 'My darling Christie' about the 'cruel treatment' that he was receiving from Mr Weller. But he continued: 'That we shall come together eventually if it please God to spare the lives of us both I have no doubt. I am very patient and determined and I have no fear whatever of your truth and constancy.'[9] His faith was not misplaced; opposition was finally overcome, and the wedding fixed.

Shortly before the wedding, and after, it would seem, some small difference between them, Thomas wrote to Christiana:

My own darling love,
    That ever we should be otherwise than 'd'accord' on all points and at all times seems the strangest thing in the world when I am absent from you. But between two such sensitive beings as we are there must necessarily be now and then some little – what shall I call it? pique – pet, cloud – slight evanescent disturbance of harmony – but I am sure nothing that a little frankness, mutual forbearance, exercise of patience and good sense, will not dissipate and scatter to the winds almost as soon as formed. Let me impress upon you, my own dearest love, the necessity of being altogether open and unreserved with me. You who are generally so 'impulsive' ought to be particularly so towards me. Out with all your feelings – make, as the saying is, 'a clean breast of it'. Never talk *at* me, never use a tone of smothered bitterness. If ever I do anything you don't like, remark upon it in the instant. Trust me, if you persuade me you are right, I shall never prove obstinate or unreasonable – and it will always be a source of pride to find in you the right, even in opposition to myself.[10]

The Wellers moved from Liverpool to London during the period of the engagement, and so it was in the Parish Church at Barnes that Christiana and Thomas Thompson were married on 21st October, 1845. Charles Dickens was a witness, and afterwards made a speech at the wedding luncheon.

The couple began at once upon the European travels that were to form the restless, shifting, kaleidoscopic background to their married life. Their first child was born in 1846 at the Villa Claremont, outside Lausanne, and was called Elizabeth, though she was ever afterwards known as Mimi. In the following year they returned to England, and a second daughter, Alice, was born at Barnes.

Almost all the pictures that are left to us of the early childhood of these two little girls come from the diaries of Mrs Thompson, and in these are captured the mood as well as the facts of those years. The entries, made in a thin, sprawling handwriting, are breathless and staccato; all is hurry, movement, ecstasy, despair, crisis, and constant change. Suitcases are lost, things forgotten, lodgings sought for and as quickly abandoned; journeys are made by boat, by train, by diligence, sleepless nights are endured, fleas are encountered. Mrs Thompson dashes helter-skelter through these chaotic days, skirts and ribbons fluttering, describing everything in a torrent of superlatives, rhapsodising over the 'sweet babes', whipping out her brushes and canvas to make what she calls 'an art'. Had it not been for Amélie, the Swiss nurse, who was a devoted member of the family for many years, one suspects that the 'sweet babes' would have been left unwashed and unfed while their gay, tender and unpractical young mother painted landscapes, read Wordsworth, played the piano, and depicted her days upon the pages of her diary in great splashes of verbal colour.

In May 1848 they were at Barnes, and she noted on the 5th: 'Meant to have babes christened. Went to Barnes Church. Babes came too late and no sponsors.' So they all went home again; but five days later the diary triumphantly records: 'Babes really christened at Barnes Church.'[11] Religion, or, at any rate, the practice of it, does not seem to have played much part in the lives of the Thompsons at that stage; and this inference is borne out by the fact that they waited a year and a half to have their elder child christened.

From Barnes they moved to a house at Prestbury, near Cheltenham, where, in October 1848, Alice, aged one year, was talking both French and English, and understood, according to Mrs Thompson, which language to use when talking to the servants, and which with her parents. A dancing bear had visited the village, and the 'babes were delighted and talked all day about "l'ourse".' Alice's intelligence, her mother noted, 'is perfect. I only fear it is too advanced.'

A year later, on her second birthday, Alice's treat was a magic lantern exhibition, and we learn from the diary that the two little girls, in high excitement, were talking all day about 'la lanterne magique dans la chambre noire'.

The children's first journey to Italy was made in 1851, when Alice was four. They set out early in November from Folkestone, and after reaching Lyons travelled by boat down the Rhône as far as Avignon. There they stayed at the Hôtel du Palais National, where there was sumptuous food, flowered wallpaper, and a smoking chimney, and Mrs Thompson 'got much excited about Petrarch and Laura and could not go to sleep for a long time'.

Their destination on that occasion was Nervi, close to Genoa, and from there they moved on to Ruta, Porto Fino. In all their wanderings it was to this Ligurian coast that they returned most constantly; and this more than any other scene of that rootless childhood was home for Mimi and Alice. They frequently changed houses and moved from one village to another – Albaro, Nervi, Sori, Porto Fino – but the mountains that face the Mediterranean, the vineyards and olive groves, 'the villages and the ringing belfry', were a constant background. Mr

Thompson had probably lived either at Genoa or somewhere along this coast with his first wife, and Fanny, his daughter of that marriage, was one cause of their returning year after year to that part of Italy; for she had married at seventeen and settled in Genoa. Her husband was an Italian officer, Carlo Brocchi, who later joined Garibaldi and was killed at the battle of the Volturno. Neither Fanny nor her brother, Tom, seem ever to have lived with their father after his second marriage, although their relations with their step-mother were friendly and their two little half-sisters were devoted to them. Fanny's own marriage must have taken place not many years after her father's, and Tom, who died early and unmarried, suffered always from bad health which probably made it impossible for him to share the wandering life of the Thompsons.

CHAPTER 2

IN THE SUMMER of 1852 the Thompsons moved to the Villa dei Franchi at Sori, a house to which they returned many times in after years. It was a long, low house of rose-coloured plaster and white stucco, 'almost dwarfish on the front where the *piano nobile* is also the ground floor, but a storey higher and of stately proportions towards the sea'.[1] The garden 'passes down stair by stair and fountain by fountain to the Mediterranean rocks'.[2] Their arrival is described by Mrs Thompson: 'On entering we all wildly rushed up and down the balcony until Agostino pulled me up by mundane grievances – imperfect state of the kitchen – nothing to eat etc.'[3]

The children started lessons with their father that summer. He undertook their education himself, and by this, as well as by heredity, shaped the minds and characters of his daughters – but especially the younger one – to his mould. His influence was so great, his teaching so indelible in its imprint on the young characters, that one would gladly know him better and find, in that knowledge, a key to many doors in the mind of his daughter. But her quality of reticence, her silence, her restraint, she had from him, so that he is kept from us by a double silence – his own and hers. From the scanty material that exists Mr Thompson comes to life as a shadowy figure, not very clearly seen. He had a fine, scholarly brain, with a scholar's dislike of what is slovenly, inaccurate, or superficial; he loved his children, but was stern, expected much of them, and the word of praise came rarely. He never learned to be practical over money matters, and was apparently quite content with a bohemian and often uncomfortable way of living. For one as precise and fastidious as he in all things intellectual, Mrs Thompson's inconsequential thoughts and wild expressions of them must have been often exasperating; we find him, sometimes, patiently correcting her, as in a postscript to a letter which reads: 'Ed*if*ying not ed*yf*ying'.[4]

Alice Meynell's essay 'A Remembrance',[5] published after his death, is the source from which we can learn most about him and his influence on her. It is still not enough. There she speaks of him as:

a man whose silence seems better worth interpreting than the speech of many another . . . The delicate, the abstinent, the reticent graces were his in the heroic degree. Where shall I find a pen fastidious enough to define and limit and enforce so many significant negatives? Words seem to offend by too much assertion, and to check the suggestions of his reserve. That reserve was life-long. Loving literature, he never lifted a pen except to write a letter. He was not inarticulate, he was only silent. He had an exquisite style from which to refrain. The things he abstained from were all exquisite . . . Things ignoble never approached near enough for his refusal; they had not with him so much as that negative connection . . .

It was by holding session among so many implicit safeguards that he taught, rather than by precepts. Few were these in his speech, but his personality made laws for me. It was a subtle education, for it persuaded insensibly to a conception of my own. How, if he could not define, could I know what things were and what were not worthy of his gentle and implacable judgement? I must needs judge them for myself, yet he constrained me in the judging. Within that constraint and under that stimulus, which seemed to touch the ultimate springs of thought before they sprang, I began to discern all things in literature and in life – in the chastity of letters and in the honour of life – that I was bound to love . . .

Men said that he led a *dilettante* life. They reproached him with the selflessness that made him somewhat languid. Others, they seemed to aver, were amateurs at this art or that; he was an amateur at living. So it was, in the sense that he never grasped at happiness, and that many of the things he had held slipped from his disinterested hands. So it was, too, in this unintended sense; he loved life. How should he not have loved a life that his living made honourable? How should he not have loved all arts, in which his choice was delicate, liberal, instructed, studious, docile, austere? . . . He had always prayed temperate prayers and harboured probable wishes. His sensibility was extreme, but his thought was generalized. When he had joy he tempered it not in the common way by meditation upon the general sorrow but by a recollection of the general pleasure. It was his finest distinction to desire no differences, no remembrance, but loss among the innumerable forgotten. And when he suffered, it was with so quick a nerve and yet so wide an apprehension that the race seemed to suffer in him. He pitied not himself so tenderly as mankind, of whose capacity for pain he was then feelingly persuaded. His darkening eyes said in the extreme hour: 'I have compassion on the multitude.'

With this teacher, then, the little girls began their lessons. They worked every morning with no regular holidays but only a day off now and then for some special expedition or because they were travelling; in the afternoons they had things to learn by heart for the next day's lesson – bits of history, poetry, the Sunday collect, and dialogues in French or Italian. Sometimes their lessons were on the terrace whence they could look across the vineyards to the blue, blue sea; sometimes in the house, as on a September morning when Mrs Thompson noted in her diary: 'Dear little angels do their writing . . . at the window in the billiard room at the little green table. Little Widgers [Mimi] delights in it – she loves to learn. Badger [Alice] is more wild.'

A painful memory of this time was recorded in an essay of Alice Meynell's, 'The Child of Tumult'; but the passage was subsequently deleted, seeming to her, we may suppose, a disloyalty to the beloved father.

Tragic emotions, unforgotten and unquelled, are associated for half a lifetime with the syllable *ex*, for one who remembers a day of abandonment to all the Tempests on account of it. The lesson was elementary and the child some five years old. Having been taught that *e* and *t* spelled *et*, she was required to solve the problem of *e* and *x*. To the teacher it seemed that the second reply might well follow on the first. But to the child the fact that *x* alone was pronounced *ex* seemed a complete reason why *e* and *x* should combine to make something more. If it had been possible to explain the difficulty, there would have been no storm, but there were no words in which to convey it. Everything dreadful that could happen to a child's desperate heart seemed to befall it in the long half day during which, for obstinacy in refusing to spell *ex* the child was shut up, brought out, exhorted and regretfully imprisoned again, clinging to the knees of her chastisers.[6]

The father, in his anxiety to make scholars of the children, was inclined to forget how young they were, and to lose patience with their childishness. To the little Alice who, in her early reading of Shakespeare, pronounced 'my lord' just as it is written, he cried with a shudder: 'Never let me hear that rank vulgarism again!'[7]

But if there were sometimes hard and painful moments to be endured in the course of the morning lessons, there was much of gaiety and delight in the rest of the day. Mrs Thompson's diary gives a glimpse of her husband unbending to entertain the children at a party that they had in the winter: 'Great amusements in the eve – first magic lantern, then charades; principally acted by Tom and Mrs Palmer who were both admirable. Then magic music and dances for the children. Sweet angels looked exquisite in little muslin frocks with ribbon run in and top-knots.'

Dickens, who went to stay with them at about that time, commented upon the top-knots and various other things in a letter to his wife. He described Villa dei Franchi as a ruinous palace in a beautiful situation. 'Coming upon them unawares,' he says, 'I found T [hompson] with a pointed beard, smoking a great German pipe, in a pair of slippers; the two little girls very pale and faint from the climate, in a singularly untidy state – one (Heaven knows why!) without stockings, and both with their little short hair cropped in a manner never before beheld, and a little bright bow stuck on the top of it. C [hristiana] said she had invented this headgear as a picturesque thing, adding that perhaps it was – and perhaps it was not. She looked very well, and seems to be greatly liked here. We had disturbed her at her painting in oils, and I have rather received an impression that, what with that and what with music, the household affairs went a little to the wall. T. was teaching the two little girls the multiplication table in a disorderly old billiard room, with all manner of maps in it.'[8]

There were expeditions and picnics, people came and went, there were parties, music, reading aloud, and much talk; in all of which the children shared to a much greater extent than would have been permitted to the children of a conventional English nursery. There are little fleeting pictures; one of Mrs Thompson, on a night when the full moon floated above the shimmering sea, having the piano brought out onto the terrace and there playing Beethoven's Moonlight Sonata while the little girls listened, enraptured;[9] another, of Alice, aged five and three quarters, being taught to swim, and making very earnest and energetic efforts to learn.[10]

Mrs Thompson made a hurried trip to England to see her family in the summer of 1853, and some of the letters that the children wrote during her absence have survived. 'My dear rose of a Mama,' Alice wrote, in a huge hand remarkably well formed for a child not yet six: 'I hope you are quite well. I send you some orange flower and one of the oleander trees has a flower . . .' Her father added a note at the end of her letter. '. . . It was very tantalizing of you to speak in the way you have about your new bonnet without telling me a word either about the colour or the form. I hope it won't produce too great an effect upon the swains of Woodhatch.'[11]

The servants who formed the household during this and many later Italian sojourns were all good friends of the children, and Alice Meynell wrote of them in later years. Agostino, the cook, was the most permanent of them, for he returned every time the Thompsons came to Italy, knowing, by some means that was never discovered, exactly when they would arrive. 'His light figure with the dancer's step was always the first thing to meet them, whether on the platform of the station or among the brown porters and the screaming apple-women, the mules and whips and chaos of the port. He was there, and he was kissing the hands of the *padrone* and the *padrona*, and had their dressing cases in his hands before they had at all decided that they wanted him yet once more to be their cook. . . . He became their cook every time.'[12]

Agostino did the shopping, bringing back the provisions from Genoa 'in bags and baskets under the wings of his cloak', and Amélie, the childrens' nurse, was accustomed to say that if he had no wages he would still make a fortune out of the Thompsons by his perquisites. These two used to have tremendous rows, chiefly upon religious matters, as Agostino was a Catholic and Amélie a Swiss Protestant; they sometimes took the dispute to Mr Thompson, but he always refused to give judgement, and merely told them to be quiet. Sometimes the rows were on a larger scale, and 'every member of the little group of servants contended in the loudest Genoese against each one of the others . . . For a wild hour all was forgotten except the angers of the moment. If a door was opened on the scene of conflict the outcries of the women and the yells of the men filled the house with uproar. It was all pure anger; no fire of alcohol had anything to do with it. Except only the usual manner of swearing, which is not kind, because of the theological allusion, but has no brutal sound, there was nothing worthy of the name of bad language. The great quadrilateral quarrel consisted of the reproaches of outraged personal dignity and affection. As to the cause, it might be connected with the feather brush or the duster.'[13]

The maids were less permanent, for, although no one of them ever left the household for any reason except the end of the Thompsons' stay in Italy, they did not return each time with the unfailing regularity of Agostino. The two little girls, who talked 'the strongest Genoese even to each other in their games', were a good deal more intimate with the affairs of the kitchen than were their parents, but the only thing that they ever had to conceal from them was the presence of garlic, which was forbidden. Of this, they themselves partook, with great stealth, in the evening, sharing with the maids a dish of bread and hot water with garlic mixed in it, and rounding off the repast with oily cakes made of chestnut flower. There was Majolina, who was long remembered for her uncommon cheerfulness, and Rosina, a peasant grown old and lean and brown in the course of many years of labour in the open air. 'The festivals in the parish church were all her joy and glory, and when she tried to describe the preaching and the lights her stammer took her and her tears, and she used to cast apart her worn hands with a broken action of overwhelmed desire.'[14]

Of a different age and temperament was the young Luigia, who came to them somewhat later. To her the little girls gave reading lessons, but they found her a difficult pupil, for she never progressed beyond the point of saying 'A, b, ab', pronouncing the letters when joined exactly as when they were apart, since she could not understand that a word could end upon a consonant; baffled, and unable to think of any way of circumventing this difficulty, the children abandoned their efforts. It was Luigia, with her singing and her high spirits, who at Carnival time dressed up as a man and went down to entertain the peasants who lived at the gates; and we are told that her cheerfulness did not wilt under the penance that was imposed upon her during Lent for this transgression, though the penance was a hard one: half her dinner to be given to the poor, and her own share to be eaten upon her knees in the presence of her fellow servants.[15]

Benedetta was remembered too, for another reason. In an article written many years later Alice Meynell said:

Dear were the ants in a wide stone loggia long ago, where they came up through the cracks to take their crumbs in the sunshine, until Benedetta swept them to destruction with a broom, and said in reply to the weeping (and, too probably, the ineffectual fists) of the children that the ants were not 'Cristiani'.

The little ants, which we thought we knew so well, by variations of size and shades of manner, as to give them names, were involved and mingled in indiscriminate death like soldiers.[16]

In January 1854 the children were taken by their parents to Florence; wearing pink plush hats they trotted at their father's heels round the Uffizi Gallery and the Boboli Gardens.[17] That summer they went to England and remained there for a year, much of which was spent in Kent. The children heard with delight the call of the cuckoo, and rode in the wagons at haymaking. Many years later the elder sister recalled that time: 'We children loved the Kentish beauty of our dear England. Poetry filtered into our little hearts wherever we abode, to blossom forth in my little large-eyed thoughtful sister in the process of time.'[18]

From Dover, where the children had been left with Amélie, Alice wrote to her mother to describe the pleasures of a spring day: 'We went on the top of Shackespear's Clif and saw a sky lark. We pluck the first flowers. It was fine weather but no sun. There was a beautiful road to go to Shackespear's Clif. We sat on the bank and eat each an apple. I send you a flower. We saw the railway passing when we were on Shackespear's Clif. Exquse this short letter dearest sweet mama. I send my love to dear you and dear papa and to all. Your ever ever ever affectionate Alice.'[19]

Then they were off again across the Channel, travelling by Calais, Paris, Strasbourg, Basle, and Berne to Clarens, where they stayed for seven weeks. Here it was that the children went out with some Swiss peasants and came home to announce proudly that they had caught a fish, only to find that this was, in their parents' estimation, an act of wanton cruelty and a cause for shame. They were not spoken to familiarly for several days. Here, too, in the garden of the old *pension* by the lake, where they stayed, they saw for the first time a night-flowering convolvulus whose beauty Alice remembered ever afterwards. 'Nothing was nearer to white than the convolvulus flowers and the early moon. Swiss women used to come along the twilight road by the lake by twos and threes, to stand whispering by. The plant grew, propped up with its scores of closed buds among very dark leaves, and its scores of the flowers of the past night, also closed, but with another kind of closing. And just at the time when the petunias began to breathe their scent, and the stocks grew more distinct, the convolvulus opened its flowers.'[20]

The wheels turned again. Over the Simplon to Domodossola, to Genoa, to Nervi. The peasants were celebrating a *festa* at Sant' Ilario, a village in the hills behind Nervi, and Alice and Mimi, mingling with the crowd outside the church, were suddenly seized with a desire to prove their Anglo-Saxon superiority to the Latin children; so, rounding up a bunch of them, they chased them down through the woods and vineyards, and never paused until they reached the street of the little town.[21]

On, at the beginning of summer, to Levanto, to Rapallo, to Porto Fino, and to Genoa again. Thence Mrs Thompson departed for a month to England, seen off by her husband and several friends. 'When all went and dear Tom, I retreated to the cabin and wept.'[22] During her absence Mr Thompson was preoccupied with financial troubles. He wrote on 21st July, from Stresa, where he was staying, with the children:

> The best arrangement that Mitton could make with the York bankers was to cancel the Bond in payment of 450 pounds. The first instalment is due on 1st August . . . Though the matter is not so bad as it might have been, still to raise 450 pounds in one year is an embarrassment and I confess at the present moment I don't see how it is to be done. My poor books! I suppose they must go . . . You are not in the way of gaining any information respecting Antwerp or Bruges or Malines or any of the Belgian towns as places of residence, are you? Or Caen? Or any old French town, with Norman architecture and pleasant surroundings? Or what of Heidelberg or Nuremberg with their picturesqueness, their cheapness, their accessibility (comparative) from England – their German for the children?
>
> These are but the wonderings of a mind that 'doesn't see its way' but does see that a call of 450 pounds has to be met.[23]

Somehow the problem must have been resolved, for no more is heard of resorting to the cheapness of the various places mentioned. Mrs Thompson rejoined her husband and children at Stresa, where she bathed with the little girls very early in the mornings. 'Sweet morn', reads the entry in her diary for September 8th. 'Bathed with angels at 7 – waves. After breakfast rushed with them to dear wine bower (we had come home that way and Angels picked blackberries) to make sketch of it. Did a nice one – sat on the chair – a cow came in the way as I was drawing babe – she hardly moved and great cow brushed by her with her bulging sides.' The children, she noted, were reading 'every day with their Pa *Swiss Family Robinson*.'

At the end of September, packing their bags once more, the Thompsons moved to Albaro.

CHAPTER 3

THE STRETCH OF COAST by Albaro has been described by Alice
Meynell as having 'its heights in the sun and its feet in a brimming sea.
It was an olive garden, a vineyard, an orange-grove set with a broadcast
city of single houses, silver grey-roofed, shuttered from the south, their
large blank walls bright with the old white, old yellow and old rose-
colour . . . faded by a hundred thousand noons of sunshine and softly
stained by the wet sea-winds of two or three centuries.'[1] One of these
houses was the Palazzo Bagnarello, in which the Thompson family
presently installed themselves, Mrs Thompson in ecstasies over the
view from the windows, an 'exquisite Italian combination of sunshine,
campanile, pine, cypress, hill and palazzo.'[2] Dickens had stayed there
some years before and had called it 'the pink gaol', because of the iron
bars on the lower windows. The bedroom in which the little girls slept
had a vaulted ceiling painted with stars, and the hangings were of
yellow satin.

A swing in the garden occupied much of the children's time, and
their mother gave them each a large vase filled with earth which they
planted with weeds and rose slips, and tended as their own gardens.
Alice's ninth birthday, soon after their arrival at Albaro, was marked
by a present of a baby doll from their mother, who described the occasion in her diary with the usual stream of adjectives. 'Little angels and I
made paste all in a row down in a little pleasant pantry – apple tarts
with babe's name encircled by leaves.'[3]

Five days later the poor little nine-year-old had to visit the dentist in
Genoa for the extraction of a tooth. 'He said the blessed soul had better
have chloroform – he gave it to her. I held its blessed head. He pulled
three times – then she screamed violently and fell off the chair. I went
quite mad with agony and fear – he gave her some more, and then
pulled out another tooth. When it was all over the angel lay quite
insensible and white and cold like a seraph. I saw the dentist look
anxious, and his hand trembled. Oh the horror and agony of that morning! . . . She was violently sick – then we laid it on the sofa and she
opened her eyes in about ten minutes. We then carried her into his
room and laid her on the bed. Soon she came to but was drowsy and
sick. He told me there had been danger.' Mrs Thompson went out and
bought a doll with a wax head which she brought back to Alice, who
was 'enchanted and consoled'.[4]

Later, in the winter, the children were both in bed with colds, and
their mother helped them to make two puddings in their bedroom. One

can imagine that the mess and the delight of the invalids were both great. Alice suffered a good deal from colds and chest afflictions during these childhood years, and there was some fear that they might indicate a serious pulmonary weakness. The Italian remedies for this were snail broth and snail jelly, and upon these nauseous dishes the poor child was fed.[5]

About this time Alice began to desire expression for the sharply felt and troubling things that stirred in her soul. Children, who are so defenceless against the world's beauty and the world's sadness, turn naturally to utterance of such words as they have at their command for relief of their deep feelings; they have not yet learned to be inarticulate. Of these feelings Alice Meynell wrote many years later:

Wordsworth cannot say too much of your passion for Nature. The light of summer morning before sunrise was to you a spiritual splendour . . . The Mediterranean under the first perceptible touch of the moon, the calm southern sea in the full blossom of summer, the early spring everywhere, in the showery streets, in the fields or at sea, left childish memories with you . . . But the cloudy dusk behind poplars on the plains of France, the flying landscape from the train, willows, and the last of the light, were more mournful to you than you care to remember now. So were the black crosses on the graves of the French village; so were cypresses, though greatly beloved . . . Your strong sense of place made you love some places too keenly for peace . . ."[6]

So she began to write. There was 'no kind of promise in it', she said in after years, 'nothing noticeable or even excusable, except a good ear for prosody.'[7]

Mimi had already begun. Three years before, she had written, somewhat precociously:

> In the north of Asia I sat,
> Not knowing what to do
> And thinking of great Caesar,
> But his time is past.
> O Brutus and Cassius, why did you kill Caesar.[8]

Another poetic effort, which may have been by either of the sisters, charmingly recalls the Bard of Japan in the famous limerick:

> Eve, Eve, how beautiful thou art
> How I love you in my heart
> And the moonlight shines upon the sea
> And does the most beautiful reflection that can be.[9]

A slightly later one has a more sophisticated appearance, for it bears a title:

THE SILENCE OF EVE
by A. C. Thompson

The silence of the eve comes o'er the sleeping flowers
The last rays of the sun are shining on the meads
And silence spreads itself around
No sound is heard but the song of birds
That sing up in the lovely trees that shade the meadows
Their leaves are rustling in the gentle breeze.
The sun is setting in all his glory
In the lovely summer's eve.[10]

But it was more often of knights and ladies that Alice wrote, and the following year, when they were in England, she sent one of these poems of romance to *All the Year Round*. It was returned, as she had instructed, to the village post office, and Amélie went in secrecy to fetch it. The sorrow of rejection was greatly ameliorated by the thrill of finding that the editor's letter began: 'Sir'.[11]

Both children were reading voraciously at that time. Their father, by reading *Jane Eyre* aloud to them (with omissions), had given them a fervent love for Charlotte Brontë; guided by him they were ranging also through the works of Dickens, Scott, Trollope, and Jane Austen.[12] Much of what they read was advanced fare for children of nine and ten, but they were old for their age; that was a natural consequence of spending so much time with their parents, instead of being shut away in the nursery. The Thompsons had a number of English friends at Albaro – chief among them Monty Brown, the British Consul, and the Reverend Alfred Strettell, the Protestant chaplain – and there was plenty of coming and going, and much talk of politics, art, and literature, to which the children listened. They used to go for picnics at Porto Fino, loaded with books of verse, and Mrs Thompson and Mr Strettell would read aloud to them from Shakespeare, Wordsworth, Keats, and Tennyson.[13]

Politics must have been a constant topic at that time, for the Thompsons, with their frequent journeyings about Europe, could not but be vitally interested in continental affairs. The famous year of revolution – 1848 – was not long past, the Crimean War had just ended, and Cavour had manoeuvred the Italian Question into the foreground of the European picture. Feeling was high in Italy in those years preceding unification, and no doubt the children heard much talk among the peasants as well as in the drawing-room. At Alessandria the year before, out walking with their father, they had written '*brutta Austria*' in the gravel alongside the canal.[14]

They were off again in May 1857, travelling to England, accom-

panied by Monty Brown. From Turin to Susa they went by train, arriv-
ing at dusk, and then 'set off for horrible night journey over Mont
Cenis'. (The tale is told in Mrs Thompson's diary.) 'Babes and I and
Amélie and a lady and a priest at the back, Tom, poor creature, in
Banquette, and Monty in Coupée. Pouring rain all night and towards
morn as we approached summit deep snow and snow storm. Hideous
scene. I had not slept a moment. All round snow and mist like
Lapland – no road to be seen. Our wheels making the track a foot deep.
Descended to Langlebourg at the horrible savage inn. No chambermaid
or waiter. I was going into a room when I was warned off – therein was
reposing the Empress of Russia, her suite round the door waiting for
her waking.'

From there they proceeded to Aix-les-Bains, then by steamer along
the Rhône to Caloz, then by train to Lyons, and on to Paris where they
stayed the night. Next day to Boulogne, Folkestone, and, at last, to
Putney and the Wellers' house.[15] The visit was not, from the children's
point of view, a great success. They hated the suburbs of London, of
which Putney was then one, and missed the wild freedom of their life
among the vineyards and beside the sea. Louis Blanc, who was a friend
of Mr Weller's, and was then in exile from France for his extreme left-
wing political activities, came to the house while they were there, and
was heard by Alice to say, on the subject of the survival of languages:
'Ce sont les deux langues qui resteront: l'Anglais pour le commerce et
le Français pour la littérature.' The thin little girl of nine years old
noted the flourish of Blanc's right arm and the affected length he gave
to the last syllable of 'littérature', and, in silence, she hated him for the
insult to Shakespeare and the English language.[16]

Perhaps the Wellers, like the children, found the visit somewhat trying, or perhaps the Thompson restlessness broke out again; but,
whatever the cause, the family soon packed themselves up once more
and departed for Betchworth, near Dorking, where the children walked
happily in the woods, listened to the birds, and remembered Putney
with loathing and scorn. Thence, after a few months, to Southampton;
where they stayed in lodgings and Alice got fleas; and on to Hastings,
where Mrs Thompson noted in her diary: 'Babes enchanted and playing all day on sweet wet sands'. Here Alice rode for the first time, with
'intense joy', and Mr Thompson, celebrating his forty-eighth birthday,
was showered with presents by the children – handkerchiefs worked in
hem-stitch and adorned with his initials, a portfolio made of scallop
shells from Hastings, poems written by Alice, and drawings done by
Mimi.[17]

At the end of the summer they went to Jersey, then back to London,
and in September 1859 once more to Italy. Their journey, as usual,
was eventful. At Boulogne, where they stayed the night, Mrs

Thompson propped open the window with her husband's dressing-case, and departed next morning without it. Mr Thompson luckily noticed its absence in time to hurry back from the station and retrieve it. In Paris, the diary records, 'I wore my hat and striped gown and lilac shawl – People stared furiously – every man, woman and child I passed – This is something . . . to attract so much of the attention of Parisians.'

They took a *diligence* from St Jean Maunieure to Langlebourg, where they went to the inn and were taken up to 'a savage wild room, curtain dividing us from where there was a man in bed. The babes and Tom set out to walk but I could not attempt it and slept a little . . . They walked in moonlight and dew . . . for two hours, . . . poor doves.'

On the next stage, to Susa, 'the going at a fast trot down the zigzags when you are lying down with your back to the horses recklessly horrible – the swing round corners. Poor babes made a point of not sleeping.'[18]

Through such adventures and discomforts they came back to Albaro, to 'sunshine, campanile, pine, cypress, hill and palazzo', to the blue seas and Agostino's cooking.

There they resumed their usual occupations, the children doing their lessons, and running wild on the hillside with the peasant children, and talking Genoese. They had a great desire not to be thought English by their Italian neighbours, not to speak with an imperfect accent or to behave like tourists; and Alice, now twelve years old, suffered agonies of shame for the English women who still wore the long curls that were out of fashion on the Continent, and carried a guide-book and a camp stool, and talked Italian with an execrable accent.[19]

Christiana continued to paint what she called 'blessed arts', and to hold musical parties for the neighbours. Years later Alice Meynell remembered the boredom of those occasions, and the suffering: 'As to the length of Beethoven, experienced by you on duty in the drawing-room, it would be curious to know whether it was really something greater than Beethoven had any idea of. You sat and listened and tried to fix a passage in your mind as a kind of halfway mark, with the deliberate provident intention of helping yourself through the time during a future hearing; for you knew too well that you would have to hear it all again.'[20]

It was at the end of April 1860 that the children saw Garibaldi, who was staying near Albaro. They had already seen King Victor Emmanuel when he drove, one day, in an open carriage along the road past the Palazzo Zerbino, above Genoa, and had described him as looking very red and hot, and having large, ungloved hands. He had saluted the two children in pinafores, who had replied, a little previously, 'Viva

il Re d'Italia!'[21] Now, having become ardent Garibaldians, it was a
great excitement for them to see their hero, a short man with a reddish-
brown beard and moustache, sitting on a wall, looking out to sea.[22] He
had been equipping his followers from the arsenal of the National
Society at Genoa, and a few days later he set out with the two ships and
a thousand men in red woollen shirts to aid the Sicilian revolt against
the King of Naples. One may imagine the eagerness with which his
campaign for the unification of Italy was followed by the two little girls
at Albaro.

Alice, aged thirteen, was writing busily. A notebook of that time has
survived, entitled *First Endeavours* by A.C.T.,[23] and containing the
fourth chapter of a romance called *The Beauty of Asytler Abbey*.
There are also some poems, one being headed 'Coeur de Lion' and
followed by a candid little postscript: 'Truly, this is not much about
Coeur de Lion but it is as much as I am equal to.' On another page she
exclaims: 'I fear I shall fill my book too soon if I go on at this rate'; and,
again, she remarks that the poems are 'not much, truly, but better than
nothing and, if nothing else, at least writing is an occupation; it keeps
me from reading too much. I am very addicted to reading novels, and I
certainly do not pretend to despise them as I believe every girl with a
"well-regulated" mind ought to do. Alas! Papa says that when we get
regularly settled in England I shall not be allowed to write so much.
Alas, alas, what will become of me!' She has been reading more of Scott
and Dickens, is plunging through the novels of George Eliot – she calls
Silas Marner 'one of the noblest books in the world' – has sampled
Bulwer Lytton, Thackeray, and Nathaniel Hawthorne.

Reading and writing and dreaming her dreams, she had withdrawn
into a little world apart; the thoughts that found expression in this
notebook were shared with no one, and the dreams of romance were
carefully hidden lest she should be laughed at or reproved for them. She
was ashamed, seeing herself sometimes as her father would see her if he
knew what passed behind her large, thoughtful brown eyes. 'I am the
most extravagant, romantic little fool in the world', she wrote one day.
'A free confession of a fact which I repeat to myself a hundred times a
day. *Dio lo sa*.'[24] But in another mood she knew that the things she
wrote were more than the scribblings of a romantic child; she recognised the compelling urge that drove her on to seek for a means of
transmitting thought and experience, that roused in her that longing
which is common to all creative artists, to achieve immortality with her
work. 'Oh', she wrote, 'that each great noble thought which strives for
utterance in my mind could be made immortal by my pen that others
might feel them too! Ambition! Without it improvement, progress,
would stop. But the time will come, *must* come, when men will read
these words, ay, these *very words* which I write *now* glad to find that

even as a child I dreamt of *fame*. Wild dreams! Dreams of a child who does not know the world!'[25]

They journeyed to England again in the spring of 1861, Mrs Thompson being anxious to see her mother, who had been ill. Of their arrival she wrote in her diary: 'Hideous appalling London. We took carriage to Fulham through the most distressing squalour, meanness, dirt and vulgarity.' Mr Weller had taken for them a dismal house in Fulham so that they could be near him; but fortunately their stay was short, and they soon moved to Hastings, where there was riding, and Mrs Thompson described her daughters as looking 'extremely picturesque in their shirts and black skirts and Spanish "black hats", feather and pompom – little white collar turned over and white wristbands – pictures against blue sky.'

Shortly before Christmas that year Amélie, the beloved Swiss nurse, died, to the great sorrow of all the family, and especially the two girls. Mr Thompson sent them to look at her as she lay dead, telling them that it was right and that they would never forgive themselves if they did not do it.[26]

They crossed the Channel again the following year, at the outset of a tour that was to take them by slow stages through Belgium and Germany. Bruges, where they stayed for a month, so won Mimi's heart that on leaving she wrote in her diary: 'Dear, exquisite, lovely, sunny, smiling Bruges, goodbye! Goodbye, fair city of happy, ever happy, recollections. Bright, gabled Bruges, we shall not look upon thy like again.'[27]

In Düsseldorf they were taken shopping by an English woman who had lived there for some years, and long afterwards Alice recalled the complacency with which her compatriot still spoke her abominable German. She 'directed her coachman and ordered her things for a whole morning, and in abundant German, without a single declension of noun, adjective, or article, and without any genders whatever.'[28]

From Cologne they went by boat down the Rhine, to Bonn, Koblenz, Bingen. At Marienberg they stayed to take the waters, bathed in the early morning, and followed a strange diet of grapes, sour milk, breadcrumbs, and a *Kraut* preserve; all this under the influence of a couple called Nichols, who ran the spa, had odd ideas about health, dabbled in spiritualism, and were to turn up again several times in Alice's life. On the way home they stayed at Brussels and visited Waterloo, where an old man offered himself as their guide. He told them that he was Sergeant-Major Mundy of the Seventh Hussars, and had fought in the battle when he was twenty-seven. He showed them the hedge under which he had lain all night, having received a wound; they met also an old woman who said that she had tended the wounded after the battle.[29]

On their return to England they went to Bonchurch in the Isle of Wight, where they took a house and settled down for a stay of quite unusual duration.

CHAPTER 4

THE DELL, at Bonchurch, was the first settled home that the Thompsons had had in England since they married. Even then they stayed for only a year, or less; but the flavour of their life during that time was different from that of their usual frequent journeyings and breathless halts in lodging houses. The feeling of permanency encouraged Christiana to make a garden where there were grass steps bordered with tall white lilies; she called it – as one somehow knows that she would – the Celestial Garden.[1] Nothing could make her other than bohemian – her huge, untidy, brightly coloured ideas struggled like exotic birds under the nets of convention – but during this time at Bonchurch she made an effort to regulate her life and that of her daughters so that they conformed in some degree to the customs of her time and class. In 1864, when they arrived at The Dell, Mimi was eighteen and Alice seventeen. Their childhood had been, as we know, unconventional in every way, and it had not mattered very much except that the little girls had sometimes suffered, when with other children, from knowing their clothing to be conspicuous or inadequate, and from feeling themselves different, which, to a child, is among the keenest kinds of anguish. But now it was another matter, for the two girls, just growing up, must be launched into society, and this demanded a settled residence, a circle of suitable acquaintances, and a measure of conformity with the rules laid down by the formidable dowagers who governed the social world. The girls must have the right sort of clothes bought for them, they must go to dances and make themselves agreeable to the right people, and their mother would certainly be expected to entertain a little for them. To these necessities Mrs Thompson surrendered; but her opinion of society is bluntly and amusingly stated in her letters to Alice, who, in the winter of 1864, was visiting her aunt at Dorking. A ball was to be given in a big house near Bonchurch, and Mimi and her cousin, who was staying with them, were invited. Alice, who had not yet made her début, received from her mother and sister news of the preparations that were in hand, and sighed to be there.

Mr Thompson at first objected to the idea of taking the girls, but his wife had decided that he should, and after a few days was able to write triumphantly to Alice: 'Loze [their pet name for him] is going to take them. Mr Opposition has come round because I said nothing about it.'[2]

There followed, on New Year's Day, 1865, an account of the ball.

Well, the H's ball was splendid – no expense spared – a profusion of pink wax lights and a flow of champagne – but poor me! About 12 I was so utterly exhausted I had to go up into the bedroom and there lie covered up till 2.30 in a torpor. I don't think I can go to any more. Even at the Cheapes' everyone was pitying me seeing my condition. I seemed at the H's to be listening for a week to hideous galops, waltzes, etc. drumming up thro' the floor, all of which Mimi and Mary pronounced delicious; the tunes are exquisitely suggestive to them – not so to me. Also every now and then poor Miss Johnson was brought up to be sick by her Mama. The dresses were splendid. Really what lavish absurdity to the tired looker-on! the whole thing is silly in the extreme. I am sure I should not think the same if the dances were such as peasants dance in the glorious southern lands – but in society they are false and frightful and the flirting and stuff ditto. I don't wish to be uncharitable but to the dispassionate observer beholding the affectation and vanity, this is the inevitable view to take of the whole concern . . . I wore my grey dove with tulle as before, and red camelias – pretty when viewed at home but bald and poverty-stricken when contrasted with the fur-belows of society.[3]

A month later Mimi was writing to her mother, who had perhaps gone to fetch Alice home, to tell her that the Hamboros at Steep Hill Castle were to be 'At Home' the following Monday: 'so get Alice seen to, her yaller tarlaton can be made up in time surely. My pink, no doubt, will pass muster . . . I hope little Alice is glad of the dance so near.'

Of the rapturous evening that Alice spent we have her own account from the diary which she was keeping at that time, and in which she wrote down everything that she thought and did with artless candour, and sometimes with startling honesty.

Wore a ravishing yellow tarlaton of the palest possible tint by night, made exquisitely, with a plaid écharpe (principally yellow and red) over one shoulder, a red rose with its leaves in my hair and one at my waist. I never had such a charming costume and never looked so well . . . Danced every single dance . . . glorious fun. To this dance there were no *drawbacks*. My partners regularly fought for me. There was a scrimmage on my account for every dance. 'Miss Thompson is always at the centre of a battle' said C. Kelly, seeing me surrounded by rival claimants. 'I am afraid it is my bad memory' said I modestly. 'It comes of being so attractive' said Charlie politely, and an acquiescing murmur went thro' the group . . . Captain Sewell . . . many times watched me going round, and told Douglas how well I danced (who told me). And indeed everyone says so. I had no regular flirtation, and no particular compliments, save that truest of all, that all the men quarrelled to dance with me . . . I sat out no dances. Danced twice running with no one. I did enjoy it . . .[4]

The Alice of this diary is very different from the girl of four years ago who was writing poems and dreaming of fame on a Mediterranean shore. She has stopped writing and she reads nothing except the foreign news in the newspaper; there is nothing in these pages that record her life at Bonchurch to suggest that she is in any way different from the other girls of seventeen with whom she walks and giggles and exchanges secrets. She has been admitted to the grown-up world, to society, and she is intoxicated with its delights. Some childish vision of love has burst upon her view and fills her dreams of the future; all her thoughts are of young men, all her ambition to be loved. She has suddenly discovered that she is pretty, and is enthralled with her power of evoking admiration; clothes fascinate her as never before, hats enchant her. She is much too honest to pretend to herself that she is not satisfied with her appearance. 'I sported a dear darling tiny mite of a velvet bonnet', she writes one day; 'violet, the rest of my attire black – so pretty.'[5] And another day, more thoughtfully: 'The girls here all think me very staid and matronly as I have taken to wearing a bonnet constantly, and sometimes a shawl, and generally very dark colours. The fact is this attire becomes me a million times more than any other – the jaunty style does not suit me in the least.' But on another day, in a mood of despair and self-reproach, she exclaims: 'O how much nicer are good women than merely pretty or merely clever. And to think that I am neither of the three!'[6]

It seems that there was some kind of tutorial establishment at Bonchurch at that time, and the boys from there were present at all the parties of the neighbourhood and were a good deal with the Thompson girls and their friends. Little bunches of them would wander off for walks together, or visit the shops, or sit in somebody's garden, chattering and teasing and endlessly vying with each other in repartee. They were a merry crowd: Alice records in her diary how they 'raised the echoes with our shouts of laughter'; and another day 'Sophy was very mad and funny and made me laugh. We certainly made noise enough.' The names of these boys are scattered through the pages; sometimes it is one, sometimes another who has the most space on several consecutive days. There was Haly, who used to fix his blue eyes upon her in long gazes that made her cheeks grow hot, and who, she confessed in her diary, had embraced her one night 'in a shadowy garden'. Of this incident she gave some hints to her friend Miss Nairne, and the next day, seized with remorse, wrote: 'I do hate and despise myself so for having told Miss Nairne about his naughty behaviour. She got it out of me, and of course it seems to her more ungentlemanly than it was, because I *did* encourage him just a *little* bit, and that I did not tell her. It is not quite kissing and telling, but something very like it, and very dishonourable.'

There was Charlie Kelly who, with his friend Money, took the Thompson sisters to the town one day: 'Money made Mimi a present of a cross at a shop which is rather shocking. Charlie confined himself to a packet of very good toffee for me.'

There was Tom Baker, with whom she walked home in the dark one spring evening, and afterwards wrote: 'Now in this journal I *invariably* write down everything, neither exaggerating nor suppressing ever, so all the truth must out.' All the truth was that while he whispered sweet nothings in her ear, she 'talked women's rights energetically'; then he squeezed her fingers as they lay on his arm, and she, recording that her heart fluttered at his touch, adds, with a delicious sense of guilt, 'What a wicked girl I must be!'

There was Holdsworth, who was the most merry of the boys, and to whom she used to sing 'Si vous m'aimez'. With him, after he left Bonchurch, she corresponded; and he, detecting a warmth in her letters, wrote that he was 'very spoony' on her, and thought that she understood and returned his feeling, but that he was too young to marry, and felt it might be better if he did not come and see her for a time. Alice, evidently with a guilty suspicion that she might have been too forward, wrote in a fury, taxing him with impertinence, and assuring him that she never wanted to see him again. He, humbly apologising, caused her to say: 'Now I perceive what a wicked letter that was I wrote on Saturday . . . How my conscience pricks . . . I have my desire – I have been loved. And splendidly have I received that love. Both he and I are miserable. There, Alice, enjoy your triumph, you little hard, heartless thing. I enjoy it in tears. I enjoy it in sackcloth and ashes.' They did not meet again; but she, reflecting upon his youthful avowal, wrote: 'To think that I have been loved does my heart good however flimsy and immature that love was. At seventeen it is very sweet to think that you have been queen over a human heart however short your reign may have been.'[7]

Her special favourite, however, was a certain Arthur Sewell,* who had already disappeared from the Bonchurch scene when the diary begins, though some of his family were there. It seems that she had annoyed him by showing too much attention to that same Tom Baker whose whispers she had drowned with talk of Women's Rights. For Arthur she says would 'go through fire and water'; but he, 'with all his frankness, is an icicle.' This she saw as the tragedy of her life, and remarked after attending a wedding: 'It is almost impossible that I should ever have the inventing of bridesmaids' dresses'; and on another occasion: '. . . my marriage day which can never be.'[8]

Like many another girl of seventeen before and after her, she liked to see herself as a mature and saddened woman, rather wicked, and wholly wise in the ways of the world. 'Climbed into a field,' she notes, one day

---

* Arthur Sewell (1841-1947), son of Robert Burleigh Sewell, solicitor, of Newport, Isle of Wight. At this time he was a Choral Scholar at New College, Oxford. After graduating he took Orders, and for a time conducted private schools, at Leamington Spa and Weymouth. He was appointed priest-in-charge at St Ann's (now St Aldhelm's) Radipole, near Weymouth, and then, until his retirement, was rector of Sutton Veney, Wilts.

in April, 'where I picked cowslips and tried to think myself an innocent little girl again with no love affairs. But alas! My long womanly gown caught in every bramble and I was obliged to keep my parasol up in pity to my complexion, and altogether I felt myself but a faint, feeble copy of that innocent little Alice.' But then suddenly there comes a flash of her delightful, devastating honesty, which compels her to admit how young she is. 'I have been reading *Fatima* and I *don't* quite think I know what love is.' And, again, she describes her thoughts as she walked one night in the moonlit garden: 'Oh, how lovely the moon was! I was not quite sure whether it was more delightful to wander about all alone dreaming romantic dreams undisturbed or to have had a companion – a very amorous one of course . . . I should say on the whole none.'[9]

During this time at Bonchurch she and Mimi were confirmed, and the experience made a deep impression on her. 'This day of days!', she noted. 'For surely until my death-day my confirmation day is the most sacred of my days – save my first communion which will be soon (God willing).'[10]

She made her first communion five days later, walking to church through a snow-storm though it was the end of March. 'Received the Holy Sacrament . . . I was so nervous that I could not hold the chalice. What can be so distracting to the thoughts as nervousness? I could not fix my thoughts on anything, but I was greatly impressed, thank Heaven . . . To Church alone in the evening.' Two weeks later, on Good Friday, she wrote: 'Good Friday has never been such a reality to me before as it has been to-day. This should be so after my confirmation. In the evening to Church at 7 p.m. It pelted – that was no hardship whatever because I like walking in the rain. Even if it had been, I was repaid by the wonderful consolation I found there in the softening of my hard heart – even if it were only for a moment. I hope it will be for longer than that.'[11]

Her confirmation was the beginning of her regular attendance at Church, and this was to grow more frequent as the months passed. One has a feeling from the diary of the great loneliness of this girl, of how deeply separated she was from her parents and her sister, although she loved them greatly. It was a loneliness that had begun almost before she had left her childhood, and that was to remain with her until she died. It was one of her sorrows that even her tender and loving heart could not save her from being always a little apart from the world, even from those she loved most; and she felt it as a failure in herself. She began now to see dimly how her loneliness might be lessened and her life given shape and purpose, but she was groping in the dark and there was no one to help her; the clergyman who prepared her for confirmation was someone to whom she could talk and from whom she could seek

help, but it is doubtful if her difficulties were as yet sufficiently well for-
mulated to present to him; and anyway, in a few months her family was
to leave Bonchurch, and she would not see him again.

Shortly before this time Christiana Thompson had become a
Catholic. Of the stages by which she came to the Roman Catholic
Church we know nothing, for she, who talked so much of other things,
talked little of her interior life. In her diary she described her reception
into the Church, and added: 'Returned home and told no one.' Her
husband and daughters were all, at that time, if not actually unsym-
pathetic to the Catholic Church, not disposed to look upon it
favourably, so she seems to have kept her opinions to herself.

Once, however, she had to appeal to her husband for help, having
got entangled in an argument with an Anglican clergyman called
Gregory. Mr Thompson wrote to her in London advising her on how
to extricate herself gracefully from this situation. In the circumstances
this was magnanimous of him. 'I am very strongly of opinion, on consideration, that you had better not reply to Gregory in the way you
intend but say to him that you had written a reply but that you found
the subject grow so much upon you that you think you could not do
justice to it and that any shortcoming on your part in conducting a
discussion with such a practised writer as himself might only damage a
cause, etc.' So as not to leave him entirely unanswered he advises her to
'state the few simple broad facts on which Catholicism rests – and
which are well put in "End of Controversy"* – in the preface I think,
but I haven't the book here.'[12]

Christiana's own letters during these years contain only one
reference to her Church, and then, writing to Alice from Richmond,
where she has gone on a visit, she says: 'I have found out the Chapel
here. It is very dear tho' plain. I went last eve to Benediction which was
of course exquisite.'

Commenting on the vicar at Bonchurch, Alice remarked that 'his
manner of doing the service was so decent . . . no aping of popery.'[13]
And another day, when she had been with her mother to look at a
Catholic Church in the neighbourhood, she wrote, with what may have
been intended either as irony or sadness: 'I felt a lost young heretic
passing the holy water.'[14]

At the end of April 1865 the Thompsons left Bonchurch. It had
been planned that they were to go for a fortnight to London, and then
to Germany; but a financial crisis – neither the first nor the last in their
lives – occurred, and prevented them. Alice, bitterly disappointed,
wrote: 'I certainly am a fool to say that I hate and detest money when

---

* John Milner's *The End of Religious Controversy*, published in 1818. This work
forcefully presented the R.C. case in a series of letters addressed to an Anglican divine,
and went through many editions.

the loss of it deprives one of so many pleasures.'[15] It was arranged that they should go instead to Henley-on-Thames, a plan which did nothing to alleviate Alice's grief at leaving her beloved Bonchurch. Her anguish was acute. She suffered as only the very young can suffer – without hope, resisting consolation – before some awareness of history and eternity has forced itself upon them and given some perspective, some sense of proportion to their sufferings. 'Day of mourning', she wrote in her diary on the day of their departure.

To-day I have shed more tears I think than I have all my life. I went round the garden and into every nook, and watered the grass with my tears. Now tears to me are most poignant agony, they are not a relief to sorrow but a mark of the utmost extremity of pain. They do not come in torrents but by twos and threes, and each one seems to crack a heart-string. Indeed I suffered. I kissed the ground and the flowers and lay along the happy grass that I should never press again . . . Now it seems to me that I must live on memories, that the sun of my life set behind the down which hid Bonchurch from my aching eyes. These are not mere words. The sorrow in my stricken soul is beyond words, beyond all expression, beyond the comprehension of happy spirits. That my life will ever be happy again I cannot believe at this moment.

She was a little cheered on the journey by being given charge of the family purse – a thing that had never happened to her before – for her father had remained at Bonchurch to complete their arrangements, and her mother was carrying a kitten which occupied all her attention. In the train on the way to Basingstoke they passed Fareham, and she noted that it was 'where *he* lives'; he, one may suppose, being Arthur Sewell.

The house at Henley filled her with dismay. It had been taken for them by Mr Weller, who had described it as charming; but his grand-daughter called it 'a hideous little plebeian cottage with no garden', and expressed the hope that they would not stay there long. Henley was 'an abominable hole', the town 'beastly dirty and the shops disgusting'; but she was not in a mood to be fair to any place while she still fiercely longed for Bonchurch. She missed the young friends who had made life merry; here, they knew no one, and there was nothing to do except go for walks, practise her music, and pour out her miseries on the pages of her diary. But she was changing again; and yearn though she might for the parties and the gay society of Bonchurch, she was beginning to realise that even that was not enough, that she wanted from life something more, which seemed to be denied to her.

How unhealthy it is to depend as I do so much on my own thoughts and moods and feelings for employment, for excitement. I ponder on them, seizing hold of the strong and feeble emotions of the inexplicable human heart and try to understand them, making a world for myself out of their shadows of which I ought to be wholly or almost unconscious. Now a young man occupied with study or business or laborious pleasures has no time to watch and ponder on every half shade of thought and feeling that flits over his heart, and if the subtle moral faculties and perceptions of his soul are kept in abeyance and perhaps never developed in this life, the more material mind, as it were, grows strong, grand and healthy, unconscious of its own growth, and perhaps in proportion as it is so unconscious. A girl, on the other hand, thrills through every nerve and fibre of her intense self-consciousness at the touch of the slightest joy or pain. If these nerves are tolerably in tune with one another she becomes a great woman – a writer, say, famous for laying bare the melancholy secrets of the female heart to the curious gaze of material-minded man; if the chords jar, she dwindles into a miserably self-conscious melancholy which feeds upon itself, or the struggle is sharper, the pain shorter, and she dies. Answer O World, man-governed, man-directed, answer for the sanity of your laws and your morals. Of all the crying evils in this depraved earth, ay, of all the sins of which the cry must surely come to Heaven, the greatest, judged by all the laws of God and of Humanity is the miserable selfishness of men that keeps women from work. Work, the salvation of the world, the winner of the dreamless sleep and the dreamless thought too, the strengthener of the mind and of the body. As to the soul, let that lie fallow, I say. What happiness did excess of feeling ever bring man? By work I mean work of the mind as well as of the body. Nature has ordained that the labour of biceps and deltoids belongs to man alone – it is his curse and his privilege – but women should have work for the mind. A girl may go mad with her own soul over needlework, but she could not do so at college, or studying for the bar or for a civil service examination. That is what I demand for myself and for my sisters . . . O my dream, my dream! When will you be realised to gladden my soul, to redeem my trampled and polluted sex . . . O my Shelley, if you were alive you would help me to fulfil my golden dream and the earth might taste happiness for once.[16]

In this bitter outburst she touched upon a subject that was near her heart always. She was to see, in her lifetime, the emancipation of women which she so much desired; but in 1865 it was a far-off dream indeed. There was every justification for the hopelessness with which she regarded any thought of a career, for she no longer believed in herself as a writer – had, indeed, ceased to be one; she had none of the talent for drawing possessed by her sister, who was now busy with her ambitions to become an artist, and no other path was open to her. 'Shall I confess that I have nothing to do?' she wrote. 'What is there to occupy me but going out, and practising?' There was no remedy for her unhappy situation except a change in woman's status; she was only one of thousands of girls with 'nothing to do'. In the nineteenth century rigid conventions and firmly closed doors frustrated, at every turn, the woman who desired to use her intellect to some purpose in the world. Resigned to what seemed the unalterable though unjust pattern of things, she wrote at the end of her passionate complaint: 'Now it occurs to me that I will never do any good in this thing – how can I? And I had better hold my jaw. But every word that I have written here has come from the depth of my soul, and is only the faintest symbol of feelings that are beyond words.'[17]

Her father joined them a few days later. She was disappointed that he thought Henley quite tolerable, and saw no reason why they should not stay there for quite a while; but his presence cheered her, and he brought a lot of books, and helped her to occupy her mind. In this new mood of hers she began to read again. Commenting on a novel of Trollope's, she said: 'Really I can't get up much interest in novels now – they are all about love, as though there was nothing else in this great world – Good Heavens.'[18]

Her despair ebbed and flowed. There were days when she was happier and found amusement. She went to a fortune-teller, who prophesied that she would marry twice, have three children, and go to Bath to end her days. She joined in the family sweepstake on the Derby, and ran down to the station in the evening to learn that the French horse, Gladiateur, had won. 'And I pocket the four bob.' But on other days she was desperate, without hope, without interest in anything, without a glimmer of happiness. She was taking red lavender, but was convinced that it would do her no good. 'If I look inwards I find tears, if outwards, rain.' She thought she would stop her diary, for even that seemed pointless. 'Of what earthly interest will it be to me hereafter to know that on such a day we went for a walk and on such a day it rained . . . and that on such a day I was half-way to melancholy mania.' Those thoughts about her spiritual life which had begun seriously to occupy her mind at the time of her confirmation were always more or less present, running like a nettle-root beneath the surface of her days. 'I am trying hard to lead a better life – to be kind and unenvious and charitable', she wrote in her diary. 'The Lord in His mercy has given me the desire – it depends of course on myself whether I shall carry it out.'[19]

And at last, in these papers recording a young girl's desolation, there comes a sentence that promises hope. It is flung out carelessly and with a note of despair, but those words written on a May evening in an ugly house at Henley represented a first step on the road that was to be the right one for her. 'I must try to cultivate that rhyming faculty again which I used to have, if it is not quite gone from me. But whatever I write will be melancholy and self-conscious as are all women's poems.'[20]

CHAPTER 5

OF THE TWO YEARS following the close of the diary – two years which were of great importance in the development of the young Alice's life – few written records remain. But as in looking at two points on a map one can tell roughly how the unmarked road goes from one point to the other, so we may conjecture the path she travelled from our glimpse of its beginning and by the point which she had reached when we next find her; and, indeed, the road is not entirely uncharted, for there are a few fragments which help in filling the gap. There is, for instance, a notebook dated 1866,[1] containing Alice's summaries of the arguments set out in John Stuart Mill's *Political Economy*. The Thompsons were in lodgings at Arundel that autumn, and evidently she was taking her studies very seriously, for she wrote a great many notes on her wrestlings with political economy, and punctuated them with comments, in parentheses, which were sometimes desperate and sometimes triumphant. "I don't quite see this', or 'Yes, I see', or 'Oh, you muddle-head!' In one place, exasperated with herself, she wrote: 'For goodness sake remember that the "operation of exchange" whether by "barter or thro' the medium of money" is "the mere mechanism by which each person transforms the remuneration of his labour or of his capital into the particular shape in which it is most convenient to him to possess it; but in no wise the source of the remuneration itself." ' And another day, wearily, she wrote: 'I really confess myself beaten by the deduction Mill draws after this. I thought I saw it but it has again escaped me. I will return to it another day for I have read it over so often that my brain won't work.'

Meanwhile, she was writing poetry. Some lines of about this time pray for her father's deliverance from the danger, real or imaginary, of immediate death.

> Lovest thou me?
> Thou knowest! Not my father, Lord not he,
> O Lord, O Love. What, call him hence,
> The tender soul I know, to Thee?
> But the revered body to the awe immense?
> He loved us so.
> He was so high, so good to us below.
> He taught us children. Ah my sweet!
> He watched us learn, and watched us grow –
> That honourable head 'neath our bereaved feet![2]

And another poem, 'In Autumn', later to be printed, with considerable revisions, in *Preludes*, indicates the sorrows that continued to beset the heart of this young girl, though she was nowhere more explicit as to the particular cause of her sadness during the autumn days in Sussex when she was writing this poem.

> The low winds moan for the dead sweet years,
> The birds sing all for pain,
> Of a common thing, to weary ears,
> Only a summer's fate of rain,
> And a woman's fate of tears.
>
> What crowds of dead and dying things,
> Poor things, your sad decay
> Will give new life to other springs
> When other leaves will blow their day,
> And other loves spread wings.
>
> I know his heart has beat to bright
> Sweet loves gone by.
> I know the leaves that die tonight
> Once budded to the sky,
> And I shall die to his delight.
>
> O, tell me, tell me, ere ye die,
> Is it worth while?
> Are life and love so heavenly –
> (His heavenly smile!)
> Do ye repent now where ye lie?[3]

Plainly, her increased intellectual activity had not yet succeeded in banishing a certain morbidity from her thoughts, and her poems at this time mostly fulfil her own prophecy that whatever she wrote would be 'melancholy and self-conscious'. That thoughts of death were then constantly with her she tells us in a poem written many years later which looks back to that time.

THE UNEXPECTED PERIL

> Unlike the youth that all men say
>   They prize – youth of abounding blood,
> In love with the sufficient day,
>   And gay in growth, and strong in bud;

Unlike was mine! then my first slumber
   Nightly rehearsed my last; each breath
Knew itself one of the unknown number,
   But Life was urgent with me as Death.

My shroud was in the flocks; the hill
   Within its quarry locked my stone;
My bier grew in the woods; and still
   Life spurred me where I paused alone.

'Begin!' Life called. Again her shout,
   'Make haste while it is called to-day!'
Her exhortations plucked me out,
   Hunted me, turned me, held me at bay.

But if my youth is thus hard pressed
   (I thought) what of a later year?
If the end so threats this tender breast
   What of the days when it draws near?

Draws near, and little done? Yet lo,
   Dread has foreborne, and haste lies by.
I was beleaguered; now the foe
   Has raised the siege, I know not why.

I see them troop away; I ask
   Were they in sooth mine enemies –
Terror, the doubt, the lash, the task?
   What heart has my new housemate, Ease?

How am I left, at last, alive,
   To make a stranger of a tear?
What did I do one day to drive
   From me the vigilant angel, Fear?

The diligent angel, Labour? Ay,
   The inexorable angel, Pain?
Menace me, lest indeed I die,
   Sloth! Turn; crush, teach me fear again!

In October Christiana went on a visit to Hastings and Eastbourne,
leaving the two girls with their father at Arundel. As usual, there were
no settled plans for the future; but there was some talk at that time of
the Thompsons planting themselves permanently in Sussex. Mimi was

now working seriously at her painting, and it was desirable that they should be somewhere where study would be possible for her.

For Alice, the nearness of a church was a consideration that influenced her approval or otherwise of their projected dwellings at this time, and if the services were 'low' she did not favour it. Writing to her mother at Hastings she asked: 'So there's a high-looking Church? How high, I wonder; for there is none mentioned in the Church Times as having daily services, which would be a pity if we regularly settled there.' At the end of her letter she said: 'I am just going out to buy some marmalade, as Papa found our teas not over-sumptuous.'[4]

Mrs Thompson's reply announced the date of her return, and reported on the level of churchmanship of the Hastings incumbent: 'My precious little 'un, Was I not pleased to find thy letter (tho' hard to decipher) the 2nd time I went to the post this morn? Thou, and all of you, seem a hundred miles away at the least – I long to see you all and hope to do so on Friday eve. I shall write at what time to have tea ready . . . I cannot say, pretty babe, if the clergyman of the new church at H[astings] has yet arrived at the very last stage of development (according to Lucy) viz. a cope – but the church appeared arranged in high church style – and certainly very beautiful. There was no service going on when we looked in. Hastings alas! pales and hides its distinguished head beside Eastbourne – but I am rather glad to hear it (the latter) is deserted in the winter on account of the cold . . . Please pretty darling order a jolly dinner for Saturday – say, sirloin of beef and a pie of fowls – alias chicken pie.'[5]

For whatever reason, Hastings was rejected as a place of residence; and in January the family were at Sumner Terrace, Onslow Square, South Kensington, with Alice engaged in more earnest reading and note-taking: this time from Lewis's *Aristotle*. In the spring the two girls were at Pangbourne, and Alice reported to her mother on the chances of finding lodgings that would suit them all.

This place is really most lovely . . . and Mimi would like to stay but I fear the trains would disturb you very much. I tried the back room last night, and I don't think there is much difference. There don't seem to be any other lodgings, except a very small one close to the churchyard – far too tiny I should think. This must be the loveliest place in England. Such arts in the river in the evening. Such skies we have had too, and most lovely fields all about. There are two artists here who are sketching all day, each with a velvet coat and a white umbrella . . . Of course I will stay with pleasure if you decide that we had better keep this on, only I *should* like to be in Town at Whitsuntide. At one church here I am told they only have services in Lent – curious.[6]

There is a note of urgency in the postscript to this letter: 'Mimi wants boots awfully and would be much obliged for a P.O. for some.'

Back again to London for a short time, and then Alice departed for

Sussex with her mother, to look for a house in the country with a farm
nearby where Mimi could paint horses. Her chosen subject was battle
pictures, and knowledge of equine anatomy was essential for depicting
cavalry charges. She was now studying at the South Kensington School
of Art, and her long, enthusiastic letters were full of accounts of the
pictures she was painting, the criticisms she had received, and the competitions among the students. Evidently she found it difficult to con-
vince her mother that her studies would progress better if she stayed in
South Kensington than if she joined the family in their trek from one
lodging to another. Mrs Thompson had been creating 'blessed arts'
through twenty years of perpetual motion, and could see no reason
why her daughter should not do the same.

My dear little Shlei* [*Mimi wrote*]
    . . . I never thought when I *half* promised to come down on the condition
that a farm was found, that it would be so soon. You don't say how long you
would take the house for. Why not, if it suits, take it at least for two months,
and I would come down the month after next, as the summer, let us hope, will
then be fairly come and I shall be able to sit and paint out of doors. You know,
Shlei, that if I am to study I must not run about hither and thither and take
snatches of study instead of keeping on regularly. But of course if I find horses
to paint in the country I shall not get musty. I think really it will be better, all
things considered, for me to remain here yet a month and by that time you will
have found out the advantage of the Arundel place and what farms I could go
to etc. so that no *precious precious* time would be lost.[7]

Where they finally went to in Sussex, or whether they went at all, is
not recorded. Nothing had been settled when Alice wrote, some weeks
later, expressing, rather hurriedly, the hope that the 'Garibaldi'**
which she had just despatched, with other things, in a 'bloated parcel'
to her grandmother, would not arrive squashed.[8]

But they were in London through the winter, and it was during that
time that they received their first visit from Ruskin, of whom Alice said
afterwards: 'He is very solemn and weighed down by the sadness of life.
What strikes me about him is that he has no society manner, and never
says light words: not like one who is not used to be among men, but
like one who has taken life and men deeply to heart.'[9]

A short time before, Ruskin had been shown one of Alice's early
poems by a friend of the family, and had crushingly remarked: 'It is
very pretty and may be helpful to many'; but during the evening he
spent with the Thompsons Ruskin – who was one day to praise her
work as 'the finest things I've seen or felt in modern verse' – was less
discouraging, and showed at any rate a kindly interest in her ambitions.

---

*　　Their mother had a variety of nicknames, but was most often Shlei or Slocum.
**　　The name given to red blouses, then fashionable.

He was shown Mimi's drawings, and listened to Mrs Thompson playing the piano, and Alice singing 'Ave Maria'.[10]

Ruskin was among the first people to see Alice's poems, for until that year she had kept them secret from everyone, even her parents. Then she had shown them to an American friend of the family, who had read them to Mr Thompson, and 'from that day', she wrote, 'I had all the sympathy and interest of my father and mother.'[11]

Alice's health was now causing her parents anxiety, and although the letters which speak of it are undated it would seem to be then that she had to suffer the unpleasant business of having a number of teeth removed. Whether this was done in the belief that the teeth were causing her poor health and low spirits, or whether her condition was itself in part due to the shock of this drastic measure, we do not know; but evidently the number of extractions was such as to necessitate false teeth, which to a young girl must have been a most distressing thing.

There are two letters of the time from her father to her mother. 'Keep poor Alice's spirits up if you can', he wrote. 'She will feel mortified, even humiliated, for some time to come, but time will soften it much. Poor dear child, I fancy these things are done now to perfection and that she has nothing to fear as regards appearances. Of course our chief concern ought reasonably to have been when the malady first showed itself for there could be no doubt what the result must be, sooner or later. It is very sad, poor child.'[12]

Later he wrote: 'I do trust poor dear Alice's mouth will be healed before the time suggested – two months! Good gracious! We must believe that what has been done is for the best – it would be too sad a thought to entertain the slightest doubt in the present. Let us hope that the poor child has been saved much future annoyance . . . But it would have been a greater drawback to her to have kept a continuously deteriorating set of teeth. Poor dear thing! It is altogether very sad to think of it. But I don't doubt she will become reconciled to the inevitable necessity before very long.'[13]

In the spring of 1868 her mother took Alice to Malvern, hoping that the change of air and scenery would invigorate her. It was while she was there that Alice became a Catholic. Her parents had, it seems, no idea of the momentous step she was contemplating; characteristically, she was silent about what was going on in her mind, and she faced the problem and made the decision alone. How long that decision took her we do not know; but we have her own word for it that it was reached slowly and not by any sudden impulse. As to whether she found the step hard or easy, she gave no sign; but perhaps her melancholy and her poor health during the preceding winter were aggravated by anxiety in this matter. Later she was to write, concerning her spiritual journey to Catholicism:

In quite early childhood I lived upon Wordsworth. I don't know that I particularly enjoyed him, but he was put into my hands, and to me Wordsworth's poetry was the normal poetry *par excellence*. When I was about twelve I fell in love with Tennyson, and cared for nothing else until, at fifteen, I discovered Keats and then Shelley. With Keats I celebrated a kind of wedding. The influence of Shelley upon me belongs rather to my spiritual than my mental history. I thought the whole world was changed for me thenceforth. It was by no sudden counter-revolution, but slowly and gradually that I returned to the hard old common path of submission and self-discipline which soon brought me to the gates of the Catholic Church.[14]

'I saw when I was very young', she wrote many years later to one of her daughters, 'that a guide in morals was even more necessary than a guide in faith. It was for this I joined the Church. Other Christian societies may legislate, but the Church administers legislation. Thus she is practically indispensable. I may say that I hold the administration of morals to be of such vital importance that for its sake I accepted, and now accept, dogma in matters of faith – to the last letter.'[15]

That early discovery of the need for discipline grew out of an early awareness of evil, a very real sense of sin, and a clear perception of her own nature. In her later life there were those who called Alice Meynell a cold woman, all brain and no feelings, but to think of her thus is to misunderstand her utterly. Her passionate nature and the violence of her emotions frightened her, and she had no confident feelings of strength – only the realisation that somehow she must find a way to shape that nature to what she believed was its ultimate destiny. She chose discipline and control, exercised over her by the Catholic Church, and by her over body and brain; this was henceforward the keynote of her whole life. It was ever afterwards implicit in all that she said and did and wrote.

She saw no kind of bondage in her unconditional surrender to the Church as the arbiter of dogma and moral law. Many years later, in a speech concerning the emancipation of women, she expressed her philosophy in a single sentence. She would like, she said, to see the Statue of Liberty in New York harbour renamed, for it is not so much liberty as voluntary obedience that is the antithesis of slavery, and gives the truest freedom.

This submission, this voluntary obedience, was for her not a fettering but a setting free; and again and again in her prose and in her verse she gave expression to her conviction that the only true freedom is that which lies on the further side of law, and can be reached by no other path. She spoke of

the rooted liberty of flowers in breeze,

and towards the end of her life she wrote in a notebook: 'The most beautiful garden, once trim, then given to liberty. So the mind, keeping within laws and breaking into unlooked for wild flowers, within the walls and boundaries once decreed, under a resplendent sun, full of surprises.'[16] The thing is most perfectly said in 'The Laws of Verse'; and if this poem be taken to mean more than merely literary rules, it may be said to explain her life more clearly than anything she ever wrote.

> Dear laws, come to my breast!
> Take all my frame, and make your close arms meet
> Around me; and so ruled, so warmed, so pressed,
> I breathe, aware; I feel my wild heart beat.
>
> Dear laws, be wings to me!
> The feather merely floats. Oh, be it heard
> Through weight of life – the skylark's gravity –
> That I am not a feather, but a bird.

In a notebook she wrote soon after her conversion: 'I received the Church so that whatever she should unfold with time she should unfold it there where I had enclosed her – in my heart. The Evolutionary Doctrine "Sic est regnum Dei quemadmodum si homo jaciat sementem in terram"* etc. of the Church in our hearts. Those to whom this does not happen ought to fear that the Kingdom of God is not in them.'[17]

And to an American friend who had written to her about conversion she said this, almost thirty years after she herself had been received into the Church: 'I quite understand your impatience of controversial books. I have always disliked them as much as you do. The only thing that decided me was the sense that I was out of communion with the living Church – the Body of Christ – while I was not a Catholic. Once I realized this the doctrines came as a matter of course.'[18]

She was prepared for her reception into the Church by Father Dignam, a young Jesuit priest then at Worcester; and by him she was received on 20th July, 1868 at St George's, Worcester. Of that day, and of the commitment that she thus made of her whole life, she wrote in 'The Young Neophyte':

> Who knows what days I answer for today?
>   Giving the bud I give the flower. I bow
> This yet unfaded and a faded brow;
> Bending these knees and feeble knees, I pray.
> Thoughts yet unripe in me I bend one way,
>   Give one repose to pain I know not now,
>   One check to joy that comes, I guess not how.
> I dedicate my fields when Spring is grey.

---

* 'So is the Kingdom of God, as if a man should cast seed into the ground . . .' (Mark iv, 26)

O rash! (I smile) to pledge my hidden wheat.
   I fold to-day at altars far apart
Hands trembling with what toils? In their retreat
   I seal my love to-be, my folded art.
I light the tapers at my head and feet,
   And lay the crucifix on this silent heart.

CHAPTER 6

A FEW LETTERS of the Thompson family survive from that summer of 1868, chiefly those written by Mr Thompson and Mimi to the absent ones at Malvern. Father and daughter were both preoccupied, the latter with her painting, the former with money troubles; but both expressed in every letter their anxiety about Alice. In May Mr Thompson wrote to his wife: 'I am greatly distressed to hear such bad accounts of Alice. Of course an ample trial must be given to the air and water of Malvern. I can't believe but that they must prove beneficial. We will see.'[1] And a few weeks later Mimi was writing: 'I have fixed to come to you on Monday . . . I hope I shall be able to cheer up Alice a little. How miserable it must be for you to see her in that deplorable state. I feel certain that Italy is the only place for her.'[2]

Mr Thompson was packing up the house in South Kensington which they had had since the previous autumn, so as to let it in the hope of making a little money. One of those mysterious financial crises that were scattered so thickly through his life was upon him, but this one was of a more alarming nature than usual, and he was taking drastic action. 'I deposited Plate this morning with an Uncle of mine', he informed his wife; adding sadly, 'Alas! I don't know how it is, but I do think that money in my hands is doomed – has some property of melting away. However we must hit upon some means of counteracting this tendency.'[3]

At the end of July, harassed by a butcher's bill and faced with the necessity of making plans for the future, he sent another cry of distress: 'I am much cut up at the prospect before us – to recommence the old hugger-mugger and knocking about at my age will not be pleasant. And the change in the whole scale of our expenses will make itself felt very disagreeably, I fear . . . Poor dear Alice! I thought she was at all events looking better and more cheerful. It is a disappointment to hear that she is neither.'[4]

Mimi, who was staying with her grandmother in Fulham, wrote that she was concerned to hear that Alice was living on a vegetarian diet, 'she who requires all the nourishment she can get'. The diet may have been recommended by the doctor, but it seems more likely that Alice had been persuaded to take to it by Mr and Mrs Nicholls, the strange and rather bogus pair under whose guidance the two girls had lived on grapes and sour milk at the watering-place on the Rhine some years before, and who had now turned up at Malvern.

Christiana wrote to report that Alice had been riding a donkey, and

Mimi told one of her friends who wrote back to say that she was 'so amused at the idea of that splendid creature on a donkey. She said it was surely an impossible combination'.[5]

While the posts between Malvern and London carried these anxious questions and answers about Alice's health and spirits, she had made a friend with whom she was able to share her ideas and talk of her ambitions as she had never done before. This was Father Dignam, the priest who had received her into the Catholic Church. It is possible that they had met before Alice went to him at Worcester for her instruction, but if so their acquaintance can only have been of the slightest; it seems more likely that they met as strangers. Father Dignam was a highly intelligent and cultured man who loved poetry, had read widely, was interested in architecture and music, and had a good voice.* To him she showed her poems, and he helped her with encouragement and perceptive criticism, urging her to write also in prose, and expressing great faith in her future as a writer. He was then thirty-five, and, judging from a portrait of about that time, a strikingly handsome man. The friendship, with so much understanding, so many interests shared, gave them both happiness for a time; but it grew, on her side at least, beyond the bounds of friendship and thus brought Alice the sharpest sorrow of her young life. No love could have been more hopeless, no vision of happiness more surely unattainable. A month after her conditional baptism in the Catholic Church Alice left Malvern for London; in October the whole family departed for Italy, not to return for almost two years. During that time she and Father Dignam corresponded intermittently, writing about her work, about books and theology; after her return to England the inevitable and complete break came. Father Dignam, having asked leave to go abroad, was given an appointment in Boulogne, and they wrote no more.[6]

This love and the suffering that was inherent in it were not, for Alice, sterile; perhaps no experience that deeply touches the heart is that. Out of this painful period of her life there came the first of her really fine poems. She sought to relieve her anguish by expression, and scorned to allow that expression to fall below the best that she could do. The sonnet 'Renouncement' which she wrote at this time has been more often quoted than any of her others. But another poem also was inspired by the separation from her Jesuit friend.

AFTER A PARTING

Farewell has long been said; I have forgone thee;
    I never name thee even.

---

* Augustus Dignam, b. 1833, entered the Society of Jesus 1856. Well known as a retreat conductor and spiritual director, he was editor of the *Messenger of the Sacred Heart* and director of the Apostleship of Prayer, and was the author of several books.

But how shall I learn virtues and yet shun thee?
　For thou art so near Heaven
That Heavenward meditations pause upon thee.

Thou dost beset the path to every shrine;
　My trembling thoughts discern
Thy goodness in the good for which I pine;
　And, if I turn from but one sin, I turn
Unto a smile of thine.

How shall I thrust thee apart
　Since all my growth tends to thee night and day –
To thee faith, hope, and art?
　Swift are the currents setting all one way;
They draw my life, my life, out of my heart.

At the time of this separation she wrote on a scrap of paper: 'I am parted from thee without any hope of earthly reunion. But only by this obedience, this abnegation, can I keep a clinging, distant, endless hold of thee. I cannot altogether lose thee when I have the strength to renounce thee. But if I committed the sin of claiming thee, then indeed my loss of thee would be eternal and irrevocable. Thou, innocent, saintly and pure, if I fled to thine open arms I should be parted for ever from thee, thou opposite of sins. And a kiss would divide us as neither lands nor seas can ever do.'[7]

Back at Albaro that autumn the Thompsons renewed old friendships, called on new acquaintances, went to musical parties, played cards and tombola, and tried, without success, to interest their neighbours in charades. Of one of these neighbours, a retired General, Alice afterwards wrote this description:

One terrace, far up, with its lemon trees in pots, bore the heavy form of the General, playing dominoes with a neighbouring proprietor . . . He was a patriot, and took some interest in the contemporary history of the incomparable country on his right hand and on his left. He had his face to the south; he even made a vessel out now and then with a telescope as she held on her way to the countries that centuries ago had mingled Arabic, Portuguese, and French with the speech of the country people.

Gioconda, his wife, had her back to everything. Her rooms were so high that she might have looked down upon the dominoes far below had she looked out at all. Her back was turned to the sea and the south, to the ships, to the islands and Africa; and she looked neither to the folded mountains to the right and the marble peaks beyond, where the sun rose, nor to the long range of promontaries to the left, where he set. She looked neither at the glittering day when the land-wind blew, nor at the soft day of sea-wind, sea-grey, sea-green, and cloudy sea-blue. Gioconda sat with her back to the window with its partly closed shutters . . . and worked all day with beads.[8]

Mimi set up a studio and went on with her painting, while Alice filled her notebooks with poems. Often she wrote down the central idea in prose first, then odd lines, then a whole rough draft of the poem, which she would work upon and polish until she was satisfied that she could make it no better. Her critical faculty had developed fast, and she was now much more aware of the strengths and weaknesses of her talent. She was feeling her way towards that wonderful spareness that was the beauty of her later poetry, cutting and shaping, and striving for economy of words and compactness of thought. She felt deeply the glory, the anguish, and the responsibility of her vocation. That November, at Albaro, she wrote 'Pygmalion: The Poet to his Poetry', in which she was thinking of the future flowering of her talent:

There is no body without its spirit or genius. – EMERSON

Thou art to live; I am watching thee.
I have laid my patient chisel away,
And watch thee somewhat wearily.
How do I know what the mouth will say?
How do I know what the eyes will be,

 – What must they be? For I suppose
The brows I made (white brows so blind),
The lovely eyelids that I chose,
Lending my hand to my inner mind,
One certain colour must enclose.

I know not what the voice will sing.
I only made the quiet breast,
And white throat with much labouring.
I only wrought and thought my best,
And lo, a new voice shall out-ring.

God knows, and knew it, fast locked in
By my own hand, who knew it not.
Have I not made the little chin,
This face and dear mouth, and begot
The voice that needs must tune within?

I am blind, I am deaf, who wrought them so,
Who loved them so. This growing one
Hath her own future there. Ah, woe!
I hardly guess what I have done.
More is gone from me than I know.

I claim the unguessed mysteries
Which make this cold white figure warm.
My life! Child, did I not devise
In dreams thy dreams, carving thy form
— Thy secrets, when I made thine eyes?

God knows. I chiselled each cold limb
With loyal pain. He has given my mind
Less light than my true hand; but dim
Is life. I wait all I shall find,
And all that I shall know, in Him.

In April they went to Florence, travelling by *vetturino* as far as La Spezia, and staying, on the way, at Sestri Levante.[9] Mimi wrote in her diary: 'There is no way of travelling like this, in an open carriage; it is so placid; there is no hurrying to catch trains and struggling in crowds, no waiting in dismal *salles d'attente*. And compare the entry into the towns by the high road and through the principal streets, perhaps through a city gate, the horse hoofs clattering and the whip cracking so merrily and the people standing about in groups watching us pass, to sneaking into a station, one of which is just like the other.'[10]

They stayed in a hotel on the Lungarno, and looked from their windows across the river to the dome of Santa Maria del Carmine and the tower of Santo Spirito, and, beyond them, the grey-blue hills topped by convent belfry and cypress tree. Later they moved to the Villa Lamporecchi, on the hillside overlooking Florence, and there they remained until the autumn, Mimi studying with Giuseppe Belucci, Alice reading, writing, and visiting churches and picture galleries.[11] Quite a number of the poems that were subsequently published in *Preludes* were written at this time, including the beautiful 'Builders of Ruins', in which she acknowledged the ability of the passing years to bestow the higher beauty upon the too perfect works of man. Two stanzas from towards the end of this long poem sum up her theme.

Our purpose is distinct and dear,
　　Though from our open eyes 'tis hidden.
Thou, Time to come, shalt make it clear,
　　Undoing our work; we are children chidden
With pity and smiles of many a year.

Who shall allot the praise, and guess
　　What part is yours and what is ours? —
O years that certainly will bless
　　Our flowers with fruits, our seeds with flowers,
With ruin all our perfectness.

In October they left Florence and went on to Rome, staying at Perugia on the way, and arriving in the Eternal City in darkness and pouring rain.[12] During the ensuing year, from their apartment at 56 Via Babuino, Alice visited Roman churches, climbed the Palatine Hill, watched the barb-racing in the Piazza del Popolo at Carnival time, made the Ascent of the Scala Sancta on her knees, saw the Colosseum by moonlight, and fell in love with the incomparable light of Roman skies. It was an exciting time to be in Rome, for it was the time of the Vatican Council, when the episcopate of the world gathered in larger numbers than ever before. A few extracts from the diary[13] that she kept during the spring of 1870 give the flavour of those days.

Ash Wednesday, March 2nd. To the Fratte for Mass at St Joseph's altar, cinders etc. Most divine day. Poor Papa had little operation performed on an eyelid, and could not go out. Mama, Mimi and I drove to S. Sabina on the Aventine which has been the station church* for Ash Wednesday ever since St Gregory the Great. . . . We saw – we women through a window – the orange tree planted by the hand of St Dominic. Father Burke** was there, getting leaves for ladies, but I had not the courage to ask. How fascinating was the glimpse of the sunny Convent garden with the sweet Dominicans walking studiously and the white silent Cloister. Oh, if I were only a monk!

Friday, March 4th. Lovely day. Mass at the Fratte. Then Papa, Mimi and I drove to S. Peter's to see the Holy Father visit some of the Altars for an Indulgence. We got near the Swiss Guard, and saw beautifully. The Pope [Pius IX] came first attired in a white garment with a train and a red thing on his shoulders. He visited first the B. Sacrament, then an altar in the part which is walled off for the Council, then S. Peter opposite to which we stood, then the Confession*** finally. He was followed by a large number of Cardinals, among them Card. Bonaparte****, strikingly handsome, with a perfect Bonaparte face, only a better head, and many bishops, who made the visits with him. The Holy Father looked well and stout, but pale and certainly infirm when one sees him walk . . .

Saturday 5th. To S. Andrea as usual. With Mama to the Miss Smiths' to practise glees. I forgot to mention that I accompanied Mama to their musical party on Thursday. I hardly knew myself in society again. The very fashions have completely changed since I mixed in the giddy throng. I wore a pale blue silk train and bodice with white chintz and tulle over – very pretty – red camellias. Mama's playing causes great enthusiasm. I sang with success and applause, in good voice and not nervous, 'Il Désir' and 'Take back the Heart'.

* Station church: The Roman churches at which, in early Christian times, the Pope celebrated Mass on the weekdays of Lent.

** Father Tom Burke, O.P., a famous Irish Dominican, who was sent from Rome while still a deacon to establish strict observance among the English Dominicans.

*** The high altar, over the tomb of St Peter.

**** Lucien, grandson of Napoleon's brother Lucien, Prince of Canino.

Sunday March 6th. To Holy Communion at the Gesù e Maria. Mass at midday at the Fratte. In the afternoon with Mama and Mimi to the Borghese gardens to pick flowers. Most delicious. A sweet, silent, grey day, sound going a long way, a sort of trance in the fields, purple with anemones and violets, half-dead fountains with their gnats, the air heavy with daisies. And one part was exactly like the Elysian fields, sombre and sweet and beautiful and breathless and lifeless. Here might walk the shades of the sad great Heathen whom Dante saw. In returning I went into S. Maria del Popolo and came in for Benediction. Then to the Gesù e Maria to Exposition and Benediction . . .

Tuesday March 8th. Mass at the Fratte . . . The delight of a letter from Father Dignam – short, he is so busy, but *very* sweet. He is drowned in Lenten work. He tells me to go on with my letters, as they are just what he wanted. My heart jumps up when I see his handwriting . . .

Wednesday March 9th. . . . Up early and to Mass at the Gesù e Maria. Home to breakfast, (I am not allowed to fast) cut my finger to the bone and rushed off to Miss Lloyds who had offered to take me to see the Hospital of S. Michele with the Franchis. Miss Elizabeth and I walked all the way there through a very dirty Trastevere, unpicturesque and dismal enough. This hospital is the great white one on the bank of the Tiber opposite the Aventine. It is an immense place, and struck me as altogether out of proportion to the number lodged there or the work done. Perhaps in a time of fever all the space may be required, however, for we must not forget that in Rome illnesses go by seasons. It is divided into two great halves having each its interior court filled with orange trees, and great loggia running round every storey, white, bright open and airy, all cheerfulness and sun. We went first to Monsignore's rooms, bare but elegant, where he received us with extreme courtesy and sent a man to show us everything. We . . . went down to the old men's refectory to see the poor *anziani* at their eleven o'clock dinner. (This hospital seems almost or entirely devoted to the care of old and incapable people and children.) . . . They looked sad old men, but what old men don't look sad in these places? I think it would be kinder and wiser to give out-door relief and let them live with a certain amount of woman-kind.

They then went with the Mother Superior and two Sisters through the women's part, the infirmaries, dormitories, and schoolrooms.

One old woman who had been there sixty years (what a life, what a life!) and had become stone blind from shock and fright in '48, bewailed aloud that she sat there day by day and year by year with nothing to do. Could she not spin or knit, we said. 'Spin or knit' she cried in scorn, 'I who did embroideries in gold and in white that was my passion! Yes, embroideries – work of the most costly and difficult. That *was* a pleasure. Not a candle shall the Madonna have from me – no, not a gold *moccoletto*. Why won't she cure me? The beautiful *recami* in gold.' 'Well, God wanted no more of the *recami*; have patience. *Così vuole Iddio*' said the Mother. But she would have her scold at the Madonna, showing, however, by her bright face and merry words that she was in heart really resigned . . .

Friday March 11th. . . . In the afternoon . . . I had 5 leeches which succeeded better than I wished. From about 3 p.m. when they came off until nearly morning the little holes they made ceased not to *couler*. I must have lost an enormous quantity. Garment after garment and cloth after cloth was soaked and sopping through and through. A sickening sight . . . And I was imprudent enough to go out in the evening to the Freemans' to practise glees with Mama . . .

Tuesday March 15th. In the afternoon Mama and I honoured with our presence a kettledrum at the Hodgsons'. I would have enjoyed it had we known more people, but is it not hateful to sit with females talking over one's head and past one's nose and through one's chignon with that polished ignoring of a stranger's presence which so well distinguishes and becomes the British female? For is there not a way—and does not a well-bred Italian or Frenchwoman well exhibit it – of shewing a polite consciousness of a strange lady's presence without a word or a direct look? The Hodgsons devoted themselves to us as much as they could and introduced a lady to us who introduced a Portuguese man with whom I got on very well – an intense Catholic. He asked to be allowed to call so I asked him to come to-morrow when we have a little reception. It was a pretty kettledrum, ornate with flowers and fragrant with nice tea and sweet with charming cakes. And the three shy Miss Hodgsons looked very nice in three violet silks making tea. Mama and I looked *most lovely*! That is a nice assertion. But really Mama did, and I looked my little best. But Rome in the sunshine and tramontana looked too glorious. Oh the golden golden lights, the azure shadows, themselves lights, the liquid sky serene with perfect beauty, the domes and campaniles sharp and distinct yet melting, visionary, light as air! . . .

Wed. March 16th. . . . In the evening we had our little reception – Mr Sidley, Conolly, Mann, Epico; my Portuguese, Don Antonio de Almeida, Miss Hardy. Practised our glees . . . Mama unwisely and rashly mentioned to Papa what she considered the admiration of the Portuguese for me at the Hodgsons', the consequence of which is that Papa has lost no opportunity of sneering at the little man in my hearing in the most exaggerated manner, which riles me. I can see as little cause for laughing at the poor man as for talk of 'admiration' . . .

Friday March 18th. I saw a very funny Council incident in the shape of a bishop sliding down a buttress of the Colosseum of a great elevation in a most undignified manner, after wall-flowers. I was a little scandalized – then pleased at such simplicity. You would not find a Spanish bishop doing that . . .

Sunday. Seven Dolours, * *April 3rd*. Holy Communion at the Gesù e Maria. After breakfast with Miss Lloyd and Walkers to S. Maria in Via, the little Church of the Servites where this feast was kept. It is a day of great devotion for me as I wear the scapular and practise that rosary. There was a Pontifical High Mass with execrable music.

* The Seven Sorrows of the Blessed Virgin Mary: a feast having its origin with the Order of the Servants of Mary (Servite Friars), and extended to the universal church by Benedict XIII in 1727.

In this year, 1870, Mimi had her first success with a picture, her *Magnificat*, in which her mother was the model for the Blessed Virgin. The picture was accepted for the Pope's International Exhibition.[14]

In the evenings at Via Babuino when there were no visitors Mr Thompson read Roman history to his daughters, and sometimes Joseph Severn, the friend who had watched at Keats's deathbed, would come and take tea with them.[15] For Alice it must have been a very moving experience to meet that old man and to hear him talk of the poet who had been dead fifty years and whose work she loved so passionately. She visited the grave of Keats, in the Protestant cemetery, and remembered how he had said as he was dying that he felt the flowers growing over him, as she recorded in her early poem 'On Keats's Grave', written in 1869, but not published during her lifetime.

.   .   .   .

> Down from the low hills with pines
> Into the fields at rest, the summer done,
> I went by pensive ways of tombs and vines
> To where the place I dream of is;
> And in a stretch of meditative sun
> Cloven by the dark flames of the cypresses
> Came to the small grave of my ended poet.
> — I had felt the wild things many a dreamy hour
> Pushing above him from beyond the sea,
> But when I saw it
> It chanced there was no flower;
> And that was, too, a silent time for me.[16]

In May 1870 the Thompsons left Rome and returned to England, travelling by Florence, Padua, Venice, Verona, the Tyrol, and Bavaria. There was much country that was new to the girls, and many things to be seen in Germany, but Rome still had them by the heart, and they could scarcely arouse enough interest to look.[17]

CHAPTER 7

IN LONDON the Thompsons settled down again in Sumner Terrace, Onslow Square, and Mimi went back to her art school. Except for a long summer visit to Henley, and a briefer one to Ventnor, there was no more travelling until the autumn of 1873 when Alice and Mimi (the latter also now a Catholic) went on a pilgrimage to Paray-le-Monial. It was the third centenary of the apparitions of the Blessed Virgin to St Margaret Mary Alacoque at that place.* They embarked in a special boat, crowded with pilgrims, at Newhaven, and had a rough crossing to Dieppe. From Paris, where they spent the night and were fleeced by their hotel, they went on by train; the crowd was so great that the sisters were separated and travelled in different carriages. Alice describes the journey and the pilgrimage in a letter that she wrote afterwards to a friend.[1]

I lighted on most interesting fellow pilgrims. An old priest, the wittiest man I have met in my life; a wild Irishman – a capital fellow, on whom his Reverence exercised his unequalled quiet satire perhaps too keenly; two young Englishmen, two other gentlemen, a lady and myself filled the compartment . . . Mimi and I are compelled to own that we women were entirely beaten by the men, especially the young men, in enthusiastic and untiring devotion. It is not too much to say that my whole view of life and of society is altered by what I have seen among the men on this pilgrimage. This day, however, although we performed the prescribed devotions – litanies, hymns, prayers for England, the whole Rosary, and an hour of silence for preparing for the sacraments – our priest made us very merry for the whole rest of the time. And, long as the journey was, we did not feel a moment of weariness . . . We were expected at Paray at 7 but it was at least 10.30 before the little unknown city all sprinkled with lights came into view. It was a mellow night of moon and stars and soft air. The whole population not only of the town but apparently of the countryside lined the roads to greet us, everyone carrying a lighted taper, and on the platform a Bishop in full canonicals, mitred, stood to receive us. England and France have met by many varying representatives in many varying scenes and times, but there was a meeting of the two countries which had an interest of its own. This was when a French and an English bishop ran into each other's arms, each trying to kneel first and to raise the other.

They went in procession up the hill to the basilica, where they were

---

* The revelations of St Margaret Mary were the initiatory cause of the modern devotions to the Sacred Heart of Jesus. The devotion was not officially recognised until 75 years after her death, but became one of the most popular manifestations of Roman Catholic piety.

given a blessing by the Bishop; afterwards they dispersed to billets in the town. The two girls had a room in the house of a shoemaker, where they lay down, having no night-clothes as their luggage was at the station. Alice was devoured by fleas and passed a miserable night without sleeping. In the morning she went out early to Mass, and afterwards attended a service at which the Bishop of Salford, Dr Herbert Vaughan (the future cardinal) was preaching. The sermon over, the pilgrims were marshalled again into processional order, with the Union Jack at their head, and defiled down the great nave. Alice's own words shall describe what followed.

As I went singing along between the dense lines of men and priests who were to fall in behind us ladies, one of these on my right struggled to the front, and my hand was taken, and Father Dignam's voice cried, 'Alice, my child, where are you lodging?' I lost all presence of mind, and remembered the woman's name too late for him to hear I fear, for I could not stop the procession; and that is all I saw or heard of my Father. It is like a dream and a painful memory.[2]

How she must have searched the faces of her fellow pilgrims that day and on the journey home, and how this agonising momentary meeting must have reawakened her sorrow! Of the ensuing night, when she lay awake with her thoughts, she says only, 'I did not sleep *at all*.'

They stayed in Paris for three days on the way home at a quiet little hotel near Nôtre Dame des Victoires, and Alice noted, after their return: 'I had no wheels until I got safe home, when I did not mind them.'[3] ('Wheels' was the name she gave to the particular kind of migraine headache to which she was subject all her life.)

The poems she was writing during the next few months show how deeply the pain of that incident at Paray-le-Monial had entered into her heart. In her notebook, following her usual practice, she wrote in prose the idea which later evolved into the poem 'The Visiting Sea': 'As the tide comes flooding the shore, so your love brims the near and outward places of my soul; but it washes places you know not and shall not know.'

'Thoughts in Separation', too, belongs to this time:

> We never meet; yet we meet day by day
>   Upon those hills of life, dim and immense –
> The good we love, and sleep, our innocence.
> O hills of life, high hills! And, higher than they,
> Our guardian spirits meet at prayer and play.
>   Beyond pain, joy, and hope, and long suspense,
>   Above the summits of our souls, far hence,
> An angel meets an angel on the way.

Beyond all good I ever believed of thee
   Or thou of me, these always love and live.
And though I fail of thy ideal of me,
My angel falls not short. They greet each other.
   Who knows, they may exchange the kiss we give,
Thou to thy crucifix, I to my mother.

She longed for counsel from someone whose critical judgement she could trust, and having made the acquaintance of the Irish poet and prose writer Aubrey de Vere, she wrote to him. This was the beginning of a correspondence in which, over the course of several years, de Vere gave her a good deal of advice and useful criticism.

Dear Mr de Vere,
   I am doing an unconventional thing in writing to you, but you will understand. I am in great need of some friendly guidance in the art I have chosen and loved for years and years, and I should value your criticism, I cannot tell you how much. Have you time, then, and inclination, to jot down the sincerest and strictest things you can say on my little book of lyrics? You shall tell me candidly if this is too great a bore, or if you have something better to do, and I shall not be mortified, believe me. Many things that you said at Lady Georgiana Fullerton's have opened my eyes to my own great ignorance and to the errors of taste and judgement which mar my work.
   I will wait for your yes or no before I send you the MS.
         Believe me,
          Faithfully Yours,
          Alice Thompson[4]

She also wrote to William Allingham, poet, and friend of Coventry Patmore. She had sent him some verses, hoping for publication in a magazine, but misunderstanding his connection with it; and he apparently supposed that she had sent them for his criticism, and wrote to inquire if this was the case. She answered that she would not have ventured to trouble him with her work for that reason. 'Nevertheless as you have it, and if you have time, cut it up. Praise does my art no good. But hard words about my "sickliness, want of tone, indefiniteness of expression" (indefiniteness of thought I won't admit) "jerkiness, subjectiveness" (you see I have had critics) and so on – produce corrections after the shock has passed off.'[5]

All her life she judged her own work without mercy, and desired that others should judge it only by the very highest standards. To be satisfied with what she knew was second rate seemed to her a betrayal of her art. 'Newman', she wrote in her notebook, 'can write verses unworthy of himself without a pang because he is a poet fifthly, sixthly, and seventhly in the order of his high vocations. It is far otherwise with me.'[6] If, however, at any point in her life, her religion and her art seemed to lay upon her conflicting duties, there was never any question

The Thompson sisters, Mimi (*left*) and Alice

Thomas Thompson, father of A.M.

about which would triumph. She would never, for any reason, write something less than her best; but she could always choose the other alternative: silence.

She deplored the excuses that were made in the name of art for those who ignored their duties as human beings. 'We may remember', she wrote, '(certainly not with pride) that all kinds of impunity if not immunity have been proposed by critics and biographers, and the world in general, for admired poets. The cruelties of one poet, the random licence of another, the treacheries of yet another, the breaking of bonds that left a fellow-creature broken – all this and more has been pardoned for the sake of a lyric; to the degradation, at any rate, of the pardoner.'[7]

Aubrey de Vere showed some of her work to Coventry Patmore, and he, who in a far, unimagined future was to give her what she called 'the greatest friendship of my life', wrote her a funny, stiff little note, which began: 'Dear Madam, If you publish your verses you will give me much pleasure in sending me a copy. The specimen Mr Aubrey de Vere showed me struck me as uncommonly good. It was not only good promise but good performance.'[8]

But before Alice's poems had begun, in print, to win her the renown of which she had dreamed in childhood, her sister, Mimi, achieved sudden and startling fame as a painter. In 1873 the Royal Academy had accepted a large oil painting by her of a battle scene, and now, in the following year, they took another painting of hers, *The Roll Call*. Its success was immediate. On 'Varnishing Day' she was questioned and congratulated by a number of celebrated people, and at the Private View the Prince of Wales expressed his desire to buy it. The picture had been commissioned by a Mr Galloway of Manchester, who at first refused to give it up; but the Queen, after ordering it to be brought to Buckingham Palace so that she could look at it, persuaded him to yield his right of purchase. The crowds before the picture were so great that a policeman had to stand there to control them; and the newspapers made much of the young female artist who had painted so terrible a scene of war.[9]

Social invitations, as well as numerous commissions for pictures, were the natural outcome of Mimi's sensational success, and many London hostesses, especially those in Catholic society, welcomed the two sisters to their houses: Lady Londonderry, Lady Herbert of Lea, and Lady Georgiana Fullerton* were among them. A letter from Lady

* Georgiana Charlotte Fullerton (1812-1885), novelist and philanthropist. Founder of the Poor Servants of the Mother of God; author of *Ellen Middleton, Grantley Manor, Too Strange not to be True,* and other popular novels. She enjoyed in her lifetime a considerable reputation for sanctity, and for a time after her death there was talk of her beatification.

Georgiana has survived in which she piously asks a priest to pray 'that Miss Thompson and her clever sister who wrote poetry might not be spoiled'.[10]

Spurred on, perhaps, by her sister's success, Alice at last resolved to seek a publisher for her poems. When he heard of her decision Aubrey de Vere wrote to tell her:

> I was very much interested at hearing you had made up your mind on the subject of publication. There is much to be said for and against very early publication. I believe that when we discussed the subject I was rather on the side of waiting a little. But if you have determined the other way it may turn out for the best. A young poet is somewhat the slave of what he has written so long as it remains in his desk. When it is once published he feels more free, as it were, to strike out [in] any new style or to modify his earliest one in any way that may seem best.[11]

The book was published in 1875 by H. S. King, under the title of *Preludes*, and was illustrated with drawings by Mimi. Alice Meynell said many years afterwards: 'My first book of verse was accepted by a publisher only because my elder sister, who had just made a great reputation as a battle-painter, was kind enough to illustrate it.'[12] Perhaps the publisher had enough discernment to value the work of the younger sister as well as the elder; but in later life she would never allow that there was much merit in that little volume. Viola Meynell says of the poems in *Preludes*:

> Hardly without a feeling of treachery can a member of her family pronounce their achievement already fine, so thorough was her own repudiation of them later, so gladly did she make any convert to her own view. For in maturity she liked in her own work only that which had more compact thought in it; her mind used itself later on harder thoughts in her poetry, as it had always been apt to do in her prose; and to please her in those later years praise had to have a very recent date.[13]

Nevertheless, praise was bestowed upon those poems by Tennyson, by Patmore, by Aubrey de Vere, and Sir Henry Taylor;* and Ruskin, writing to Mrs Thompson, said: 'I really think the last verse of that song ("A Letter from a Girl to her own Old Age") and the whole of San Lorenzo and the end of the daisy sonnet the finest things I've seen or felt in modern verse.'[14]

The book contained some forty poems, the greater number of which had been written between 1870 and 1875. It is true that they lack the 'compact thought' of her later work, but they show how her talent was developing in that direction, how she was all the time achieving greater

---

* Henry Taylor: 1800-1886. Friend of Southey and Wordsworth. His tragedy *Isaac Comnenus*, 1828, was a failure; his *Philip van Artevelde*, 1834, was a great success in book form, but a disaster on the stage.

economy of words, greater discipline in her use of language, leaner and sparer flesh upon the bones of her thought. These early poems differ from all that came afterwards in being much more personal; they reflect her life, her heart can here be seen, and it was never so again; her later poems were more intellectual than emotional, born of an idea rather than a feeling.

There are some images of extraordinary felicity, as, for example, in 'Spring on the Alban Hills', where she describes the distant view from the Campagna:

> Rome in the ages, dimmed with all her towers,
> Floats in the midst, a little cloud at tether.

There is the beautiful 'Advent Meditation':

> *Rorate coeli desuper, et nubes pluant Justum.*
> *Aperiatur terra, et germinet Salvatorem.*
>
> No sudden thing of glory and fear
> Was the Lord's coming; but the dear
>   Slow Nature's days followed each other
>   To form the Saviour from His Mother
> — One of the children of the year.
>
> The earth, the rain, received the trust,
> — The sun and dews, to frame the Just.
>   He drew His daily life from these,
>   According to His own decrees
> Who makes man from the fertile dust.
>
> Sweet summer and the winter wild,
> These brought him forth, the Undefiled.
>   The happy Springs renewed again
>   His daily bread, the growing grain,
> The food and raiment of the Child.

And, finest flower of this early bunch, 'Regrets', in which she uses the image of the ebbing tide as she used that of the flowing one in 'The Visiting Sea'.

REGRETS

> As, when the seaward ebbing tide doth pour
>   Out by the low sand spaces,
> The parting waves slip back to clasp the shore
>   With lingering embraces, —

So in the tide of life that carries me
    From where thy true heart dwells,
Waves of my thoughts and memories turn to thee
    With lessening farewells;

Waving of hands; dreams, when the day forgets;
    A care half lost in cares;
The saddest of my verses; dim regrets;
    Thy name among my prayers.

I would the day might come, so waited for,
    So patiently besought,
When I, returning, should fill up once more
    Thy desolated thought;

And fill thy loneliness that lies apart
    In still, persistent pain.
Shall I content thee, O thou broken heart,
    As the tide comes again,

And brims the little sea-shore lakes, and sets
    Seaweeds afloat, and fills
The silent pools, rivers and rivulets
    Among the inland hills?

In the summer of 1875 the Thompsons went to Italy, where they visited Alice and Mimi's half-sister, Fanny, at Genoa, and stayed with Mr and Mrs Ross at the Villa Castagnolo, Lastra a Signa, between Florence and Pisa. Great celebrations were being held that year in Florence in honour of Michelangelo; these they attended, watching the procession which went from Santa Croce across the Ponte alle Grazie and up to the hill of San Miniato, where the wide square, with its magnificent view over Florence, had lately been completed and named the Piazzale Michelangelo.[15]

Back in England the following summer, the two sisters were summoned to visit Tennyson at his house near Haslemere, and Alice was reproved by him for omitting to send him a copy of her book, although other poets, as he said, 'made his life a burden with their sendings'. The conversation did not flow easily, and when Alice asked him to read 'The Passing of Arthur' it proved to be the wrong choice, since he thought it less good than some of his later works. However, he did read it, in a broad accent which his hearers at first thought to be affectation, but later discovered to be that of his native Lincolnshire.[16]

Alice was now doing a little journalism, writing occasional book reviews for *The Tablet*, and also visiting, and writing notices on, some of the art exhibitions. A letter from the editor of this paper, dated 11th April, 1876, says: 'There is nothing whatever to alter in "Daniel". There is very seldom likely to be anything requiring change in what you write, but if there should be you may reckon on my telling you at once.'[17]

Among the reviews of *Preludes* had been one in the *Pall Mall Gazette*, quoting the sonnet 'The Garden'. This review was read by a young man called Wilfrid Meynell, who was working as a journalist while living with Father William Lockhart,* the rector of the Fathers of Charity, at St Etheldreda's, in Ely Place, Holborn. Meynell, then twenty-five years old, had been born in Newcastle, the son of a colliery owner, and the seventh of eight children. His family were Quakers, but when he was eighteen he became a Catholic, and soon afterwards came to London, determined to make a living in journalism; there, with other young men who had no home in the city, he lived in St Etheldreda's clergy house, helped with the work in the parish, and wrote for the magazine which Father Lockhart edited, as well as contributing to other papers and periodicals.[18]

The sonnet by the young poet Alice Thompson so impressed Meynell that he said to Father Lockhart, 'That is the only woman I should want to marry.'[19] Father Lockhart already knew Mrs Thompson, and promised the young man that he would take him to one of her Wednesday afternoon 'At Homes'; but he was slow to fulfil his promise, and in the meantime Wilfrid Meynell wrote to ask Alice if she would care to contribute some verses to Father Lockhart's magazine, *The Lamp*, and to the *Irish Monthly*. She answered, and he wrote again, apparently mentioning his hope of coming with Father Lockhart to the Thompson home.[20] To this she replied on 11th April, 1876:

Dear Mr Meynell,

I never see the *Irish Monthly*, so if you can spare a copy containing your sonnet, I should very much like to read it.

Pray do not let your coming depend on Fr Lockhart's many engagements. Your review of *Preludes* gave my father and mother so much pleasure that you need no other introduction. We are always to be found on Wednesday from 4 to 7 o'c.

I forgot to ask you never to tell Mr de Vere that I had reviewed either his own or his father's works in the *Tablet*.

Believe me,
Faithfully yours,
Alice Thompson[21]

* William Lockhart: 1820-1892; a cousin of Sir Walter Scott's son-in-law and biographer. B.A. Exeter College, Oxford, 1842. Received into the Roman communion 1843, two years before his revered master J. H. Newman. Entered the Rosminian Order (the Institute of Charity) 1845.

He came, the visit was repeated, they corresponded; he sent her poems for criticism, and they wrote to each other about their work. In May she was sending him some autographs of her 'most valued correspondents': 'A signature of my dear Ruskin's, one of Sir Henry Taylor's, one of Coventry Patmore's, whose exquisite poetry I hope you know and love.'[22] A few days later, in answer to his question about one of her poems, she wrote: 'That line in "A Young Convert"* – I am always glad to be told *where* my obscurity lies. I mean that not only present actual things but all the secrets of the future are signed with the cross at the moment of baptism, and among those secrets are a love which is not yet in existence and an art which is not yet developed.'[23]

In July, after more visits from Meynell, she sent a criticism of some poems: 'I have said very frankly what I think of your poems but you must console yourself for the bluntness of my criticism by the perfect sincerity of my praise.'[24]

At the end of that summer Alice and Mimi went to Italy, staying, as they had done the previous year, with their half-sister Fanny at Genoa, with the Monty Browns at Porto Fino, and with Mrs Ross again at Villa Castagnolo. From Porto Fino Alice wrote to her mother:

My dearest little Mama,
  We have made enquiries here in the hope that something for you might turn up, but they tell us there are no houses of any kind whatever to be had in this direction. As to the Castle itself it is lifted out of the reach of outdoor noises and there seem to be few or no indoor noises except a clock which does not bother one at a certain distance. Today at dinner I shall begin to talk about the chance of your coming to Italy and I am sure that Monty will ask you here. I must say I long to see you with your paints in this place. You would not be in the least *gênée* by dear little Mrs Monty who is like a sweet little girl of twelve. As to the beauty – it is a relief to think you know the place, because *no* words can attempt to describe it. We are on a very steep high promontory looking over to the coast of Chiavari and Sestri on one side and over the open sea beating against magnificent rocks on the other, and the promontory makes one of the horns of the little landlocked harbour of Porto Fino; into this little village and into the depths of the pellucid and unspeakably blue sea we look almost straight down through precipices of aloe, vine and olive. The colour of the sea and of the mountains simply baffles description. How you would enjoy it, my Mama! In coming here we could not be persuaded to try the boat so we walked; it is by no means a long walk, with rests. Mimi has begun two panels. She particularly wished me to tell you that she is sleeping well again now, and I am sleeping better. The fact is one must fight shy of tea and coffee in this air . . .
  Dear little Fanny was loth to let us go even for a few days. I cannot recommend her house for quiet. The railway makes the deuce of a noise and there

* Subsequently renamed 'The Young Neophyte'.

are cocks, and Nino is an early riser. She has eight lanky cats who try to come in at the windows all night.

Thanks for the *Tablet*. An occasional graph would be welcome. I don't think we shall be able to tear ourselves away from Genoa on the fifteenth.

There is a beautiful Church in the village and the *festa* bells yesterday came up across the little bay too delightfully.

I assure you one forgets what colour is. I have seen this sea many times before, but it is really staggering. The depth here is immense, which adds to the colour. It has been too fresh just lately for bathing. I fear we shall not get any. I think we shall return to Genoa about Wednesday.

> Best love to Papa . . .
> Ever your affectionate
> Alice[25]

Another letter, from Lastra a Signa, described a day in Florence when she and Mimi had revisited some of the churches and picture galleries, and had called on Bellucci, with whom Mimi had studied seven years before. 'Mr Meynell', Alice said in this letter, 'sends me the *Academy* regularly and other literary papers now and then, but as to political news I have been until now quite in the dark. Mrs Ross takes the *Daily News*, however, and I was able to post myself up.'[26]

The days of that Tuscan autumn were happy and light-hearted. It was very hot, and the girls helped with the grape-picking, which began while they were there. In the evenings there were often young Italians dining at the villa; they were a merry company, singing songs with a guitar until past midnight. Alice had her photograph taken, and wrote to her mother: 'Everyone was so in love with my summer hat that they made me be taken in it.'

They left Italy still basking in golden weather, and arrived back in London on a foggy October night, bravely trying, in the hansom cab that bore them home from Victoria station, to keep up their spirits by singing Italian songs.[27]

CHAPTER 8

THAT WINTER, after her return from Italy, Alice was still seeking and receiving help from Aubrey de Vere. In a letter of November 1876 he wrote: 'You take suggestions as well as Henry Taylor does; but you must remember also the bargain that he and I have always made relatively to the suggestions of the other, viz. that the *Author* is always to retain a full confidence that he must really be the best judge; that a great reliance is to be placed on the *first* inspiration; that *suggestions* are to be regarded as *suggestions* only, not recommendations; and that, where the Author doubts, he should stand by what he has written . . . So pray never regard any suggestion of mine as offered with any great confidence on my part. When you have considered them you are much more likely than I to know whether they are good or bad.'[1]

The advice which she received she passed on to Wilfrid Meynell, who frequently asked her for her criticisms on his poems. 'Every really poetical idea', she wrote to him, 'has one certain shape and length which fits it, and no other. Aubrey de Vere is always hammering at this in all his frequent letters to me, and he is right. (He is not a strong poet, but he is an artist in these matters).'[2]

She sent him two of her own poems, one of them the sonnet 'Renouncement', which, either for literary or personal reasons, had not been included in *Preludes*. In the accompanying letter she mentioned Father Dignam, though not by name, as one who had greatly loved her poetry. 'I know that you will not care for them at the first reading. The greatest lover of my work used to say that he was obliged to read a piece of mine nine times. But I should be loath to inflict such a task on everyone. This sonnet . . . is the recasting of a lyric which I wrote about eight years ago.'[3]

The *Irish Monthly* published a poem by her, 'Singers to Come', and de Vere wrote to congratulate her on it. 'In imagination, sentiment, and in much of its diction, and many of its cadences, I think I like it *the most* of all the poems of yours which I have read. There are few of our modern poets who might not have been proud of writing it. And now – after all this laudation – comes the offensive part of my criticism . . . If you will only correct it carefully, chiefly in avoiding roughnesses which do not come to you by nature (so many parts are so musical) but by Browning, you will at least double the value of the poem.'[4]

At Christmas Wilfrid Meynell sent her a sonnet and a present of some very luscious soap, which seemed to them both a great extravagance. She wrote to him: 'Yes, indeed, Mr Meynell, I prize your gift and your sonnet most truly. Of all the dear presents and letters and greetings which have come to me in a heap this Christmas from the undeserved love of my friends, the unique gift of a Christmas sonnet so tender and so religious was the most welcome. God bless you always Alice.'[5]

Wilfrid Meynell's visits to the Thompson home (now in Tregunter Road, Earls Court) had become frequent, and he and Alice had exchanged photographs. On New Year's Day, 1877, they became engaged.

Meynell related many years afterwards that he would not have thought it proper to propose to her, their situations being somewhat different and he having no money; but she told him that it was unfair of him to come so often and make her so fond of him, and then not to ask her to marry him. At that point they embraced, and all was understood between them. 'So', his story always ended, 'I never proposed to her.'[6]

Father Lockhart wrote to her that same day:

My dear Child,

I will not let an hour pass without expressing my deep sympathy in all I have heard today. It has wholly taken me by surprise. It has however confirmed the opinion I had formed of you and your sister that you were unworldly and unspoiled by the praise of the world. You have determined to link your lot with one who is chivalrous in honour, tender in pity and love and who will be faithful to the end and true as steel in weal and woe. For him you have been willing to forgo a more brilliant but not, as I believe, a happier lot. My only anxiety is to know that you have your father's and mother's blessing.

> May God bless you both,
> Yours affectionately,
> W.L.[7]

She answered him the next day:

Dear Reverend Father,

Many thanks for your blessing. My future husband will, I am sure, make me a better woman than I have been hitherto.

With kindest regards and good wishes for the New Year.

Believe me, Dear Reverend Father,

> Respectfully and gratefully yours,
> Alice Thompson[8]

There was nothing of brilliance or glamour in the man she had chosen that could have affected Alice's choice. Wilfrid Meynell had very little money, an unimpressive social background, and no startling good looks, though he was a young man of pleasant enough appearance. He was intelligent, invariably kind and good-humoured, and was a perceptive critic of literature and art. Years afterwards she commented on the wisdom she had shown in choosing him deliberately as the man who would be not only the best husband for her, but also the best father for her children. She had for him a great affection, tenderness, and esteem; she recognised his extraordinary goodness, kindness, and simplicity of heart, and was won by these things. In the course of their engagement her letters show how she came to love him more every day.

Meynell, on his side, now and for the rest of his life, adored her with an unselfish devotion, and his pride in her work was untinged by any sense of invidious inequality through the years of her brilliant success and his own relative obscurity. Many years later, when he had published a book called *Aunt Sarah and the War*, he wrote to acknowledge a letter of appreciation about it which had suggested that his wife too had had a hand in it. 'You are quite right', he wrote, 'as to the dual authorship. For, though Alice did not see the book till it was in type, every word of it comes from the lessons I have learned from her and I hope that this is fully expressed in the lines of dedication.' He goes on to say: 'It was thirty-eight years ago yesterday that I put to her the question on which my fate depended, unconsciously taking advantage of her inability to say anything but "Yes" to any heart-felt request. But, looking back, I think that God has rewarded, in both our lives, that act of extraordinary magnanimity.'[9]

In a different way, Wilfrid Meynell had his own successes. That Francis Thompson's poems were ever given to the world was entirely due to him; and he helped to shape and guide the careers of others besides Thompson. The rôle he played was always outside the limelight – he suggested, advised, instructed – and he was satisfied that it should be so. For that reason his figure appears somewhat shadowy, and gives, perhaps, an impression of nebulousness. In fact, he was a man of very definite and strong character, of firm opinions and sound judgement. He was always master in his house, and his wife deferred to him in everything, even in literary matters; but the fact remains that they were both writers, she a great creative artist whose work would live, and he never more than a journalist. The inequality of talent and achievement might have come between them and wrecked their marriage, but it never even threatened to do so; and that it did not, though in a certain measure due to both of them, was perhaps more especially to the husband's credit.

Towards the end of his life Wilfrid Meynell wrote his own epitaph:

> When my last fires of life burn low
> (I who have loved all fire-light so)
> When hence you bear my load of dust
> To the grave's pit, as bear you must,
> Remember that naught perisheth

In all God's universe but Death.
Weep not, though tears be holy water,
Tears of a wife, a son, a daughter,
Think of me only when you laugh;
And if you write my epitaph,
No name or date be there, but rather
'Here lies her husband and their father.'[10]

There were difficulties to be overcome at the beginning of their engagement, for Mr Thompson thought Wilfrid Meynell's financial prospects too uncertain, and was opposed to the marriage. Alice's first letter, written before her father had been approached, radiated happiness and foresaw no troubles: 'You will be glad to hear that my sweet little Mama who returned yesterday consents to our engagement freely and happily. I don't think my father has been told yet, so that I cannot yet say whether we can have the proposed talk on Wednesday. I will tell you when I see you. You won't let me be talked to *all* the afternoon by Dr Hamilton and Mr Goode, will you?'[11]

Two days later she writes more seriously, on the subject of money, spoken of between them as 'soap', an allusion to the present that he had given her for Christmas. Father Lockhart, anxious to help the young couple, had offered Meynell the editorship of *The Lamp*, his own Catholic magazine, the salary for which would augment, though slightly, the small income which was all that Wilfrid could depend on.

My dearest Wilfrid,
Mme de la Croix talked to me a little this afternoon, and I am sorry to hear that the difficulties about 'soap' are so very serious. It is not a thing I like to talk to you about so I write instead. This project about *The Lamp* I certainly like, but you know this could only be one of other things. My father would never consent to my marriage with nothing to trust in but that. Don't be hurt or discouraged, will you? Trust my constancy; and think hard of some plan to make *some* kind of soap possible to us.

You say that you care more about letters than I do. Until we are married you *will* care a *little* more, it is true, and for about a year after; and then it will be I who care most, for all the rest of the time God leaves us together.

Take care of Father Lockhart's letter; it praises you and therefore it is much more precious to me than to you.
　　　Goodnight my Wilfrid,
　　　　　Ever your affectionate
　　　　　Alice[12]

That night there was a stormy interview with Mr Thompson, and next morning she wrote:

My father is calmer, he speaks of you with the esteem which you can never fail to win. Write him one of your own charming letters; let him see something of your heart. I *hope* you slept. Do spare yourself, for love of me. Yes, indeed I will write to you every day.

My love, your dear dear tears shed for my own past sorrow seemed to me the most exquisite thing ever dreamed of. I wish from my heart that I had never loved before; I will try to take courage one day and tell you what it really was; you will believe that I *intended* no wrong.[13]

The father still withheld his constent to the marriage unless Meynell could promise greater security, and he forbade Alice to enter upon an indefinite engagement. At twenty-nine, it may be thought that Alice was old enough to set aside her father's wish in this matter since her own mind was made up; but the year, let it be remembered, was 1876, when even the most rebellious of daughters would think it a grave thing to defy a father's ruling; and she was a dutiful daughter. The young man was in despair. Alice wrote to him at five o'clock on a winter's morning with tenderness and with anguish:

My Dearest,

I have been sitting up with my sister to keep her fire burning; that is why I am imitating you in my date; and I must write you this line before I go to bed for a short sleep. Be courageous, be hopeful for my sake, and pray, pray understand, my own Wilfrid, how it is that I am bound to refuse you my word for an indefinite engagement. It is simply that my father forbids it, and I am obliged, by my conscience and by my promise, to obey him. But I am yours with all my will, as you know, and I have been praying hard during this night that I may have the happiness of marrying you. If only I were worthy of you! That I am not has cost me tears tonight that came from my heart, and I so seldom cry. Let *that* be the one object of your prayers, that I may grow worthier of your love.[14]

The next day, she wrote to him:

Why are you so unhappy? It breaks my heart. I give you my word of honour to wait for a year if we cannot marry sooner. I would say more if I might. I gave a promise to Papa that I would not make an indefinite engagement, and I will be true to the letter of this promise, but not beyond.

If, she continued, at the end of a year there were even a remote prospect of their marrying, she could renew the promise.

Be full of hope; pray with me; but above all trust me. Do not again say the heart-piercing things which are in your last letter. They bathed me in tears last night and this morning, and tears are rare and difficult for me. I love you more every day . . . And I *will* make you a good wife. I am full of faults but grace and love will be stronger than these. At least I am very affectionate; this has been my temptation and danger hitherto, but now it will be my delight and duty.[15]

At last Alice's father relented, partly, it seems, thanks to the intercession of Father Lockhart on behalf of the young couple. On 8th January Alice wrote to Wilfrid:

Good morning my Love, I am afraid your breakfast table had no letter from me as I wrote too late. I left Father Lockhart to tell you about last night, and indeed I was not present at his interview with my father.

The *only* difficulty seems to be a financial one, and certainly if God wishes us to marry, that will come right. Only, dear Wilfrid, I would like to be your *young* bride. You are yourself in the flower of youth and I should wish to begin the dear life *à deux* in my own full flower.[16]*

Later the same day she wrote again to report the latest development.

My father will allow me a hundred and fifty pounds a year, I find. Poor dear Papa, he cannot do more, but it is so little that I shall have the happiness of depending on you almost entirely, you see. The lawyer is coming to make my will! I had intended to leave everything to the Holy Father, but the last few days have given me more sacred interests even than his . . . My father is better and calmer. He seemed to be almost angry with me in spite of the obedience which has cost me so much, and yesterday things were sad indeed. I had done what I thought just to both, and both my dear ones were in tears for me. But I think I have conquered my father by force of obedience and unchanged affection. He spoke to me kindly this morning, and the clouds are lifting.[17]

In the midst of these tears and troubles and hopes deferred there was no lessening of her concern for her art and his. 'As to your sweet verses' she wrote, 'the *directness* of the penultimate stanza is what I like about it. I don't like "iron" chain, nor do I like the running together of the first and second lines; but the ending of the stanza is charming.'[18]

Mrs Nicholls, wife of the eccentric dietician who had been friendly with the Thompsons for some years, now made some indiscreet remarks to Wilfrid, who asked Alice for an explanation. 'About what Mrs Nicholls told you [*she wrote*] of a very slight and passing fancy I had a year ago. The gentleman in question used to walk with me every day from Mass (besides writing nearly every day) and on the last occasion when I was on the point of leaving town he asked me to prolong the walk a little and began to enquire into the state of my heart, when I let him see *unmistakably* that the proposal which I supposed was coming would be of no use. You see how little seriousness there was in what I said to Mrs Nicholls. Afterwards, when my former admirer began to come to our house again, perfectly healed, I believed, and when Dr Nicholls made those severe comments on my behaviour, he was not really paying me attention.'[19]

Alice's letters through those weeks of their engagement are tender, gay, full of her new-found happiness and the joyful prospect of their life together. Daily – sometimes twice in a day – the post carried her

---

* Wilfrid was five years younger than Alice.

messages from Tregunter Road to Ely Place; a selection from them tells of that time without the necessity of any comment.[20]

January 11th, 1877. You make my mornings so happy with your letters. But do not again sit up to write. Wilfrid, I wish you would make one sacrifice for me, and that is the occasional sacrifice of your sacrifices. Mortify your desire for mortification now and then. And stay half-an-hour longer in bed when you do not feel quite well.

15th January. My Wilfrid, It would have been sweet to be at Mass with you this morning. Will you come another Sunday and go with me, or meet me there?

Do you know, I should like Father Russell to know that Aubrey de Vere liked *Future Poetry* so much and said that there were 'few living poets who might not be proud of having written it.' I know that Father Russell himself could not care for it in any way, and probably none of his readers did, so Mr de Vere's opinion would console him.

Papa has had a kind of relapse into displeasure as to our engagement. He sent for me last night to ask me to break it quite off, but I told him I am pledged for a year. You do not think much of that arrangement, I know, but believe me it is an anchor. What reply could I have made but that?

Dreadful London Sunday without love-letters!

January 16th. All your letters are sweet, but the one of this afternoon surpasses them all. You know that you are free to come tomorrow. Are you indeed afraid of loving me too much? That does not frighten me; but do as you think best.

January 17th. I cannot tell you how glad I am that your editor likes my little article! He praises it far more than it deserves, but as he pays magnificently in comparison with other papers I am delighted that he should be pleased in proportion.

Think hard of some other book for next week. Would it be too late to review Ashby-Story's *Boudoir Ballads?* They are already in their second edition. But if I review them I shall be obliged to be *rather* severe on them.

22nd January. It hurt me also to say goodbye last night. The relic is most precious. It was most dear of you to think of sending it to me. *What* supper, Wilfrid? There is a studied reticence about that 'I have had some supper' which excites my suspicions of buns and ginger beer.

Papa was very much impressed by your Macmillan success and sincerely pleased. But, dear Wilfrid, do not again tempt me to such a long tête-à-tête. Papa was a *little* angry – not with you but with me for it is always the lady who is held responsible. When I think of your cold and lonely room I cannot bear to send you from me.

Don't be very late tonight.

Could you not sometimes take me for a little walk? I have no one to walk with.

Goodbye, goodbye, goodbye. Until tonight.

       Your Alice who loves you

January 23rd. Read 'Love Among the Ruins' and 'At the Fireside'. I think they are among the loveliest things that Browning ever wrote. But Alfred Austin does not think that he is 'specifically a poet at all'!!! I don't think A.A. has the faintest spark of poetic appreciation. He can reason about poetry with dismal justice, but he cannot feel it any more than a man who has no ear can feel music however well he may understand counter-point.

January 24th. I think you might be better employed at five in the morning than in reading 'Atalanta' and even than in writing to me! No more hungry nights, Wilfrid, or I shall doubt that you *really* love me.
    Yours conditionally, Alice

In their search for ways of making money they had thought of starting a magazine. Mimi had offered to help by drawing for them, and Alice had optimistically suggested that they might have among their contributors Tennyson, Matthew Arnold, Browning, and Ruskin. But Alice's request to the last-named met with such discouragement that the project was killed off. 'Alas', she wrote to Wilfrid, 'I have a disappointment for you, poor boy. By this evening's post came a nasty crabbed crushing letter from Ruskin, putting an end to every shadow of a hope that he will write for us. He takes up the word "Review" which I used instead of "magazine" and harps upon it all through the letter. He is very glad I am engaged, but very sorry I am going to be a Reviewer as it is a profession impossible to follow with honour unless I were an *archangel* "and he will not go beyond angel even for me". He then adds that I ought to have guessed his feeling on the subject and ends by wishing me a happy marriage "and a better trade".'

2nd February. Poor Papa was so sleepless last night that I sat with him until 3 o'clock and read to him, then I had such cold cold toes that I could not sleep. I hope my Wilfrid rested better . . . I generally put aside my blind and look out towards Holborn to bid you goodnight.

3rd February. You do indeed give me 'proofs' and 'signs' also, and it was delicious to get three letters today.

5th February. No 'talk' has yet taken place but Mama told me that Papa had received a 'sweet little note' from Father Lockhart which seemed to touch him and which made her cry.

7th February. Be strong for me, my dear Love, and help me not to break my poor little rule again. I should need your pen to answer the letter you brought me. God bless you for it a thousand times.
 My Love, the sonnets speak your heart more perfectly than you know. Darling, darling sonnets that first showed me the poet's heart and then gradually the lover's. How can I love them enough?
 I want you very much to pray for me just now.

13th February [some occasion to which Alice attached importance loomed.]
Hat, over-coat, dark red cravat, and if I may enter into details, lighter trousers

coming well down at the back of the foot. Also, boots which *fit* and have not toes a quarter of a yard broad. Studs at the wrists (once or twice you had *no* buttons or studs at all; today I think you had ordinary shirt buttons). In fact, my pet, you must take your brother at his word, and send him *one* tailor's bill at least. It will please him I am sure.

15th February. I went to afternoon tea at another house where there was a gathering of very jolly young artists and we had some fun. Then I smoked a cigar with Lalla.* But if you don't like me to smoke I will give it up entirely.

17th February. This morning it occurred to me that I had made a stupid mistake in my notice, so I invaded the *Yorick*** office hoping to catch you there at twelve o'clock but you were not there, and Mr Darling was very much distressed that I should see the blackness of the staircase. I hope he was not really unhappy at my incursion, but I could not bear that my article should appear with the blunder. He was very nice to me . . .

Darling, new hat and cravat and boots and everything,
Your Alice

24th February. Dearest Wilfrid, I have no stamp, and it is too late to get one, so you will be obliged to pay twopence which is better than being sad.

24th March. The sixteenth be it! But Mama and Mimi are dead set against St Etheldreda's so I must decide for the Servites*** and I will write to Father Lockhart to ask him to marry us there. White dress, four bridesmaids and a limited family breakfast.

Remember to have an eye on brass fenders – two, for narrow fireplaces. If the *Architect* really pays 2 guineas a column, I shall receive from this and *Yorick* seventeen or eighteen guineas after these pictures. Could we not then buy those celestial curtains?

28th March. [She has been ill in bed and has struggled through her column reviewing French pictures for the *Architect*.] Papa has been *too* kind. He has hardly left me and it was touching to see how he stuck up my brass things in sight of the bed to amuse me.

Mr Thompson, now reconciled to the marriage which he had opposed so strongly, was once more close to his younger daughter and was showing by various small acts of kindness his regret for the strain that had been between them. On 29th March Alice wrote that he had been helping her with preparations in the little house that was going to be their home. She had decided that it would be better to stain and varnish the drawing-room floor so that the matting need not cover it all. 'I have just returned from both the Registrars and the business is concluded. The earliest day on which we can be married is 20th which is dread-

* Alice Meynell's cousin, daughter of her father's sister, Elizabeth Smithson.

** A paper edited by Richard Darling, a friend of Wilfrid Meynell's.

*** The Servite priory church in the Fulham Road.

Wilfrid Meynell, 1877,
water-colour by Adrian
Stokes

Alice Meynell, 1877, water-
colour by Adrian Stokes

Alice Meynell about 1880

fully near the press days at the Exhibitions, is it not? What is to be done?'

In fact, they were able to bring forward the wedding date, and it was fixed so that it would not interfere with the reviewing of the Exhibitions, which was such an important source of income to them.

Shortly before the wedding Alice wrote to tell Wilfrid that a priest, Padre Bisio, had spent an hour with her father that morning, and that she believed arrangements were being made for him to be received into the Church. 'I cannot believe it until it is done. Do ask all the dear fellows where you are to pray for him *hard*.' This letter ends, 'Ever your own (on mortgage for the present) Alice.'

In the event Mr Thompson did not become a Catholic at that time, but several years later, not very long before his death.

Wilfrid Meynell and Alice Thompson were married by the Bishop of Nottingham, Dr Bagshawe, at the church of the Servite Fathers on 16th April, 1877. The bride wore the gold rosary of Mary, Queen of Scots, which was an heirloom in the Meynell family.

Two months later Mimi, who had become engaged in March, was married to Major William Butler, an officer in the Army.

CHAPTER 9

THE MEYNELLS' FIRST HOME was at 11 Inkerman Terrace, Kensington. The house was very small, but they were delighted with it; and Alice Meynell, after giving much thought to the subject of furnishing and interior decorating, noted the results with satisfaction in an article in *The Mirror of Literature*.[1] 'Darkened ceilings would reflect no light, so that we should recommend a cream-tinted ceiling, to match a matted floor, and, with this, Morris' branch-pattern paper, brightened and accentuated by plenty of brass, of Chinese turquoise blue in the ornaments, and by black wood. This arrangement reflects plenty of light, whilst it preserves the advantage of a darkened background for figures, pictures and ornaments. We can speak by experience of the harmony and repose of such a room, and of the charming cheerfulness of its colour.'

Their home began at once to be, as it was ever afterwards, whatever its geographical situation, a meeting place of the literary world. Alice's old friend Aubrey de Vere was a frequent visitor, and to a party in the first year of their married life came Robert Browning.

Wilfrid and I [*Alice wrote in her diary*] met Browning at one or two Private Views and were introduced to him by W. Bell Scott.[*] As I had never sent the great poet [*i.e. Browning*] a copy of my book at the time it was published, Wilfrid took advantage of the pleasant acquaintance to send him a 'Preludes' which drew from him a most kindly and encouraging note; and hence my invitation to him to call – readily responded to.

Everyone exclaims, at a first sight of Browning, 'how unpoetical!' To my mind, however, the most masculine of poets expresses himself far better by his healthy *bonhomie* than he could do by dreamy distraction, however sincere it might be. He is invariably jolly and never betrays self-consciousness for the fraction of a moment; this in itself proves a peculiar and rare greatness and grace. When he does talk of himself he can smile at his own peculiarities – witness the following: The Chinese ambassador has been one of the Lions of the London season this year. Browning told me that he had met him, on which I made some remark on the sweet expression and bearing of His Excellency. Browning laughed and told me that this sweet-faced man had been sent on the mission to England in order that his passion for decapitation might be checked as he was in the habit of cutting off too many heads even for Chinese fashions. 'I also heard' continued Browning 'that he was the most popular poet of his time in his own country so we exchanged a little professional talk. He told me

* William Bell Scott: 1811-1890. Poet and painter; published five volumes of verse, now forgotten, but highly esteemed at the time. He is remembered chiefly for his association with the Rossettis.

he had published four volumes and asked me how many I had given to the world. I was ashamed to tell him. Being entirely ignorant of the nature of the Ambassador's poetical labours, I asked one of his suite to tell me what kind of poems he wrote. 'Well' said he, 'they are *chiefly enigmatical*!' 'At last' said Browning, with his jolly laugh, 'I felt I had found a brother!'

Browning's son has a picture in this year's Academy which has had some fair success, and that it should gain a certain amount of commendation has apparently been a matter of solicitude to father and son. 'You see' said Browning to a friend of ours, 'a good deal is expected of him – because he had a clever mother.' I am quite sure from what I have seen of the poet that he said this – and it is certainly a sweet and humble saying – in perfect sincerity.'[2]

Aubrey de Vere gave them an introduction to Sir Henry* and Lady Taylor whom they visited at Bournemouth. 'I hope you will like my young poet friend Alice Meynell' de Vere wrote to Lady Taylor, who was his cousin. 'To me she is very interesting but you will find her shy.'[3] While they were at Bournemouth they met Lady Shelley, the poet's daughter-in-law, and Alice wrote in her diary: 'She has a refined, thinking, intelligent face. To me it is a memorable thing to be visited by Shelley's daughter-in-law.'[4]

Husband and wife were both working hard at the journalism which was to fill their lives increasingly as their family grew and the need for money became always greater. In the summer of 1878, when Alice was expecting her first baby, her husband sent an article to Edmund Yates, editor of *The World*, with a letter that explained his reasons for wanting to earn more; Yates replied in these kindly terms: 'I have too vivid a remembrance of the occurrence of such "events" in my own youth, when my pockets were very poorly lined, not to sympathise with you and to endeavour to be of what assistance I can to you. But I don't see my way to publishing the enclosed . . . Don't be discouraged, but try again.'[5]

Their son was born on 19th October and was christened Sebastian, and the Inkerman Terrace household, then consisting of one servant, was augmented by a nurse. A year and a half later, on 24th March, 1880, their second child, Monica, was born. To the young mother, who suffered much during her pregnancies and had long and difficult confinements, Mimi wrote, 'Make a joke of your pains – a good plan.'[6]

A journalistic venture of that year was *The Pen, A Journal of Literature*, which appeared weekly under the editorship of Wilfrid Meynell and died an untimely death after seven numbers. One of them contained an unsigned article by Mrs Meynell on Dante Gabriel Rossetti, who wrote to a friend: 'I think I told you that a thing called *The Pen* had descanted flatteringly on me, as I heard. I have since seen

---

* Sir Henry Taylor, author of *Philip van Artevelde* and friend of Tennyson and Wordsworth.

it, and it is very good (I know not by whom at all), but I regret to find that I have killed off *The Pen*, as its writing days ceased with that number.'[7]

During the brief and precarious lifetime of the magazine Aubrey de Vere wrote to Mrs Meynell: 'I am really unhappy at hearing that *The Pen* is in a critical condition. It would be sad indeed if a journal so likely to do great good were to perish, and sad also if you and your Husband were to have had all your trouble for nothing. If the enclosed sonnet . . . can do any good as a contribution . . . pray give it to your husband.'[8]

In the following year Cardinal Manning asked Meynell to take on the editorship of the *Weekly Register*, a Catholic periodical which was chiefly concerned with ecclesiastical affairs. It was to be a familiar feature of the Meynell household for eighteen years, coming to be known by the affectionate name of The Reggie, and creating a sense of crisis on Thursdays, when husband and wife both worked desperately against time to prepare it for the press. In its pages appeared the first of many articles that Alice Meynell was to write on the poetry of Coventry Patmore, and the discriminating praise that she gave him so pleased the poet that he wrote to thank the editor, saying that he had 'seen other articles in which there has been as much commendation but perhaps none in which the commendation has been so good in quality, or has had so flattering a correspondence with the *intentions* which inspired the poems criticised.'[9]

Some idea of the industry of the wife and mother, who had already her household to attend to, may be gained from a list of the periodicals to which, at that time, she was contributing fairly regularly: *The Spectator*, *The Saturday Review*, *The World*, *The Scots Observer*, *The Tablet*, *The Magazine of Art*, and *The Art Journal*. All this besides the book reviewing, proof-reading, and translations of papal encyclicals which she did for her husband's paper. Many of her outside contributions were notices of art exhibitions, and some of the catalogues of those she visited and wrote about at that time have survived, with swift, humourous comments pencilled in the margins. Against *The Judgment* by Burne-Jones, whose work she disliked, she noted: 'So difficult to tell the damned from the blessed'; and at a later exhibition she wrote beside his *The Star of Bethlehem*: 'Angel trained to carry his feet perpendicularly'.

In 1881 the Meynells moved to a larger house, in Phillimore Place, still within the borough of Kensington, and another servant was added to the household at a weekly wage of five shillings and five-pence. The wages, the weekly cost of food, the extra items of expenditure, were all written down by the housewife in the intervals of being a journalist; sums were done, averages worked out – painful and boring duties to her always. And sometimes she would note down among the accounts some small fault of which she had been guilty, and of which she must make confession. In one place she broke off her arithmetic to write, in exasperation, 'As I have a space, let me go into a householder's troubles. We have been a year and ten months in this charming house of ours, 21 Upper Phillimore Place, which is in every way adapted to make a servant comfortable, and I am a most gentle and considerate mistress, yet I have had *nine* different cooks, five housemaids, one coming twice and making two changes, three nurses, one of them coming twice.'[10]

Alice's father died in 1881. Except for the period of strain immediately before and during her engagement she had always been very close to him. Their correspondence has not survived; but there remains one letter written by Mr Thompson to his younger daughter not very long before his death which shows how constant was their communication and how much it meant to him. 'Of course', he wrote, 'my mind runs to you. I can't tell you what a blank it is when I find no letter by the side of my morning cup of tea.'[11] Alice's sorrow for a beloved father was deepened by her always over-scrupulous conscience, which brought to her the memories of what she felt had been failures of love towards him. Many years afterwards, Viola Meynell tells us, one of her children, finding her in tears, inquired the cause and learned that she wept for a day when she had refused him her company for a walk.

It seems that despite the long years of no communication Mrs Meynell must have known where Father Dignam was at that time, or perhaps she wrote to him through the Jesuits at Farm Street. But certainly she wrote to tell him of her father's death, and also of her marriage; for his answering letter has survived, dated 26th May, 1881. After condoling with her on the death of her father, he continued: 'And you, my child, are married! I had heard of it I know now, but it had gone again so completely from my thoughts of you that I was startled. I am glad of all you tell me – many of the happiest marriages I know of are proportioned as to ages as yours, and I never regret hearing that and I felicitate you on what has proved so great a good to you. Your Mother (whom I believe I love best of all of you though I know her so little) was able to watch your father's dying bed and she is, I trust, still well . . .'[12]

Their second son, Everard, was born the year after they moved to Phillimore Place; and two daughters, Madeline and Viola, followed, to make a family of five. Perhaps it is not surprising to find Aubrey de Vere inquiring of Mrs Meynell: 'When will you have time for writing poetry again?'[13] and concluding a letter to Meynell 'With kindest remembrances to your Wife, who I hope finds time occasionally to write poetry.'[14] Undoubtedly the demands of her young and growing family, and the necessity of using her art in a more profitable way, were factors that contributed to the silence that now fell upon Mrs Meynell's poetry – a silence that was to last for thirteen years. But these alone would not have been sufficient reasons to silence one who was in heart and soul and blood a poet, and it seems that the long pause was a deliberate, chosen, premeditated thing.

In *Merry England* in 1884 there appeared her sonnet 'Unlinked', which had been written some time before.

> If I should quit thee, sacrifice, forswear,
>   To what, my art, shall I give thee in keeping?
> To the long winds of heaven? Shall these come sweeping
> My songs forgone against my face and hair?
> Or shall the mountain streams my lost joys bear,
>   My past poetic pain in rain be weeping?
>   No, I shall live a poet waking, sleeping,
> And I shall die a poet unaware.
>
> From me, my art, thou canst not pass away;
>   And I, a singer though I cease to sing,
>   Shall own thee without joy in thee or woe.
> Through my indifferent words of every day,
>   Scattered and all unlinked the rhymes shall ring,
>   And make my poem; and I shall not know.

Writing in the *Fortnightly Review* several years afterwards Coventry Patmore expressed his admiration of her prose in the very highest terms, but said of her poetry that though it was true, beautiful, and negatively almost faultless, it did not 'attain the classical and only sound standard . . . Mrs Meynell's thoughts and feelings seem to be half suffocated by their own sweetness and pathos, so that, though they can speak with admirable delicacy, tenderness, and – that rarest of graces – unsuperfluousness, they cannot sing. With extraordinary power of self-judgement, she discovered this fact while she was as yet a mere girl, and, disdaining to do anything which she could not do, not only well, but best, and notwithstanding the encouragement to persevere in poetry which she received from a large and high class of critics, she gave up the attempt and has hardly since written a line.'[15]

A proof of this article was sent to Mrs Meynell for her comments before publication, and as she did not remark upon this statement of Patmore's it must be concluded that she agreed with it. In a letter of 1901 Wilfrid Meynell wrote to his wife: 'He [*Charles Lewis Hind, editor of "The Academy"*] says he thinks your work lies in prose not in verses. You say the same. I don't. They are incomparable.' It was the poems written in the second phase, culminating in the outpouring of the last two or three years of her life, that Alice Meynell liked; and but for the insistence of her husband, and of others whose judgement she valued, she would have gladly allowed the earlier poems to go out of print and pass into oblivion.

Merry England, in which the sonnet 'Unlinked' appeared, was a monthly magazine started by Wilfrid Meynell in partnership with the publishing firm of Burns and Oates in 1883; but after the first year it was owned solely by him. It sold at a shilling, and eventually acquired a distinguished list of contributors; but a good deal of the contents, especially of the earlier numbers, had to be written by the Meynells themselves, and Wilfrid has described the disguises that he used. 'Besides my pen-name of "John Oldcastle", to break the monotony I sometimes signed Francis Phillimore, and when I edited and adapted two or three anonymous articles published in Catholic magazines a hundred years earlier I gave them the signature A.C. Opie (which meant a copy).'[16]

It was by sending an article and some verses to *Merry England* that Francis Thompson began the friendship with the Meynells but for which his poetry might never have been given to the world. The story is too well known to need retelling, yet no account of Wilfrid and Alice Meynell can be complete without at least a brief version of it. Thompson, the son of a north-country doctor, had become, at twenty-nine, part of the tragic flotsam of the London streets, taking laudanum, sleeping in doss-houses, ragged and unkempt. He had read *Merry England* since its beginning, and in February 1887 he decided to send some contributions to it. Accompanying them was this letter:[*]

Dear Sir,

In enclosing the accompanying article for your inspection, I must ask pardon for the soiled state of the manuscript. It is due, not to slovenliness, but to the strange places and circumstances under which it has been written. For me, no less than Parolles, the dirty nurse Experience has something fouled. I enclose stamped envelope for a reply, since I do not desire the return of the manuscript, regarding your judgment of its worth as quite final. I can hardly expect where my prose fails my verse will succeed. Nevertheless on the principle of 'yet will I try the last', I have added a few specimens of it, with the off-chance that one may be less poor than the rest. Apologising very sincerely for any intrusion on your valuable time, I remain,
>> Yours with little hope,
>> Francis Thompson

Kindly address your rejection to the Charing Cross Post Office.[17]

---

[*] Francis Thompson usually wrote the definite article as ȳ, but I have everywhere substituted 'the'. [J.B.]

Meynell, overworked and never very businesslike about his correspondence, thrust the packet into a pigeon-hole for examination at
some later date, and then forgot about it. Six months later he came
upon it, recognised the merit of the work, and desiring to print the
article and one of the poems wrote to Charing Cross Post Office, but
got no reply from Thompson, who had long since ceased to look for
letters there. In April 1888, more than a year after receiving Thompson's packet, Meynell printed his poem 'The Passion of Mary' in the
magazine, hoping that the poet would see it and communicate with
him. It happened as he expected; Thompson wrote, and finally came,
himself, to Meynell's office, a thin, nervous man, ravaged by drug-
taking, no shirt under his coat, no socks, and gaping shoes. With tact,
gentleness, and great compassion Meynell set about doing what he
could to save this broken man whom he recognised as a genius. He persuaded him to go to a doctor, and after he had been for a time in
hospital sent him to Storrington Priory, in Sussex, where he lodged
with the White Canons and slowly regained some measure of mental
and physical health. Wilfrid Meynell's reward for the time, money, and
patience that he lavished over the course of many years on the often
exasperating Thompson was the undying devotion of the poet, and the
knowledge that he had made it possible for great poetry to be written.
The payment for his lodgings, the purchase of shirts or boots, which remained to the end of his days a charge upon the Meynells, meant often
a real sacrifice; but it was done ungrudgingly.

Meanwhile the multitudinous activities of Wilfrid and Alice continued unabated. Items of news were collected and turned into
paragraphs (known as 'pars' or sometimes 'sparrows') for the papers;
stacks of proofs covered their tables, letters were lost and found again,
answered or forgotten; amid the confusion Alice Meynell's beautiful
prose – terse, melodious, thought-laden – flowed on, and the money
slowly trickled in to be turned into heat and light, servants' wages, and
food and clothes for the five children in the nursery.

In the summer of 1886 a rare holiday was snatched, and was spent
on 'the bird-beset coast of Holy Island'. During that stay Alice came by
chance on the cottage where Grace Darling had lived, and where her
sister lay dying. 'Her cottage stood a little way from the sea, a north-
eastern sea, the waves of which faced westwards, and near evening
showed long radiant lines of foam shining with late sunlight . . . As the
writer arrived and stood looking at Grace's relics in the parlour, her old
sister had already fallen ill, and a clergyman's voice was heard praying.
Then sounded that noise of weeping – the 'clamour' of women – which
tells that there is no more need for quiet, reticence or feigning.'[18]

The poignant sorrow of a child's death came to Mrs Meynell in the
following year. A son, Vivian, was born to her on 3rd March, and died

five months later. In one of her most exquisite essays, she was later to write of the feelings of a mother alone with her baby: 'A newly-born child is so nursed and talked about, handled and jolted and carried about by aliens, and there is so much importunate service going forward, that a woman is hardly alone long enough to become aware how her own blood in her child moves separately, beside her, with another rhythm and different pulse. All is commonplace until the doors are closed upon the two. This unique intimacy at night is a profound retreat, an absolute seclusion. It is more than single solitude; it is a redoubled isolation more remote than mountains, safer than valleys, deeper than forests, and further than mid-sea.'[19]

The loss of the child so beloved was enough to wring from her this cry of agony:

We have something to forgive God for. Does that seem a blasphemy? I say that with the little knowledge He has given us and the short sight, we have something to forgive the Creator who makes husband and wife grow one only to smite them in two again . . . who prodigally overdoes and exaggerates the love in a mother's heart and then forces her to watch a child's long agony. If we saw all we should have nothing to forgive. But He makes us see little and He must wish us to forgive Him. It is easy to forgive; to be forgiven is not easy; shall man alone play that noble part, and so be more noble than God? Will not God, too take our pardon? We forgive Thee, our Maker, for Thy infinite inventiveness in planning the anguish of human life.[20]

Later she used the idea of man's forgiveness of God for a poem 'Veni Creator', published in the *Scots Observer* in 1890:

> So humble things Thou hast borne for us, O God,
> Left'st Thou a path of lowliness untrod?
> Yes, one till now, another Olive-Garden.
> For we endure the tender pain of pardon:
> One with another we forbear. Give heed,
> Look at the mournful world Thou has decreed.
> The time has come. At last we hapless men
> Know all our haplessness all through. Come then,
> Endure undreamed humility: Lord of Heaven,
> Come to our ignorant hearts and be forgiven.

CHAPTER 10

IN 1888 Wilfrid and Alice Meynell bought for £1,321 a piece of land in Palace Court, Bayswater, upon which they commissioned Leonard Stokes to build them a house, a step that was made possible by Alice's inheritance of a sum of money from her father. The building of this high, gabled, red brick house cost them £2,500, and it was completed and ready for occupation in the following year. It was one of the first houses to be built in Palace Court, but with the advent of neighbouring buildings it was given the number 47.[1]

Mrs Meynell's many contributions to the *Scots Observer* were crowned at that time by the publication, in March 1889, of her essay 'The Rhythm of Life'. The editor, W. E. Henley, himself a poet and a man of great intellect and discriminating judgement, called it 'one of the best things it has so far been my privilege to print'; and it was certainly among the finest things Alice Meynell wrote in a long lifetime of fine writing. The wisdom which she had gained from living – which, indeed, can be gained in no other way – her faith, her apprehension of the human heart, shaped the thoughts here expressed in a spare, limpid, musical prose; her paragraphs contain no superfluous word, and none that could be replaced by another without loss. One reading does not disclose it all, and even a second leaves some subtleties not yet within our grasp; not because of obscurity (which she disliked and avoided) but because of the concentration and compactness of thought. In this, as in so much of her work, there is a certain sadness, an implicit suggestion of sorrows that lay not in her ultimate view of life but in the living of it, day by day. She was an artist, acutely sensitive, hurt beyond the common measure by the world's suffering, and moved to a sometimes intolerable ecstasy by its beauty; so that perhaps it could not be otherwise with her. Yet she was aware, as she showed in this essay, that happiness or its reverse are often inexplicable.

If life is not always poetical, it is at least metrical. Periodicity rules over the mental experience of man, according to the path of the orbit of his thoughts. Distances are not gauged, ellipses not measured, velocities not ascertained, times not known. Nevertheless the recurrence is sure. What the mind suffered last week, or last year, it does not suffer now; but it will suffer again next week or next year. Happiness is not a matter of events; it depends upon the tides of the mind. Disease is metrical, closing in at shorter and shorter periods towards death, sweeping abroad at longer and longer intervals towards recovery. Sorrow for one cause was intolerable yesterday, and will be intolerable tomorrow; today it is easy to bear, but the cause has not passed. Even the burden of a spiritual distress unsolved is bound to leave the heart to a temporary peace; and remorse itself does not remain – it returns. Gaiety takes us by a dear surprise. If we had made a course of notes of its visits, we might have been on the watch, and would have had an expectation instead of a discovery. No one makes such observations; in all the diaries of students of the interior world, there have never come to light the records of the Kepler of such cycles. But Thomas à Kempis knew of the recurrences, if he did not measure them. In his cell alone with the elements – 'What wouldst thou more than these? for out of these were all things made' – he learned the stay to be found in the depth of the hour of bitterness, and the remembrance that restrains the soul at the coming of the moment of delight, giving it a more conscious welcome, but presaging for it an inexorable flight . . .

The souls of certain of the saints, being singularly simple and single, have been in the most complete subjection to the law of periodicity. They endured, during spaces of vacant time, the interior loss of all for which they had sacrificed the world. They rejoiced in the uncovenanted beatitude of sweetness alighting in their hearts. Like them are the poets whom, three times or ten times in the course of a long life, the Muse has approached, touched, and forsaken. And yet hardly like them; not always so docile, nor so wholly prepared for the departure, the brevity, of the golden and irrevocable hour. Few poets have fully recognised the metrical absence of their Muse. For full recognition is expressed in one only way – silence . . .

. . . Man – except those elect already named – is hardly aware of periodicity. The individual man either never learns it fully, or learns it late. And he learns it so late, because it is a matter of cumulative experience upon which cumulative evidence is long lacking. It is in the after-part of each life that the law is learnt so definitely as to do away with the hope or fear of continuance. That young sorrow comes so near to despair is a result of this young ignorance, so is the early hope of great achievement. Life seems so long, and its capacity so great, to one who knows nothing of all the intervals it needs must hold – intervals between aspirations, between actions, pauses as inevitable as the pauses of sleep. And life looks impossible to the young unfortunate, unaware of the inevitable and unfailing refreshment. It would be for their peace to learn that there is a tide in the affairs of men, in a sense more subtle – if it is not too audacious to add a meaning to Shakespeare – than the phrase was meant to contain. Their joy is flying away from them on its way home; their life will wax and wane; and if they would be wise, they must wake and rest in its phases, knowing that they are ruled by the law that commands all things – a sun's revolutions and the rhythmic pangs of maternity.

In the summer of 1889 Meynell received from Francis Thompson his 'Ode to the Setting Sun', the first major poetical work that he had attempted since the doctors had begun trying to break him of the laudanum habit. The excitement at Palace Court was such that it seemed necessary to communicate it immediately to the poet, so that the Meynells, with a young friend, Vernon Blackburn, took the train to Sussex to congratulate him.[2] Thompson was slowly dragging himself out of the abyss; but it was a hard struggle, and health for him could never be complete again; the effort to live without the drugs which he had come to depend upon caused him agony, both mental and physical, and there were times when he lapsed back into the laudanum habit again, followed always by bitter remorse. His letters speak constantly of the ills that afflicted him more or less all the time – nausea, dyspepsia, giddiness, insomnia – and he wrote to Meynell of his 'villainous mud-hut of a body'.

A lodging was found for him in London in the following winter, near to Palace Court, and for the next two years he was part of the Meynell household. He came and went with no regard for time, and took no account of the days of the week; he shared the littered library table where the two journalists already worked, sometimes helping them with their proof-reading but more often working at his own compositions, and interrupting their labours with conversation or cries of distress about the loss of a pencil or an exercise book. He was writing poetry steadily at that time, as well as occasional essays, and he had begun work upon the group of poems addressed to Mrs Meynell and called 'Love in Dian's Lap'.

Thompson loved Alice Meynell with a love which was too undemanding to be called hopeless, since he never came near enough to hope to abjure it. He loved her from afar, spiritually, ethereally, and on the plane of the intellect, saying to her in his poetry the things that he could never say to her in speech. He felt for her, too, – while it in no way conflicted with his more romantic feelings – something of the love that he would have given to a mother.* She, for her part, cherished his poetry (though she valued it less highly than did her husband), and was fond of him, exasperated by him, and thought of him rather as though he were another child to be taken care of and worried about with her own children. The situation was not, it seems, a cause of anguish to Thompson, for he had long understood that he would always, in that sense, be alone, and he accepted it.

'It was my practice', he wrote in his notebook, 'from the time I left college to pray for the lady whom I was destined to love – the unknown She. It is curious that even then I did not dream of praying for her whom I was destined to marry; and yet not curious; for already I had previsioned that with me it would be to love, not to be loved.'[3]

His admiration for her work was unbounded. In 1890, when her 'Veni Creator' was published in the *Scots Observer*, he wrote to a friend:

The poem is a perfect miniature example of her most lovelily tender work; and is, like all her best, of a signal originality in its central idea no less than in its development. It is quoted, by the way, in this week's *Tablet*. In the current

* His mother had died when he was twenty.

Scots Observer she has a little sketch (the product, I hope, of her holiday) finished like an ivory carving.* This, like all the articles she has at times contributed to that paper, should go down to posterity among the very choicest prose-morsels in the language. I hope it was the result of her holiday because unless done under conditions of unusual health, it will have made her ill, as the production of these gems always does. That is why they are so lamentably few. Even after she has written her various art-criticisms on the opening of the London art galleries, she is generally in bed with violent headache; and her ordinary journalistic work is sufficient tax on her frail health. Her soul has indeed 'fretted the pigmy body to decay'; but fragile she must always have been. Her youthful portraits show a beautiful, spiritualised face, with musing, saddened eyes; the head in most portraits drooped as with the weight of thought. Yet the mournful sweetness of the countenance is preserved from anything weak and poetessish (Mrs Meynell is a poet – something very different from that unendurable creature, the poetess) by its continued quiet. A face which is a poem as beautiful as any she has written. Nor is this prejudice. In the first of these portraits which I saw I did not recognise her. Yet I at once cried to myself 'What an ideal face that would make for a female poet!' It is a rare thing. Most women of genius – Mrs Browning, George Eliot, Charlotte Brontë – have been decidedly plain. Mrs Browning, indeed, alludes to her husband's penetration in seeing beyond 'this mask of me'; and Charlotte Brontë, as you know, shows herself painfully conscious of her plainness. Mrs Meynell will not attain any rapid notice like them. Her work is of that subtly delicate order which – as with Coleridge, for instance – needs to soak into men for a generation or two before it gets adequate recognition. Nevertheless it is something to have won the admiration of men like Rossetti, Ruskin, Rossetti's bosom friend Theodore Watts,** and, shall I add, the immortal Oscar Wilde.[4]

In this letter – a very long one written over a period of several months to Canon Carroll, a friend of Thompson's father – he wrote about Vernon Blackburn, the Meynells' young friend who was music critic of the *Pall Mall Gazette* and a sub-editor of the *Tablet*. He said that he valued Blackburn's judgement much: 'In the first place he generally represents Mrs Meynell's judgement, who is his guide and friend in everything – and such a guide and friend no other young man has. In the second place he has an excellent judgement of his own.' He mentioned that the Meynells had been for a holiday, and that Vernon Blackburn's mother – known to all her friends as 'Madam' – had edited the *Register* during their absence. 'You saw, I suppose, Mr Blackburn's admirable little article on Henley in a recent *Tablet* – the very best thing he has yet done. It marks his literary puberty, if I may use such an expression. His style is not yet original, it is strongly influenced by Henley himself. But every young painter graduates from some school . . . and Mr Blackburn has used his master's style with an in-

---

*   'A Remembrance'.

** Later known as Watts-Dunton.

dividual vigour and cleverness which makes it a compliment to Henley to be so imitated. It is very distinguished work for so young a man. He is only twenty-four.'[5]

It was when the Meynells were about to set off for the holiday just mentioned that Thompson wrote to Wilfrid Meynell: 'I cannot let you leave without writing to you to thank Mrs Meynell for the gracious note which she sent me. I had no opportunity of expressing my thanks personally; for I hate displays of feelings in company. If she derive any pleasure from the knowledge that she has given pleasure to others, – but that must be a thing of everyday with *her* – then you can tell her that she has given me deeper than pleasure. I sincerely hope that the weather will improve for the holiday you so much need.'[6]

That winter Thompson wrote 'Sister Songs', addressed to Monica and Madeline Meynell. With characteristic shyness he deposited the manuscript on the mantelpiece at Palace Court, with a note saying: 'If intensity of labour could make it good, good it would be.'[7]

Often Francis Thompson's communications with the Meynells were made by letters which he would leave behind him, particularly if he were expressing special regard or attempting to explain some incident in which he thought he had given or received a hurt. Such a one he wrote to Mrs Meynell from the British Museum in September 1892.

Dear Mrs Meynell,
It is a small matter and hardly, I suppose, worth taking a second thought about in your mind. Yet as I seem to have offended you, and as to offend you *is* the most grievous of things, you must pardon me if to *me* it is a grave matter. I mean the misunderstanding of this afternoon.

I wish then to say that I did nothing except with the design to consult your wishes. When I came in this morning, you told me that I was punctual to my time, but that you must go out; and asked me not to mind. It was clear, therefore, that you remembered our overnight agreement, and that there was no need for me to remind you of it. And it was clear, too, that you understood me to have come early in the morning for the express purpose of keeping my agreement, and that there was no need for me to explain my desire that you should go through *A Portrait* with me. Yet you came back from your shopping, and never signified your willingness to go through it; you saw me finish my letter to Madam, and sit down patiently to wait, yet you still made no sign of readiness. Now, delicacy forbade *me* to ask *you*; because it was you who were conferring the favour, not I. Consequently, once I had made sure that you remembered my request, and knew what I had come for, I felt that I could not delicately, in the absence of any encouragement or signification of willingness from you, press from you a favour which it seemed probable you had repented. If nothing had passed between us since I entered the house, of course it would have been my part to remind you of the overnight agreement. But your own words forestalled that; and so it seemed to me that the only thing I could courteously do was to wait until you signified your readiness to fulfil the agree-

ment which you had already signified your remembrance of. No such signification of readiness came from you before we went down to lunch: and, I repeat, I
did not like to ask you, lest I should be pressing on you the fulfilment of a
promise you had repented. When we went down to lunch without your having
intimated any readiness to commence the task you had agreed to overnight, I
felt convinced that you shrank from it for some reason – perhaps sheer
boredom – and, to say truth, I felt sharply wounded. For if there is one dread I
have perpetually before me it is to presume on your good nature and toleration.
When I went upstairs after lunch, my eyes fell on the proofs lying in your
place. Then, I thought, I understood the matter. You were anxious to get your
essays revised, in order to send them to C[oventry] P[atmore], who had, you
told me, telegraphed regarding them. I was very sad that I should have pressed
on you my own selfish affair, when, as I now found, your own work was pressing on your hands, while mine could wait indefinitely. So I determined that the
only way I could repair the unintended selfishness I had been guilty of, was to
take my leave of you under some pretext, and so spare you the task of keeping a
promise wrung from you in the kindness of your heart, but which interfered
with what you desired to be at work on. Great was my consternation when I
did this, and found that you resented it. I meditated whether I should draw
back, since I had angered you where I meant only to consult your hidden
wishes. But I saw that you were so cold and estranged from me, that the going
through of the poem would have been a constrained affair for both of us. So I
left.

It seems to me that the more I strive to please you and serve you and think
always what may be your pleasure, not mine, the more I alienate you from me,
so far as a lady so sweet can be alienated from anyone. If you understood one
thing, I think, you would have judged me better in the past. It is this. I am
unhappy when I am out of your sight; and would pass every hour, if I could in
your exquisite presence, only to feel the effluence of your spirit in contact with
mine. But *you*, of course, can have no such feeling in reference to me; and
would often gladly be without my presence when my love for you prompts it,
and your good nature prompts you patiently to bear it. Now my sense of this
inspires me with a continual timidity about inflicting my society on you in any
way, unless you in some way signify a desire for it. Hence such misunderstandings as that of today.

Let this be sufficient, and let it not come between us. I know how it must tax
you to endure me; for you are a friend, a mother; while I, over and above these,
am a lover – spiritual as light, and unearthly as the love of one's angelic
dreams, if you will – but yet a lover; and even a Seraph enamoured must be a
trying guardian-angel to have to do with.

Ahi! soavissima Madonna Alice, avete pietà di me!

> Ever yours, most beloved lady,
> Francis Thompson[8]

And again:

My own dear lady and mother,

How did it come about that what began between us in confidence this afternoon ended, somehow, in constraint and reticence? I could not understand it at the time; I could only feel that, while I was tenderly grateful for your dear kindness, I had somehow fallen out of touch with you after the first moment. And I was miserable to feel it. I have now come to the conclusion that the fault was all on my side. Though I said otherwise at lunch (for I hate parading one's private ills before strangers), I had slept little last night, eaten nothing in the morning, and was able to eat little at lunch. So that I felt utterly spent, and unable to stand the strain of emotion, or to respond to your spirit with the instinctive perception I am accustomed to have for it. I trust you, honour you, and love you more than ever, – O believe: it was simply that paralysis of the heart and emotions which follows a prolonged strain upon them. Pardon me, and do not let it rest there. Confidence has gone too far not to go farther, or die altogether. Give me an opportunity tomorrow, if possible; at any rate the sooner the better. And I will open to you, if you wish it, my most secret soul; that on my side you may never misunderstand me through distrust or want of knowledge. That I promise you. On your side, be all exactly as you will. It is marvellous to me how I missed grasping your sweet and sympathetic purpose this afternoon; but I did. Let it not persuade you to believe me anything but your loving child, friend and sympathiser.

Francis[9]

But a happier one enclosed his poem 'In her Paths':

Dear Mrs. Meynell,

Your sudden arrival on Tuesday prevented me from answering your letter – the letter from Anglesey – but I resolved nevertheless, as soon as *The Register* permitted, to tell you by note how delighted I was to receive that letter. Indeed, after you left, I felt as if it were night, with a great hole in the heavens where the moon ought to be. What I had intended to forward in answer to your letter I forward now. The concluding words of it, 'friend and child', reminded me of some lines written at the time I was composing *Amphicypellon*. They were written hastily, to relieve an outburst of emotion; and, not thinking there was any poetry in them worthy of you, I never showed them to you. But when I read those concluding words of your letter, I remembered the lines; and resolved to transcribe them, that you might see you could not have addressed me more according to my wish. . . . I hope you are going to have no more headaches, 'wheel' or otherwise; but to be just happy for a while, now the *Register* is done. And that tomorrow, for once in a way, and Saturday, you will do just what you like and take pleasure in doing; If, indeed, it is possible for you for one day to drop that inveterate habit of thinking so much of other people, that you put yourself away in a corner and forget that you have left yourself there. And since I think you must have had far too much of my company forced upon you during the last fortnight, if I leave you now as much as may be without me you must ascribe it solely to my anxiety for anything which might fatigue you; not to neglect, of which I am incapable, or weariness which no man – I least – could feel in your companionship.[10]

IN HER PATHS

And she has trod before me in these ways!
I think that she has left here heavenlier days;
And I do guess her passage, as the skies
    Of holy Paradise
    Turn deeply holier,
And, looking up with sudden new delight,
One knows a seraph-wing has passed in flight.

The air is purer for her breathing, sure!
    And all the fields do wear
    The beauty fallen from her;
The winds do brush me with her robe's allure.
'Tis she has taught the heavens to look sweet,
    And they do but repeat
The heaven, heaven, heaven of her face!
The clouds have studied going from her grace!
The pools whose marges had forgot the tread
Of Naiad, disenchanted, fled,
    A second time must mourn,
    Bereaven and forlorn.
Ah, foolish pools and meads! You did not see
Essence of old, essential pure as she.
For this was even that Lady, and none other,
The man in me calls 'Love', the child calls 'Mother'.

The Meynell family was increased by another daughter in 1890. She was christened Olivia; and it was to her that her mother was one day to write the poem in which she recalls the Creole blood that had bestowed upon the child her beautiful brown eyes.

TO OLIVIA, OF HER DARK EYES

Across what calm of tropic seas,
   'Neath alien clusters of the nights,
Looked, in the past, such eyes as these?
   Long-quenched, relumed, ancestral lights!

The generations fostered them;
   And steadfast Nature, secretwise –
Thou seedling child of that old stem –
   Kindled anew thy dark-bright eyes.

Was it a century or two
   This lovely darkness rose and set,
Occluded by grey eyes and blue,
   And Nature feigning to forget?

Some grandam gave a hint of it –
   So cherished was it in thy race,
So fine a treasure to transmit
   In its perfection to thy face.

Some father to some mother's breast
   Entrusted it, unknowing. Time
Implied, or made it manifest,
   Bequest of a forgotten clime.

Hereditary eyes! But this
   Is single, singular, apart: –
New-made thy love, new-made thy kiss,
   New-made thy errand to my heart.

Katherine Tynan, the Irish writer, who was a devoted friend of Alice Meynell, was godmother to the new baby. She wrote to Wilfrid: 'I hope dear darling Alice is getting up strength quickly, and I hope she won't be bothered with any more babies for a long time to come.'[11] But scarcely more than a year later she was writing again: 'Wilfrid dear – I am rejoiced at the new boy's safe arrival. I think on the whole you'd better now have no more boys and girls. You have a comfortable family for a young couple already.'[12]

The 'comfortable family', consisting of three boys and four girls, did in fact come to an end with the arrival of the 'new boy'. He was christened Francis, and Thompson was his godfather. To Meynell, the poet wrote: 'I hardly, I fear, gave you even commonplace thanks for the favour you conferred on me in choosing me for your little son's god-father. Even now I am utterly unable to express to you what I feel regarding it; I can only hope that you may comprehend without words. As for the quietness with which I took it on Saturday – for the premeditated of emotion in speech I have an instinctive horror which, I think, you share sufficiently to understand and excuse in me.'[13]

There were illnesses and accidents among the older children that caused great anxiety to the parents in the next year or two after Francis's birth. Monica was gravely ill with pneumonia, and for a time her life was in jeopardy. It was then that Francis Thompson wrote 'To Monica thought dying'.[14]

Later, Sebastian, at school at Ramsgate, also had pneumonia, and Alice Meynell hurried there to be with him through his illness.[15]

Viola, leaning too far over the banisters at Palace Court, fell thirty feet to the hall below, where she lay unconscious. She had to be in bed for ten days after the accident, and her mother described the unexpected resignation of one so young. 'And yet during every hour of the time the little child is not only gay but patient – not only impulsive but steadily resigned; sparing of regrets; reluctant to be served; sweetly and piously thankful; inventive of tender and affectionate little words that she has never used before. "You are exquisite to me, Mother" she says at receiving some little attention.'[16]

It was Viola, too, who suffered another accident described by her mother. 'A little wild girl, brilliant and stormy in temperament, and unaccustomed, as one would think, to deal in any way with her own impulses, a child whose way is to cry out, laugh, complain, and triumph without an instant's reflection, dashes, in a run, her face against an un-noticed door, and is cut and immediately covered with blood. "Tell Mother it's nothing! Tell Mother quick that it's nothing" cries the magnanimous child as soon as she can speak.'[17]

At a time when two members of the family were ill Mrs Meynell wrote to a friend: 'I have kept them in bed and nursed them – very badly. Among all the things I do badly that is the thing I do most stupidly.'[18]

Of the children in full health in these early years there is a report in a letter from Alice to Wilfrid, who was away from home: 'These rascals are pretty troublesome in your absence, but I don't let them stop my work. And between their badnesses they are uncommonly dear. Edith helped me yesterday to control them when visitors came, but the nurse gives up the struggle. She is so spiritless that I shall not regret her so very much. We went on Saturday to Mrs Cameron's office and I trust she will find me someone.'[19]

And during this absence of Wilfrid's another letter tells of how much she missed him. 'My darling darling priceless pet, how much I look forward to seeing your dear face, I trust looking well, not dark under the eyes. I laughed much over your two dear and charming letters. It was one of my few grins since you left. Ever your most loving James.'[20]

Nicknames were much used in the family. Alice was often 'Johnson' as she was useful as a dictionary, and sometimes 'James', for what reason is not know. Olivia was 'Lobby', or sometimes 'Beelie'; and Viola was 'Prue', perhaps after Steele's second wife. Madeline was always 'Dimpling'.

Her practical ministrations as a mother were never very skilled; nursing, sewing, mending: she was in varying degrees bad at all these things; but in love, in gaiety, in gentleness and understanding she was unsurpassed, and her children adored her. She was often abstracted, inattentive, busy, being forced to gain the solitude she needed if her work was to be done by absenting her mind from the room where six or seven children played and talked and wrote; but when her work was finished no one more readily shared their games and stimulated their laughter. Viola Meynell has described the diversion thought out by her mother of putting a child into a trunk, pulling it through doorways or along passages, and making them guess where they were before opening the lid. Alice Meynell herself wrote at that time of another game:

It is a special desire of a family of children that their mother should go to their beds at night; But in order that they may have assurance of her visit, which takes place after they have fallen asleep – or, as they phrase it, 'in the miggle of the night' – they ask her to leave a sign. When the custom began she left a trace, unmistakable but not otherwise delightful. She hung the little garters over the looking glass or put the trodden shoe, that tells so much of a child's day, upon a nail in the place of the nursery picture . . . For fear the visit to unconscious hosts should leave no marks, the children sometimes put up a paper in a conspicuous place with the reminder 'Please make a sine.'
But the 'sign' could not long continue to be a mere sign and no more. Yielding to a human temptation, the mother . . . began to devise a sign in the shape of a biscuit or a fruit. And it is the reflex pleasure of thinking that a little creature will wake alone and feel for his 'sign' that amounts in time to a veritable preoccupation of the mind. It has to be at least confessed; when her friends, perhaps, respect her abstraction, rashly assigning a literary cause, she is wondering whether it shall be a Carlsbad plum or two black currant lozenges.[21]

The children's world was never set apart from that of their parents, and although there was always a nurse who, nominally at least, ruled their lives, they strayed at will from nursery to library, and liked to feel that they were not excluded from the work that went on there. The older children would be sent to post the letters and sometimes allowed to accompany their father to his editorial office; errands were run and cups of tea brought to the harrassed and hard-working parents. Of this latter mission Alice Meynell told a story of one of the children: 'A little girl . . . was wont to bring a cup of tea to the writing-table of her mother, who had often feigned indignation at the weakness of what her Irish maid always called "the infusion". "I'm afraid it's bosh again, Mother" said the child; and then in a half-whisper, "Is bosh right, or wash, Mother?" She was not told, and decided for herself, with doubts for bosh. The afternoon cup left the kitchen an infusion, and reached the library "bosh" thenceforward.'[22]
Beneath the table at which their father and mother worked the children edited their own magazine, which they called *The Bere*. This title came from a remark by Clement Shorter when he started *The Sphere*. Asked what had prompted him to do this, he replied, having a severe cold, 'Oh, it was a bere whib.'[23] They often appropriated for its

columns the comments, which they heard quoted in the house, of other writers upon their parents' productions. When these comments seemed to her to praise too highly Monica sought to counteract what she feared to be their harmful influence by sharper criticisms in letters which she, in common with all the children, was accustomed to leave about the house for their mother. 'I hope you will in Time give up your absurd thoughts about literture . . . Just because Mr Henley and those sort of unsencere men say you write well simply because they know if they don't flatter they'll never get anything for their papers.'[24] And, on another day: 'My dear Mother, – I hope you will never write such a bad article again as you did for the Art Journan the other day, if you do I shall really begin to lose trust in your litreture. You know I love you but it really takes off a little of my liking for you when you write such unconventionan wash as that article if it is worthy of being called an article. From your most indulgent daughter Monica.'[25]

The impression of frailty which Mrs Meynell gave to those who knew her – though she must, in fact, have been endowed with a good deal of strength and will-power to carry her through what must be done – filled her family and friends with a great desire to protect her, and even a seven-year-old daughter wrote to her father during one of his absences: 'Mother had very bad wheels last night and she has got them still. We are trying to keep her quiet from the babies.'[26] Those agonising hemi-cranial headaches, preceded or accompanied by the typical migraine symptom of flashing lights or wheels before the eyes, were frequent with her; the enduring and, in so far as it was possible, ignoring of them called for a good deal of fortitude. Her occasional references to them in her letters are always half humourous, and one suspects that they were often borne with no mention at all; only a casual sentence in one of her essays has a hint of grimness. 'Every woman who has headaches has them in distinct varieties known to herself, which she will be wise not to describe.'[27]

A few letters to her husband when he was away from home give glimpses of the daily life of Palace Court. 'Monnie wept overmuch this morning at going to school (geography) but she went nevertheless, looking rather ill. I shall go to fetch her. Lobby [Olivia] slept twelve hours solid except for one meal which she took with her eyes shut.'[28] And on one occasion when Meynell was visiting Francis Thompson, who was then at Pantasaph, in North Wales, being cared for by the Franciscans there, Alice wrote: 'My Darling, I feel as though I had written the whole Pall Mall Gazette today! You should tell me more of yourself, especially the sleep. Dear Viola has a bad finger, but it is much easier at the time I write. It was squashed under the perambulator in which she was wheeling Francis. He was not hurt. That magnanimous Viola thought of nothing but telling me that it was "much better" when I came in and found her almost faint. I have her in my bed tonight and she is there now, quite smiling.'[29]

Whenever they were apart they wrote to each other daily, and Mrs Meynell, of course, sent news of how her work progressed, as well as items of a more domestic nature. Sometimes Francis Thompson was in London, and then, if Meynell were absent, he was pressing in his offers of help with the journalism. Sometimes his presence speeded the task, and sometimes it did not. Here is a random selection of the 'good' days. 'My own Love . . . F.T. and I kept our noses to the grindstone well yesterday.' 'I think I have done a good day's work. Francis Thompson and I sit opposite each other in extreme gravity. He is *exceedingly* good and offered to play with the children and take them out all day.' 'Never again shall I fear taking the *Reggie* for you; I am going in it at a canter with both hands down. But another time I shall ask you not to send copy to the printer but to let me have it; there has been some duplication already and I expect to see more in the proofs today. I am perfectly capable of turning out an amusing *Register* with no help except that of F.T.'[30]

The *Scots Observer*, in which 'The Rhythm of Life' and various others of Mrs Meynell's essays had appeared, had become in 1890 the *National Observer*, and Henley, continuing as editor, bombarded her with requests for contributions. These she supplied as often as she could, but the high standard to which she was faithful in prose as in poetry precluded rapid or abundant essay-writing. Her subjects were varied – 'I think you would write well about a broomstick', Henley told her – but she never wrote without having something definite, original and valuable to say. In 1892 she was approached, through Henley, by John Lane, the publisher, who wanted to reprint some of these essays, and it was agreed that some others should be added to them and the book produced in the following year. Lane also wished to publish a volume of her poetry, which would consist chiefly of the poems contained in *Preludes*, now almost twenty years old, with one or two more not previously collected. These included 'Renouncement'. There was no newer work to add to these except 'Veni Creator', written in 1890.

It was at first proposed to publish the two volumes simultaneously; but while the plan was still under consideration Alice Meynell wrote to her husband: 'Lane wants to put the poems off to the spring. I said I would ask you. He has not set his heart on it, but he says the prose book will cause a general demand in the notices "What about the poems?" and that they ought then to be announced as forthcoming in the spring. That gives me time (if you think well) to work on them *really*. Henley has been reading *Preludes* and he seems to have told Lane that he thought them very unequal. I gather that he did not say it in so many words.'[31]

Francis Thompson was much distressed at this idea of Mrs Meynell's that she should revise her early poems, and he wrote to her:

Dear Mrs Meynell,

At the risk of offending you by what you may think officious interference, I take up my pen to implore you to meddle as little as may be with the text of *Preludes*. In principle, I think the modern foible of poets for revising in maturity the poems of their youth to be not only most perilous for the poems tampered with, but a capital sin against that art which the process is designed to serve, and by which you set such store. It is fatal to *keeping*, and keeping is surely all in all to art. You would not retouch your youthful portrait into the contours of mature womanhood, though they be absolutely more perfect. And all poetry to a certain degree, but such as *Preludes in excelsis*, is a portrait. It is a portrait of your youthful self. By re-modelling it according to the mind of your maturity, you will destroy its truthfulness to the thing you were, without making it truthful to the thing you are . . . In the name of your art, which you are going about to betray under the notion of safe-guarding; in the name of your poetry, which we loved for what it was, not for what it should be or might have been; in the name of the white sincerity which you have never before falsified; in the name of your admirers, whose instinct you have not doubted in the case of others; I conjure Alice Meynell to leave us Alice Thompson. Unimproved, unsophisticated, with her weakness and her strength as we saw, accepted, admired and loved her.[32]

CHAPTER 11

THE YEAR 1892 saw the flowering of a close friendship between Alice Meynell and Coventry Patmore. Eight years before, her percipient comments on his verse had drawn from him the letter already quoted, and now a further article by her in the *National Observer* on his work had brought them together. The Meynells visited Patmore at his house at Lymington, in the New Forest: sometimes both Wilfrid and Alice, sometimes Alice with some of the children, sometimes herself alone. Patmore, on his visits to London, became a frequent guest at Palace Court, and in the intervals of their meeting they corresponded regularly.

Coventry Patmore was then a man of sixty-nine, married to his third wife. His first wife, whom he had married in the year of Alice Meynell's birth, had died after sixteen years of immensely happy marriage, leaving him with six children. She was immortalised in his best known work, *The Angel in the House*. A year after her death he married again; but this marriage, too, lasted only sixteen years, during the last part of which his wife was an invalid. Owing to her poor health it was felt that someone young and energetic was needed as a companion for the girls, and Harriet Robson, a friend of Patmore's eldest daughter, was engaged to be governess to the younger children, and to help Mrs Patmore with running the house. By the time the second Mrs Patmore died Harriet had been with them for ten years, and Coventry Patmore had grown very fond of her. When the conventional year had elapsed they married, the bridegroom being then fifty-eight and his bride some twenty-five years younger.

At the time when Patmore's friendship with Alice Meynell began, although he was approaching seventy, he was still a handsome man, vigorous, arrogant, intolerant, and capable of great charm. Edmund Gosse described him thus: 'He was exceedingly unlike other people. But his face possessed quite as much beauty as strangeness. Three things were particularly noticeable in the head of Coventry Patmore – the vast convex brows, arched with vision; the bright, shrewd, bluish-grey eyes, the outer fold of one eyelid permanently and humorously drooping; and the wilful, sensuous mouth. These three seemed ever at war amongst themselves; they spoke three different tongues – they proclaimed a man of dreams, a canny man of business, and a man of vehement physical determination.'[1]

Like the Meynells, he was a convert to the Catholic Church, though he had come to it later in life than they, after the death of his first wife.

His prose writings were mostly concerned with philosophy and theology, and in these, as well as in his longer poetic works, *The Angel in the House* and *The Unknown Eros*, he returned again and again to the theme of the parallel between the love of God for the soul and the love of husband for wife, with a strong emphasis on the physical side of the union. Osbert Burdett, in *The Idea of Coventry Patmore*, says: 'His real contribution to Western mystic literature is to supply the emphasis, elsewhere lacking, on the divine nature of human love.'[2]

That Patmore fell in love with Alice Meynell almost at once is evident, and he made no secret of his devotion to her. That he who, in his writing, had so emphatically praised the beauty of the bonds of marriage should now, in the last years of his life, love outside those bonds was a terrible irony; but whatever torture it caused him he was willing to endure rather than forgo the company of the beloved. He was astonished and fascinated by the clear, brilliant, penetrating intellect which he found in this most feminine of women, and was charmed by her beauty; while she, on her side, was overjoyed that the man of whose greatness she was so certain should desire her friendship, knowing that she could offer him no more: and on that basis their relationship lasted for some three years.

It must be said that it was a curious friendship, especially when viewed against the background of the social conventions of that time. It was not commonly done then for a man and woman who were not related and not childhood friends to call each other by their Christian names; but already in 1892 Patmore was writing to Wilfrid Meynell and referring to his wife as Alice; while she, in the same year, writing to her husband when he was away from home, said: 'My Love! No letter to cheer a working girl on her Friday morning! Hurry up, little Willy! Coventry never misses a day.'[3] And despite the fact that Alice Meynell visited the Patmores at Lymington quite a lot during the years 1892-95, she and Mrs Patmore never addressed each other by their Christian names. On Patmore's visits to London he seems never to have taken his wife, and she is rarely mentioned in his letters to the Meynells. There is no evidence that Harriet Patmore resented her husband's friendship, though one cannot but feel that she must, at times, have felt somewhat left out of things. It is obvious, however, that Mrs Meynell must have considered this aspect of the situation, and it would be entirely alien to her nature to continue with a friendship that caused unhappiness.

As for Wilfrid Meynell, no devoted husband, surely, was ever less jealous than he! The overt admiration of Francis Thompson, of Patmore, and, later, of George Meredith for his wife was proclaimed in their poems and widely known; and he, so far from resenting their attentions, was proud that such great men should offer her the praises that he felt to be no more than her due. He, trusting her utterly and secure in her love for him, saw no reason for jealousy; and one may suppose that he derived satisfaction from the knowledge that greater men than himself would have given much to win the prize that was so securely his. Husband and wife seemed, in some curious way, to share the tributes of her admirers; and she told Meynell of their praise, not from conceit but because she knew that it would please him. So did she sometimes tell her mother the compliments that were paid to her by her critics or by readers, not valuing them greatly herself, but glad of the pleasure they brought to Mrs Thompson. The analogy is not complete, for she prized very much the regard of Patmore, Meredith, and Thompson, and cared very little for that of the general public, but the spirit in which she handed on these tributes to those who loved her was in each case the same.

On 8th July, 1892, when Alice Meynell was staying with the Patmores at Lymington, she wrote to Wilfrid: 'Coventry makes me very happy with his devoted love. He always asks me to tell you how much he loves me. He says that in some respects it is more than he has ever felt for a woman before . . . Coventry will often be in town now, he says he would at any time go a thousand miles to see me.'[4]

During another visit, in August, with some of the children, she wrote to Wilfrid:

My own Sweetheart,
   Thanks for your particularly dear letters. I missed the post this afternoon owing to the very early dinner which took me by surprise. It is quite cold but I am warmed up with fires and perpetual hot water bottles. The children are particularly well and happy. Everyone waits on them and Coventry will not allow me to do anything for them. By the way, say *nothing* to your paramours* or anybody about him. He is evidently nervous lest tongues should wag . . . Oh Sweetheart, don't be lonely.
   I was glad to get Coventry's missing letter. He says in it that you wrote to him most charmingly and that he can never repay you except by hoping that I will give you an extra kiss. He spoils me much and I get on excellently with Mrs Patmore.
   Always your more than own Girl.[5]

It was probably after this visit to Lymington that Alice Meynell took Patmore back with her to stay for the first time at Palace Court. In a letter which cannot be dated more exactly than that it was written in 1892, she wrote to tell her husband what preparations must be made before she returned, bringing the great man with her.

Tea is the one indispensable thing to the health and happiness of Coventry. Let it be ready and good, with a rusk or something . . . A nice plain dinner

---

*   A family joke about the women who expressed devotion to Meynell.

punctually at seven. Claret. Gertrude says he takes sherry also, but I have never seen him take it, I think, and we should not be able to get really good sherry, so perhaps the claret will do, or some hock (Nursteiner) for a change. He quite likes the idea of meeting Henley. Would you think of a way? He wants Henley to come and stay here, but I am to negotiate it; and I would rather the two men see each other first. Coventry also wants to see F[rancis] T[hompson]. 'Great genius' he says distinctly, but he thinks the unreserve and intemperateness are very serious faults. Anyway he wants to know him. He will spend two nights with us. He is having a little ring made for me, with your permission, which I gave.[6]

That the meeting with Henley was effected is told by a letter from Patmore to his wife, written from Palace Court.

My dearest Soul,
There was a very interesting Dinner Party here yesterday. Henley and I took to each other quickly. He wants me to go to a party at his house on Tuesday . . . I am in clover. Mrs Meynell and Greenwood are the only persons after *Obby* [*his wife*] and Piffie, [*his son*] who are able to give me the sensation of *society*.
            Yours,
              Coventry

Mrs M. say that she will be delighted to come for a fortnight ending October 10th, if you can have her and the two little girls.[7]

During an absence from home of Wilfrid Meynell, Alice wrote to him: 'I have a lovely letter from C.P. He says that he is "startled" at the thought in my work, and altogether delighted'. She reported that all was well at home, and went on: 'All you have to do is rest and enjoy yourself. You need it. But, my Love, keep the centre of your heart for me.'[8]

And on another day: 'My own Love, It was indeed a pleasure to get your sweet and cheerful card. It found me after a much better night. I hope you have as glorious a morning as we have. I decided against going to Lymington. I want a little time to make my whole heart orderly. I think he will come up all the more for my not going.'[9]

That last paragraph suggests that then, for a moment, Alice Meynell was uncertain about her feeling for Patmore. But the moment passed, leaving her secure in her devoted love for her husband and children. The following, written to Wilfrid on 2nd September, 1892, on her arrival for a brief visit at Lymington, indicates that Patmore had perhaps been too pressing in his attentions and had now accepted a rebuke. 'The Ps all very nice. C.P. most admirably all that he should be and nothing that he should not be. My dearest Love, it is not every ten minutes I think of you but often in five.'[10]

Another letter, undated except to the year 1892, was written, prob-

ably on her birthday, to Wilfrid, who was at the sea with some of the
children.

> My own Love,
>   Thank you for your letter and *beautiful* verses and flowers. By the same post
> I got a box of roses from Coventry and I think I am the happiest woman in the
> world. I am anxious to know that you are sleeping and that the chicks are
> better. I am sleeping well. Beware of letting Monnie bathe if it is at all cold.[11]

Alice Meynell's frequent letters to Patmore during the three years of
their close friendship tell, often briefly and hurriedly, of her daily life
and work, of the people she was meeting, the books she was reading, of
her thoughts on her own writing and on his.

> My dearest Friend [*she wrote to him in September 1892*]
>   Thank you very much for your letter. I am ashamed to ask you to accept
> quite a little one today. I am distracted with things to do – and things to do
> always oppress and bewilder me, though I get them done. I have my nephew,
> Patrick Butler, to take care of and dispatch with Bastian to Ramsgate, with
> clothing and other details to execute. Then I have the paper – well-prepared it
> is true, by Wilfrid, but a great responsibility. He decided to go down to
> Lincolnshire yesterday and I wrote immediately to my cousin. F.T. has not
> turned up at all yet.[12]

Alarmed lest she should make herself ill with work, Patmore offered
to come up to London and help her during this or some other absence
of Wilfrid's. Her answer bears no date.

> My dearest Friend,
>   A thousand thanks for both your most kind offers. I could not bring you up
> for the fatigue of a two days work under all the circumstances. No one but
> Wilfrid can carry it through at this time of the week and I am the only person
> who can do it instead of him, because I know the way of it; and then I require
> the whole time from the previous Saturday. There is no lack of copy, so I
> return you the chapter. I cannot tell you how kind I think it is of you to be will-
> ing to give us so important a work.[13]

And on another occasion when he wanted to spare her by taking her
place beside Meynell at the library table, she wrote:

> My dear Friend, – You must not think of that kindness of coming up to work
> in my place. I should readily accept it if it were a question of proofs merely. But
> there are the foreign papers – arriving in a batch – to look through, and an
> unaccustomed eye would take half a day over the quest for Catholic news,
> which my practised glance can do in half an hour. Then, if Wilfrid is hard
> pressed, there is an article to do in a hurry in the evening. These little things
> require no talent, but they do require a knowledge of current things, and a
> perfect familiarity with the habits of the paper.[14]

Coventry Patmore was preparing for publication in book form a collection of his essays, some of which had appeared in *Merry England*, and he sought Alice Meynell's advice on his work of revision. 'I am so very glad', she wrote to him, 'as to what you tell me of a book of your essays. I can hardly tell you what a pleasure it would be to me to read them over with you.' In a postscript to this letter he said, in reference to one of the essays, ' "Our many points of disagreement" include Democracy, Land Laws, State Socialism and other things on which I have probably more conviction than knowledge!'[15]

Later she pleaded with him for the omission of one of his essays which she thought unworthy of him. 'Does "Distinction" go into your book? Will you think twice of it? Forgive the rather presumptuous suggestion that it is not altogether worthy – as I remember it – to accompany your best prose. It is really rather ambiguous, also; and I think (still) that it is rash. Candidly, I do not understand how without having read Lowell's essay on Dryden, you can assert *carrément* that no American has distinction. If you had read it and still thought it so I should not complain. And what about Emerson?'[16]

Patmore was not persuaded; writing again when she returned the essays Mrs Meynell said:

I know you will excuse the boldness with which I have suggested one or two small alterations merely for the sake of beauty. Sometimes the word 'which' occurred perfectly correctly but not prettily several times in one sentence. I have taken it out, substituting 'whereof' or a participle.

It has been a happiness to read again, through and through, the words of the greatest intellect I have ever known. To me the truth of your teaching is much more than convincing, it is evident instantly; the only effort I have to make is to understand – a most happy effort. But why is it that some passages – a very few and all in the later book – trouble me by getting no interior assent from me at all? They are all about women.

I would ask you to remember 'Distinction' after all. Believe me, it does such injustice to living writers (so does 'William Barnes' indeed) that it is almost a confession that you do not thoroughly know the men you slight. And that is so extremely irritating to people that I am inclined to think it has caused the partial boycotting of your work.

But worse than this is the quarrel in it with the *Spectator* and the *Guardian*. Your attitude has been always one of singular dignity. I have always thought so, and I think so now more than ever.[17]

Thus candidly did she voice her opinion; it was never her way to temper her judgement in literary matters for friendship or any other reason. But 'Distinction' stayed, though one passage to which she objected was omitted. She tried, also unsuccessfully, to make him withdraw or modify his statement in the essay upon herself which placed her work above that of all other women writers, and sent him, in support of her argument, *Sonnets from the Portuguese* and some extracts from *Wuthering Heights*. 'There have been very few great women in the history of letters', she wrote, 'but Emily Brontë was one.'[18]

But the protests which Alice Meynell made from time to time against some minor point of opinion or expression were as nothing compared with the praise that she gave to Patmore's work. 'I have never told you what I think of your poetry. It is the greatest thing in the world, the most harrowing and the sweetest. I can hardly realise that he who has written it and who is greater than his words is celestially kind to me and calls me friend.'[19] And, 'I have read again with profound admiration "Dieu et ma Dame", and I see it to be the most important setting forth of your gospel which you have made in prose. As I have told you, it belongs to a region into which I have not really entered . . . I cannot tell you how . . . overcome I feel at finding "Mrs Meynell" in such a volume. God bless you, my best friend.'[20]

Shortly before the publication of her own book of essays Alice Meynell received from Patmore a vehement entreaty to cancel one entitled 'The Leg', which offended his sense of propriety. She wrote to her publisher:

My dear Mr Lane,
    Is it possible to cancel any part of the printed book?
    The fact is I have received a telegram from a judicious person to whom I sent the duplicate proofs saying 'At any cost cancel pp. 26-28'.
    As I have returned you my own proofs, I do not know what comes on those pages. I dimly guess it must be the article on 'The Leg', and that it is considered improper. I need not say it makes me turn cold to think of publishing anything that *any*body would consider improper!
    May I ask you to be so very kind, if possible, as to get me the proof again? I am sorry to give you this additional trouble, but this is an unexpected disaster!
                    Very sincerely yours,
                    Alice Meynell[21]

    To Patmore she wrote:

My dearest Friend,
    I immediately wrote to my publisher asking him to cancel the pages and to send back my proofs so that I might see what I had cancelled. So you see this was a respectable amount of blind obedience – most gladly given. If, as I suppose, it is the little pictorial article on 'The Leg' that you object to, I confess I am surprised. Never in my life have I been among people – the strictest – who would have seen the least idea of harm in it. I published it in the N[ational] O[bserver] without a shadow of misgiving, and everybody read and liked it. So you see I cannot see it as you fear others will see it, but I gladly do what you ask of me, because you ask it . . . I suppose living much in countries where men and women go bare-legged as simply as they go bare-handed here has something to do with my unconsciousness of the harm of human legs.[22]

And a few days later:

My publisher says that to cancel the pages is 'quite impossible', but that I may change the title and alter three or four lines. Shall I accept this, or stop the publication and insist upon the substitution of a new little essay, and shut myself up for a week and write it? . . . Tell me what I shall say to the publisher.[23]

The matter was at last settled to everyone's satisfaction, with the title changed to 'Unstable Equilibrium'; but not before Lane, in a great state of perturbation, had visited Palace Court to discuss it. 'Last night after I was undressed', Mrs Meynell wrote to Patmore, 'he came dashing to the door in a hansom and I dressed again and received him.'[24]

The two volumes of Alice Meynell's work, *Poems* and *The Rhythm of Life*, were published at the end of 1892. Both were enthusiastically welcomed by the critics. Francis Thompson, reviewing *Poems* in the *Tablet*, wrote:

The footfalls of her Muse waken not sounds, but silences. We lift a feather from the marsh and say 'This way went a heron'. And so with her, the emotion sheds but a single phrase to betoken what manner of wings had lonely passage athwart her soul . . . Much poetic thought can be divorced from its poetry and rendered with completeness into naked prose. But Mrs Meynell's thought is as indissolubly wedded to imagination as light to colour. We may, abstractly, conceive the existence of light without colour but did it thus exist we should cease to be cognizant of it. So, too, divorce her thought from its imaginative expression and it might exist in her mind, but it would become invisible – that is, incommunicable. As a test, let anyone attempt to explain 'Builders of ruins' to a quite unimaginative person. He will soon conclude that, on the whole, it would be a more prosperous employment to translate Aquinas into Romany. And because this poem so centrally exhibits her characteristic of imaginative thought with feeling murmuring about its base, the poem is perhaps her greatest, or at least greatest of her longer poems . . .

Foremost singer of a sex which is at last breaking the silence that followed on Mary's *Magnificat*, she will leave to her successors a serener tradition than masculine poets bequeathed to men. She has reared from them an unpriced precedent and she has given them the law of silence. That high speech must be shod with silence, that high work must be set forth with silence, that high destiny must be waited on with silence – was a lesson the age lacked much. Our own sex has heard the nobly tacit message of Mr Coventry Patmore. But by an exception rare as beautiful, the woman's calm has been austerer-perfect than the man's.

The prose volume contained, besides the essay from which it took its name, the one on her father called 'A Remembrance', critical essays on Patmore, James Russell Lowell, and Oliver Wendell Holmes. 'Domus Angusta' gives beautiful expression to a principle to which she was faithful all her life – that those who are slow, stupid, commonplace, should never be the objects of her laughter or scorn. It was a principle the observance of which must sometimes have been hard for her, for she was not by nature tolerant of stupidity, and her sense of humour, which was so swift, must often have yearned to use itself upon some foolishness or pomposity. She denied it.

The narrow house [*she wrote*] is a human nature compelled to a large human destiny, charged with a fate too great, a history too various, for its slight capacities . . . That narrow house – there is sometimes a message from its living windows. Its bewilderment, its reluctance, its defect, show by moments from eyes that are apt to express none but common things. There are allusions unawares, involuntary appeals, in those brief glances. Far from me and from my friends be the misfortune of meeting such looks in reply to pain of our inflicting. To be clever and sensitive and to hurt the foolish and stolid – 'wouldst thou do such a deed for all the world?'

Her children, urging her to join in their merriment at some person or incident that they found ridiculous, learned not by her words but by her silence what things she found inappropriate for laughter. She who had written of her father that 'his personality made laws for me' believed example to be more potent than precept, and her dealings with her children, like so much else in her life were influenced by the memory of her father's dealings with her. There was, however, this difference – that she, even in anger, was always tender with her children, while Mr Thompson had been hard.

The Pall Mall Gazette, the *St James' Gazette*, the *Literary World*, and many more periodicals and papers carried laudatory reviews. But the supreme praise, and that which she valued most, came from Coventry Patmore in the *Fortnightly Review*. Hearing that his article was in preparation, she wrote to him: 'I can't imagine anything more delightful happening to me than that you should write it.'[25] And on receiving the proof of the article, she wrote: 'I am more than delighted and more than grateful. It is so beautiful and so profound and so generous! I think I shall awake from the whole incident as from a happy dream.'[26]

It was indeed high praise that the poet gave her:

At rare intervals the world is startled by the phenomenon of a woman whose qualities of mind and heart seem to demand a revision of its conception of womanhood and an enlargement of those limitations which it delights in regarding as essentials of her very nature, and as necessary to her beauty and attractiveness as woman. She belongs to a species quite distinct from that of the typical sweet companion of man's life, the woman who is so sweet and so companionable, even because, as Thomas Aquinas affirms, 'she is scarcely a reasonable creature' . . . I am about to direct the reader's attention to one of the very rarest products of nature and grace – a woman of genius . . . In a very small volume of very short essays, which she has just published, this lady has

shown an amount of perceptive reason and ability to discern self-evident things
as yet undiscerned, a reticence, fulness, and effectiveness of expression, which
place her in the very front rank of living writers in prose. At least half of this
little volume is *classical* work, embodying, as it does, new thought of general
and permanent significance in perfect language, and bearing in every sentence,
the hall-mark of genius, namely, the marriage of masculine force of insight
with feminine grace and tact of expression. Of the 'sweetness and wit' which
are said, by Donne, I think, to be woman's highest attainment, there is in these
little essays abundance, but they are only the living drapery of thought which
has the virile qualities of simplicity, continuity and positiveness. The essays of
Emerson, of which those of Mrs Meynell sometimes remind the reader, are not
to be compared with the best of hers in these merits: moreover, the
'transcendentalism' of the American writer afforded a far easier field than that
chosen by the English lady. It is very easy to speak splendidly and profusely
about things which transcend speech; but to write beautifully and profitably
and originally about truths which come home to everybody, and which every
one can test by common sense; to avoid with sedulous reverence the things
which are beyond the focus of the human eye, and to direct attention effectively
to those which are well within it, though they have hitherto been undiscerned
through lack of attention or the astounding imperfection of common vision for
the reality of common things, is a very different attainment. Gaiety of manner
with gravity of matter, truth perceived clearly and expressed with ease and joy,
constitute the very highest and rarest of prose writing . . . In the writing of Mrs
Meynell we have brightness and epigram enough, but they are the photosphere
of weighty, intelligible and simple human interest; and they never tempt her,
as the possession of such wit almost inevitably tempts the male writer, to any
display of scorn and contempt. She has always pity and palliatory explanation
for the falsehood which she exposes so trenchantly.

Of the personal words of praise that Patmore sent to Mrs Meynell
from himself and his wife she wrote: 'I am extremely glad to know that
you and Mrs Patmore really like the Essays. But candidly I am not surprised! That is bumptious, isn't it? But I know so well what my work is
worth, in matter and manner, processes and results, and I am quite
sure that this prose has a value. I am not at all happy in republishing
the poems however.'[27]

Francis Thompson, who was in North Wales, wrote to Wilfrid
Meynell: 'I have been wondering what criticisms had appeared on Mrs
Meynell. I have seen none, except the *Fortnightly* and the *Chronicle*.
Coventry all abroad about her poetry, Le Gallienne all abroad about her
prose.'[28]

She sent Patmore news of the press notices that she received, of
interviews that she gave, and of the publication of her work in
periodicals; sometimes she sent him cuttings, sometimes she forbade
him to read pieces that were displeasing to her.

'You are naughty about *The World*!' she wrote to him, after he had
disobeyed one of these commands. 'It was just one sentence I did not

like you to see. I know you would not seriously misunderstand it, but I felt that had I written it more deliberately I should have made any misunderstanding impossible. It is where I said that a woman loves her hairpins better than graver things. Of course I meant irresponsible women, whom their graver and better educated sisters ought to protect. But indeed I don't care that you should read such mere pot-boiling. I will send you the "Tempestuous Petticoat" which I wrote yesterday, when it comes out. It is not at all rowdy and rather pretty.'[29]

This essay was printed in the *Saturday Review*, and drew from its editor, Walter Pollock, a request for some more, 'articles connected with changing fashion like that excellent "Tempestuous Petticoat".'

'I think', Alice Meynell wrote to Patmore on another occasion, 'I cannot send you *Sylvia's Journal* with an interview with me. It is too ghastly. It makes me talk frightful grammar and say things I could never have said, amongst others "Oh yes, I have written a great deal in the *National Observer*. They take anything I like to send." It sounded so insolent that I wrote to Henley to disclaim it. He had seen it, and he wrote back very kindly, asking me to try to do him an article . . . I should very much like you to meet MacKenzie Bell. He seems a good creature and much in love with poetry. He is rather paralyzed and very nervous and shy.'[30]

After Patmore had praised some articles of hers in *Merry England*, she wrote: 'Many thanks for your delightful words about my *Merry England* articles, I ought now once and for ever to lay aside all vanity and ambition and desire for recognition. Indeed I do. I send you some more little notices. The *Queen* one, which is as full of misprints as of silly blunders, is the first that has hinted at our being log-rollers, you and I. I hope you will only be amused at it.'[31]

Her letters often told of long hours of work and were written hurriedly and wearily when her journalistic labours were finished. 'I am writing in bed after a rather hard day and bad sleep. I worked until the earliest dawn of the year without Wilfrid knowing so that I might get my *Pall Mall* done and help him.' 'I have got well through the paper, in spite of having to cancel columns and columns at the last moment to make room for a pastoral.* I worked for three days and a half incessantly except for food and sleep, and I am none the worse. In fact I liked it.' 'I have just translated for *The Register* the Pope's letter to the Hungarian Bishops – without pranks. Sometimes I make His Holiness quote our poets.'[32]

The letter that tells of another busy day when, in her husband's absence, she was doing the *Weekly Register* herself, has a rather desperate sound. 'I think I shall not have a very hard *Register*. There is

---

* Pastoral; i.e., the text of a pastoral letter from the Archbishop of Westminster to his flock.

a good long law case that makes copy. Father Cuthbert* came this morning but no one had time to talk to him. You know what it is when I am mending frocks and everyone is calling me. These are all sweet duties, but sometimes I am on the verge of crying.' And with humorous exasperation she tells how an evening's work had been lost 'because three men called after dinner. One wanted to talk literature, the other wanted to talk of religion, and the third was burning to tell me of his engagement just arranged. Of course he won the day, or rather the night, and sat the others out, and he is bringing his maiden to spend the night here to make my acquaintance.' The literary man, she continues 'was a Gloucestershire rector, who reads everything and has never met any authors and is deeply interested in everything. The religious man is a nephew of the Archbishop of Canterbury, who has given up his clerical career to become a Catholic, and has been all but starving, and ready to take a place as a tram conductor. Wilfrid has found him some work. He is very nice and fond of the children.'[33]

Another undated letter to Patmore relates troubles both literary and domestic.

My dearest Friend,
Thank you very much for your good account of your journey. I was glad indeed to hear of your good rest. Here we have not been resting. The W[eekly] R[egister] was struggled through with effort. Our troubles with the boiler (imagine my writing to you about the boiler!) are not over. The water never got warm and the kitchen is in pieces again.

The *Saturday Review* wrote to me about my wretched mistakes, sending me one letter as a specimen of many casting every form of contempt upon the unfortunate paper. I replied by telling them that though I was humiliated I felt it harder to bear the thought that I had done the Saturday some little injury. Then Mr Saintsbury wrote** again. I told him I would not accept any fee for the article. His tone is very kind.

I send you a little notice from the *Review of Reviews*. Please thank Mrs Patmore for her nice letter.

Ever your affectionate Alice[34]

In November 1892, when Sebastian was ill with pleurisy, Patmore wrote to Wilfrid Meynell: 'My dear Wilfrid, You and Alice must find it very hard to get on with your next numbers of your two Periodicals. It has struck me that I might help you by sending a little article for the next number of *Merry England* – if it be not too late. Command me

---

* The distinguished Capuchin Franciscan scholar, author of the standard English life of St Francis of Assisi.

** George Edward Bateman Saintsbury: 1845-1933. Journalist and literary critic. Assistant editor of the *Saturday Review*, 1883-1894. Then Professor of Rhetoric and English Literature at Edinburgh University. Author of *A Short History of English Literature*, *Notes from a Cellar Book*, etc.

also for correcting proofs of the *Register*, or anything else I can do for her and you in your trouble. I do hope that she will take care of her dear self. She seems strong, but she may rely too much on her strength, which, perhaps is rather that of spirit than of body, and she may break down suddenly and fatally.'[35]

Not content with this, he followed it two days later with another warning: 'You will not think it meddling on the part of one who has probably had much more experience than you have had of illness and the very serious effects of long nursing if I venture to caution you against letting Alice watch too long.'[36]

But in the following spring there was the first hint of a rift in the friendship. It seems that there was some misunderstanding and it may well have been caused by Patmore's jealousy of some other friend, which was later to become obsessive. Whatever it was, the matter was put right and Alice Meynell wrote from Lymington to her husband on 5th March, 1893: 'My dearest Lad, I hope you slept and are rather better than not. I had a good journey and am very glad indeed I came for everything that might have become very tragic is made happy. It is definitely settled . . . Diamonds prevail at dinner, and low dresses. I wish I had had room for my other. Bear in mind, pet, that the biggest of all the palms wants water.'[37]

So all was smoothed out, and on 23rd March Alice was again at Lymington, and writing to Wilfrid: 'If you suppose I am not thinking of your darlingness at work through the weary day you are much mistaken. Coventry is so melancholy and nervous at my working that I am glad the Kipling is over though I enjoyed doing it* . . . We have been for a most exquisite drive and all the way I thought of my beloved Boy writing in the fender. What a delight to see you on Saturday.'[38]

When Patmore's book of essays, *Religio Poetae*, was published she wrote to him: 'I have begun the little review of your book for *The Tablet*, but I am so slow a writer that it will not be ready for this week's number';[39] and a few days later she told him: 'I am not happy about my *Tablet* notice of you. Wilfrid read it and said it would cause great excitement, so we cut the middle out of the proof. I have asked the Editor, if it is not too inconvenient, to let me re-write it for next week, but I have not heard.'[40]

Wilfrid Scawen Blunt was a close friend of Wilfrid Meynell, and he and his wife, Lady Anne Blunt, a grand-daughter of Bryon, welcomed the Meynells often as their guests in Sussex. After one of these visits Alice Meynell wrote to Patmore:

We were much interested at the Blunts'. There was so much rather ominous heredity represented by three beautiful young girls – one the great grand-

* Probably a review. Kipling published *Many Inventions* in that year.

daughter of Byron and daughter of Wilfrid Blunt; two, granddaughters of the first Lord Lytton* and of his terrible wife, and daughters of 'Owen Meredith'.**

I am no admirer of that Lord Lytton's poetry, and it happens that I wrote in the *National Observer* an unfavourable review of his last book, published immediately after his death. In making friends with his charming widow I remembered this with some qualms of feeling. She is an ideal Ambassadress or Vice-Queen. In spite of her grey hair, exquisitely arranged, she has a peculiarly modern, up-to-date kind of grace. The dresses were so lovely that one felt somewhat like a sheep that had found its way into a flock of gazelles. We spent the whole evening in composing nursery rhymes.

A discussion as to the authorship of a well known line occurred at breakfast, the line to the effect that poets 'learn in sorrow what they teach in song'. Lady Lytton is editing her husband's letters, in one of which he quotes the line as Shelley's. She had her doubts which I confirmed. Lady Anne claimed the line for her grandfather. Mr Hake,*** who is staying here, says Shelley. Can you tell me? I promised to let Lady Lytton know.

Wilfrid Blunt, strange to say, had not read 'The Toys' before. I have never seen him so moved by admiration for any poem. I am sending him all the Odes.[41]

And after a rather different sort of social gathering Alice wrote to Patmore: 'We went on Saturday night to one of Lady Jeune's**** parties – not one of her hugest crushes, but all the pleasanter for moderate numbers. I go about so little that I never know a great many people at these parties. The few I met here all had the same little compliment, "We hardly ever see you, but we always read you." '[42]

But from this time she began to go about much more in London society. It was partly, perhaps, that she acquired a taste for it which had been absent in her before, and partly that the new fame that came to her in 1893 caused her to be sought by those hostesses who liked to have celebrities in their drawing-rooms. In that year not only were her two lately-published volumes being widely acclaimed, but she also began her weekly contribution to the column in the *Pall Mall Gazette* entitled 'The Wares of Autolycus', for which, over a period of about six years, she was to write her exquisite essays. The column was

* Edward George Earle Lytton Bulwer-Lytton: 1803-1873. Member of Parliament. Secretary for the Colonies 1858-'9; created Baron Lytton of Knebworth 1866. Novelist and playwright; m. 1827 Rosina Doyle, daughter of Francis Wheeler of Lizard Connell, Co. Limerick.

** *Nom de plume* of Edward Robert, 1st Earl of Lytton: 1831-1891. H.B.M.'s Minister at Lisbon 1874-'76; Viceroy of India and Governor General 1876-1880; ambassador extraordinary and plenipotentiary to the French Republic 1887-'91.

*** Thomas Gordon Hake: 1809-1895; physician and poet.

**** Susan Mary Elizabeth, daughter of William Stewart-Mackenzie of Seaforth and wife of Sir Francis Henry Jeune, distinguished judge, created Baron St Helier, 1905.

anonymous, but discriminating readers soon began to look eagerly for her unmistakeable pieces which appeared at first every Friday and later on Wednesdays; and it was not long before the secret of the writer's identity leaked out.

A letter of this time from her sister, Lady Butler, says: 'I heard from Miss Sweetman that you were the lion at a great literary soirée lately, in London, and that someone who wanted much to approach you could not do so, so surrounded were you. I hope you enjoy these situations.'[43]

Patmore, on his visits to London, was persuaded to go with her to literary dinner parties and even to large receptions, though such things had been unknown to him for many years. His letters to his wife, quoted by Derek Patmore in his biography, describe some of these ventures into society. 'Yesterday I went to the Meynells' to luncheon, and afterwards to Sir F. Leighton's. It was "Studio Day" when all the great artists show their pictures to their friends. Leighton's great house was thronged with fashionable people.'

And another day, after attending a reception at Lady Jeune's, he wrote: 'The party last night was an immensely swell affair. Everybody of note in "Society" seems to have been there . . . Thank you, dear, for thinking of the Camellia, but, alas, it came in ruins. They won't bear travelling. Mrs M. says that the three I sent her had all fallen to pieces.'[44]

Dinner parties were arranged at Palace Court to which were invited those of the Meynell's friends who would interest Patmore – Aubrey de Vere, Lionel Johnson, John Lane. 'The Meynells are making it as pleasant as they can for me', he wrote to his wife. 'The large dinner-party yesterday – given expressly for me – was only *too* good . . . Mrs Meynell is getting all sorts of commissions to write at very high prices, and works many hours *every* day.'[45]

In June 1894 Patmore wrote to Wilfrid Meynell: 'Give my love to your wife, and tell her how *very* kind I thought it of her to run away from all her home duties and take a journey of 200 miles just to see how I was. My hand and arm much the same as yesterday, but I feel very weak. I shall take long drives every fine day till I go to town in order to recover my good looks for Sargent and my spirits for her society.'[46]

Patmore was having his portrait painted by Sargent, and Alice Meynell went with him to the studio to see the picture when it was finished. It was at his request that Sargent then drew the portrait of her which was used as a frontispiece for her collected essays. He was an admirer of her work, and when a book of reproductions of his pictures was published in 1903 he asked that Mrs Meynell should write the introduction; which she did.

Patmore's journeys to London at this time were frequent, and the return to Lymington was sometimes postponed, one suspects, for no other reason than that he could not bear to leave Alice Meynell. There is something very unconvincing about this paragraph in a letter to his wife: 'As I said nothing in reply to the Meynells' request for an extra day instead of Friday, they seem to have arranged things on the assumption that I should stay over tomorrow. They have got a very nice dinner-party. Baddeley, Greenwood and Lionel Johnson have been invited. Nevertheless, believe me, Dear, I would *rather* have returned to you tomorrow.'[47]

After one of Mrs Meynell's visits to Lymington Patmore wrote to her husband; 'Since she left me I have not known what to do with myself for want of her society.'[48]

He gave her the manuscripts of his works, *The Unknown Eros* and *The Angel in the House*; these, the greatest gifts that it was in his power to bestow, acknowledged both his love for her and her love for his poetry. Again and again she acclaimed him the greatest of living poets. To her publisher, John Lane, she wrote: 'We have just returned from a most delightful visit to Coventry Patmore. *That* is the great man of the age.'[49] And to Patmore himself: 'I hope you will forgive me for keeping your Mss a little longer. They are quite safe and I cannot tell you what a consolation it is to me to read them as I can get time. You would not deprive me of that if you knew. But I read it [*sic*] with many tears and my heart is full of sorrows.'[50] And, 'I have read the Odes yet again with a new amazement. And then, after my tears over these, I bought a frock to please you.'[51]

Of her, Patmore wrote:

> Ah sole essential good of earth,
> And sweetest accident of Heaven,
> Their best rays, on her lucky birth,
> Beamed from the planets seven.
>
> Her body, too, is so like her –
> Sharp honey assuaged with milk,
> Straight as a stalk of lavender,
> Soft as a rope of silk.[52]

In lighter mood he wrote this portrait of her in her own home which he called

ALICIA'S VANITIES

> A rustle on the staircase
> Gives the heart gay warning;
> With a laugh like many primroses

She flies the children's chase;
And she comes in to breakfast,
As bright as a May morning,
All the day's glad duties
Shining in her face.
'You are an early caller!'
'I have brought you my review,'
In haste she takes her coffee;
Then she rises, and we two
Draw our chairs towards the fender,
And I read her praise while, sweet
She smiles in contemplation
Of her fame and her small feet.[53]

CHAPTER 12

COVENTRY PATMORE AND FRANCIS THOMPSON did not meet until 1894; but long before that they were, of course, intensely aware of each other, both as writers and, in a more personal way, as friends of the Meynells, and of Mrs Meynell in particular.

In August 1892 Thompson had written to Mrs Meynell telling her that he was going to the Friary at Crawley to talk to Father Cuthbert about Patmore's religious theories.

Dear Mrs Meynell,

I hardly know whether to occupy your mind, however briefly, with a subject which I fear, from some late indications in your manner, has begun to weary and overstretch your mind with the tyrannous extent and uncertainty of the questions which it suggests. I don't quite know why I write, indeed, except that I have confided my thoughts to no-one; and before I go to Crawley I feel a necessity of confiding them to someone. I go with very serious purpose, so far as my own mind is concerned. The alleged coincidence of Fr Cuthbert's system with C.P.'s has simplified and defined immensely the central points on which I want to assure my mind. There are two points in C.P.'s teaching – so little of it, that is, as I have gathered – which I will not away [*sic*] with.

1st his doctrine on the nature of union with God and between souls in Heaven, *as it has been presented to me*, I simply reject; my God-given instincts reject it. The permanence of carnal delight in the Heavenly union would to me make it un-heavenly. Even here on earth, my own instinct as to the typical union – given also the typical woman – would be a union like that of the Virgin and St Joseph. Provided I were united with her spirit, I would be content to wait for her body till I could be united with it on the same terms – i.e. *as a spirit*, when it was assumed to the dignity of its soul. I recognise that on earth it may not be so for the many; but after – ?

2nd The opinions I have gathered – not for the first time – from the *Fortnightly* on the number of the elect. Let him bring me the tale of the stars, and I will listen to him. I do not believe in an exclusive society of Duchesses in either life. I reject the thought that Heaven is a select little spiritual aristocracy. That it *has* its aristocracy, yes – but its commonalty too. I believe in the Commonalty of Souls. I must touch here a subject I never touched before with any person but one. I do so because you, who know that my poetry contains that deeper life of me which passes within closed flesh – you must know this thing of me already, having read those Manning verses* which I do not like to read again. You know that I believe eternal punishment: you know that when my dark hour is on me, this individual terror is the most monstrous of all that

---

* Poem on the death of Cardinal Manning written by Francis Thompson at Wilfrid Meynell's request.

haunt me. But it is individual. For others – even if the darker view were true, the fewness is relative to the total mass of mankind, not absolute; while I myself refuse to found upon so doubtful a thing as a few scattered texts a tremendous forejudgment which has behind it no consentaneous voice of the Church. And I do firmly think that none are lost who have not wilfully closed their eyes to the known light: that such as fall with constant striving, battling with their temperament; or through ill training, circumstance which shuts from them true light etc.; that all these shall taste of God's Justice, which for them is better than man's mercy. But if you would see the present state of my convictions on the subject, turn to the new *Epilogue* of my *Judgment in Heaven*. (You will find it in the wooden box containing my Ms where I have lately placed it instead of the old copy. Or Mr Meynell may have brought back the book of translations, which also contains it.) There I have given the spirit of them, which is better than any letter.

In these two matters, then, I stand implacably aloof from C.P. *if I rightly understand him*. And I go to ask Father C. if his system coincides with C.P.'s in these details, no less than in its general purport. Does he, I shall ask, hold eternal punishment *by eternal suffering?* If so, does he hold, as part of his system, the minute number of the elect? Secondly, does he hold, as part of his system, that other principle which *I have understood* to be C.P.'s? Or does he hold any principle which issues in it? Lastly, if he holds either or both of those two principles, are they integral portions of the system? Will it logically fall to pieces if either of these principles be withdrawn? Should he answer all these in the affirmative – then this famous common System, though legions of Coventry Patmores stood behind it, and hordes of Father Cuthberts, shall not stand before the instincts of my own soul. I will quarry out of it what truth my mind may think good for building with; but the System itself shall be for me anathema. For what am I a poet, but that my soul's instincts may stand like lighthouses amidst the storms of thought?

Nor will I, in any case, tie my life to any system of metaphysics or mystic theology. Mystic Systems come, and may go: a life is true apart from them. If such an aid help one to realise one's life, one's aspiration; so far it is good for one. If it confuse and perturbate one's life, one's ideas, it is clearly ill for one. And one simply excretes it. I may admire: but it does not fit my nature and I will have no more of it than fits my nature. If mystic theology is ever to form part of my life, it must be what God shall teach me, not Coventry Patmore, nor another.[1]

A month later Thompson suffered a severe relapse into the taking of laudanum, from which, as is evident from his letters, he had given a personal promise to Mrs Meynell to abstain. His drugged condition on an evening visit to Palace Court had, it appears, caused Alice Meynell to rebuke him, and to follow that rebuke with a note underlining the fact that his presence in the house with the children was not acceptable when he was under the influence of the drug.

His pathetic reply expresses how deeply hurt he was, and, by implication, showed that he was angry and jealous about Mrs

Meynell's friendship with Patmore. It is dated simply 'Wednesday Night'.

Dear Mrs Meynell,

I, at least, did not on Tuesday night adopt the attitude that you had no reason to be angry with me. On the contrary, I told you that I was very sorry I had lapsed from my word to you. It is a minor matter, but I had not again broken my promise on that Tuesday when I spoke to you. I had broken it the day before, and was bitterly remorseful for having done so. You had lightened my heart and strengthened me immensely in that night's interview: for I thought that you had taken what was indeed the true view of the matter. Namely, that under a weight of suffering of which you had not, nor ever can have, any conception, I had lapsed from my word for a single day; but having got relief from God when my burden was become beyond the strength of human nerves, I had resumed my courage and was going forward again in the path that I had promised you. You had, I thought, taken this true and merciful view; and instead of visiting me with your anger, were going to pray that I might be sustained, and to encourage me by your affection and sympathy. I went to bed, comforted, and praying that God would help me on my side to co-operate with you, and to spare you any addition to your sorrows from me. But this morning I get your terrible letter, and feel that Heaven has indeed crowned the awful trouble which has been accumulating on me for the last month, by withdrawing from me your love and sympathy, which alone gave me courage to struggle against it, and try to keep my soul from the influences which were dragging it downward. God help me, for I feel blinded and paralysed. Before Heaven I tell you, that if you knew all as I know it, you would feel that never man had more claim on you for patience than I have, however hard it may be to extend it to me: and that I am indeed more sinned against than sinning. But I make no further claim on you. I bow to your decision. Henceforth I will only come to your house when business calls me there; and if you are brought into contact with me, it need not be beyond the ordinary formalities of courtesy. I will draw back into the hermit, and leave your lives free from me; and perhaps when the curse of me is removed from the house it will settle back into its ordinary condition. As you will not see me now for (I suppose) a fortnight, it will be all the easier when you come back for us to fall into these new relations which are the old.

I will send to Palace Court to-morrow the leaderette which Mr Meynell asked me for. If there is anything else he wants from me perhaps he will send a note to my lodgings.

Yours sincerely
Francis Thompson

P.S. Will you, as a last favour, keep what I send you with this, in memorial of the time before this man's shadow fell across me; when indeed I lived highly and loved you, God knows, as I still do, as purely as an angel? That may be commoner in your experience of man than in mine. I do not know. They are your letters, which I have worn in front of my heart since you first began to send me any: though two precious ones are lost. I am no longer worthy to wear them, since I have forfeited your love and respect. Will you keep them 'For sake of the dead him whose name they bear?' . . .

P.P.S. The postscript is repented of, and I have not returned you the letters. Do not think, dear lady, that I reproach you with your action. Within your knowledge you have acted perfectly justly, as you always do. And perhaps it will prove for the best in the end. Good-bye, if this should reach you in time. In my despair I was writing to Coventry Patmore. And if that note had reached him, offering him my unqualified alliance, it would have been the death-knell of all our souls. [2]

Next day, before Thompson had despatched the letter, he received a note from Wilfrid Meynell asking him to come to Palace Court. He replied on Thursday evening:

Dear Mr Meynell,

I am not fit to come in tonight. I have broken my promise to Mrs Meynell both yesterday and today. She was wrong in thinking that I had broken it on Tuesday when she spoke to me; nor did I guess that she thought so. I had broken it the day before, for the first, and it might have been the last time; broken by the pressure, night and day, of an extra-natural conflict in which you do not believe because – Englishman-like – it is outside your personal experience, as before that it was outside mine. But that Monday night and on the Tuesday following I found myself completely delivered; as if God saw that the limits of human endurance had been passed. I was full of remorse for what I had done, and resolved never again to add to her sorrows by giving her such pain on account of me. Then, on the Wednesday morning, came her letter as a crushing blow, breaking me utterly to pieces on the top of all I had gone through. I fell into wild recklessness and carelessness about my soul; and, as I have said, I broke my word to her completely both that day and today. Therefore I cannot come in tonight. But be comforted, if you can. Your letter has given me a ray of hope and comfort again; and if you can pardon and overlook what is past, I on my side will take up the task of amendment again. The dreadful conflict against the unseen will of that man at Lymington seems altogether to have passed from me; and if I am only delivered from the thought that she and you have cast me off and turned against me, I can once more regain the mastery of my own self and soul. God and her innocence help her, and God help us who are left behind. If she will write me two lines to say that she pardons me and does not withdraw her affection from me, she shall, please God, hear a good account of me when she returns. I send her, by way of explanation, the letter I wrote last night but feared to forward today.

                    Yours,
                        Francis[3]

Wilfrid Meynell, whose patience in soothing Thompson's hurt feelings, and procuring help for his battered body, was unending, felt that it was necessary to get the poet away from London for a time, and he arranged for him to go to Pantasaph, in North Wales. There he would be under the care of the Capuchin friars, among whom he already had, through the Meynells, several friends. Away in the country he would be unable to obtain drugs secretly; and Meynell thought that the air of Wales, too, would be better for him than that of London. A lodging was found for him at the gates of the monastery.

From there, on 4th January, 1893, Francis Thompson wrote to Wilfrid Meynell reporting that he thought the opium habit was broken. He wished now to go out and divert himself by taking walks, but was unable to do so because of a mishap sadly typical of the poor poet. 'I can't get out because snow has fallen, and by a foolish trick before I left London I have ruined my boots. Cowering over the fire at Fernhead Road one night, I let my boot hang too near over the bars, and before I noticed it, the tip was burned off. At first I thought it was only the tip of the sole, and so nothing was spoilt but appearances. Since I came here, however, I discover to my dismay that the upper leather is charred along with the tip of the sole; and it has come away from the sole, split, and begun to peel off, leaving the snow free to get in through the open end of the boot. So that just when I want and long for walking to act as a tonic against my debility, I am compelled to stay in the house.'[4]

No doubt Meynell supplied new boots. The poet spoke only the truth when he wrote once: 'I am an expensive taste – the most ruinous taste you ever had, my poor Wilfrid!'[5]

In that year, 1893, John Lane published *Poems* by Francis Thompson. Their preparation, shared between Thompson and the Meynells, caused much correspondence between London and Pantasaph, with discussions about the alteration of a line or the admissibility of one of Thompson's curiously unorthodox words. 'As for immediatably,' he wrote, 'it is in all respects the one and only right word for the line, as regards the exact shade of meaning and feeling, and as regards the rhythmical movement it gives to the line.' 'I send you the line altered altogether. This must do. The stanza cannot go out.'[6] And Alice Meynell wrote to him: 'The Bible has unquenchable, and I don't think it could have "quenchless". Lowell has "exhaustless" somewhere. I think one can strictly hold "less" to equal "minus" or "without", and with these the verb is impossible. I remember refusing to be taught a setting of some words of Praed's* that had "tameless" for "untamable", so you see it is an old objection with me.'[7]

Francis Thompson had written several poems to the Meynell children, and of one of these Alice Meynell spoke in this letter: 'Never has there been such a dance of words as in "The Making of Viola". All

---

* Winthrop Mackworth Praed: 1802-1839. Barrister and member of Parliament; Secretary of the Board of Control in Peel's government, 1834. Famed for his clever *vers-de-société* and mild political satires in verse. His romantic verse-tales enjoyed great popularity for a time.

other writers make their words dance on the ground with a certain weight, but these go in the blue sky. I have to unsay everything I said in criticism of that lovely poem. I think the long syllables make themselves valued in every case. But I do not like three syllables in the course of the poem – the three that give the iambic movement. I have not made up my mind as to the alternative endings. They are all so beautiful.'

In sending him the proofs she wrote: 'Here are your wonderful poems – most wonderful and beautiful. It is a great event to me to send you these proofs.'[8]

The group of poems to Mrs Meynell called 'Love in Dian's Lap', which had been written during the past three years, and two of which had already appeared in *Merry England*, were in this volume. In the beautiful 'Her Portrait' Thompson wrote;

> How could I gauge what beauty is her dole,
> Who cannot see her countenance for her soul,
> As birds see not the casement for the sky?
> And, as 'tis check they prove its presence by,
> I know not of her body till I find
> My flight debarred the heaven of her mind.

It is perhaps not inapposite to quote here, beside Thompson's public homage to Mrs Meynell, a later entry in his notebook which tells the private story of the course of his love.

I yielded to the insistent commands of my conscience and uprooted my heart – as I supposed. Later, the renewed presence of the beloved lady renewed the love I thought deracinated. For a while I swung vacillant . . . I thought I owed it to her whom I loved more than my love of her finally to uproot that love, to pluck away the last fibres of it, that I might be beyond treachery to my resolved duty. And at this second effort I finished what the first had left incomplete. The initial agony had really been decisive, and to complete the process needed only resolution. But it left that lady still the first, the one veritable, full-orbed and apocalyptic love of my life. Through her was shewn me the uttermost of what love could be – the possible divinities and celestial prophecies of it. None other could have taught them quite thus, for none other had in her the like unconscious latencies of utter spirituality. Surely she will one day realise them, as by her sweet, humble and stainless life she has deserved to do.[9]

Poems was dedicated 'To Wilfrid and Alice Meynell'. Before publication Wilfrid Meynell had expressed a wish that his own name should not appear, but only that of his wife. Thompson wrote to him:

With regard to substituting your full names for the initials, do as you please. But I cannot consent to the withdrawal of *your* name. You have of course the right to refuse to accept the dedication to yourself. But in that case I have the right to withdraw the dedication altogether, as I should certainly do. I should belie both the truth and my own feelings if I represented Mrs Meynell as the sole person to whom I owe what it has been given me to accomplish in poetry. Suffer this – the sole thing, as unfortunate necessities of exclusion would have it, which links this first, possibly this only volume, with your name – suffer this to stand. I should feel deeply hurt if you refused me this gratification.[10]

The book had a mixed reception from the critics; but a review by Patmore in the *Fortnightly* pleased Thompson greatly. He wrote to Alice Meynell: 'I am delighted with it. From first to last it is preeminently *just*; and managed to combine fine praise with discriminate and illuminating criticism of defects and limitations. "Illuminating"; for other critics note the symptoms of one's poetic maladies, he diagnoses the seat of the disease. I have got more help and self-knowledge from his article than from anything else which has appeared. Will you convey to him my warmest thanks for an article which cannot but remain a landmark in my life?'[11]

In the previous year, when *Religio Poetae* was published, he had written to Patmore: 'Your little book stands by the stream of current literature like Cleopatra's needle by the dirt-eating Thames.'[12]

Besides Thompson's own letters Wilfrid Meynell received constant reports of his health from others at Pantasaph: Father Cuthbert, and Mrs Blackburn, Vernon Blackburn's mother, who was a neighbour in the village. In the spring of 1894 these reports became disquieting, and the Meynells decided to go and see for themselves how the poet was faring. Alice Meynell wrote of this visit in her essay 'At Monastery Gates', which appeared in the *Pall Mall Gazette* and was later published in her book *The Colour of Life*:

> The poet, too, lives at the monastery gates, and on monastery ground, in a seclusion which the tidings of the sequence of his editions hardly reaches. There is no disturbing renown to be got among the cabins of the Flintshire hills. Homeward, over the verge, from other valleys, his light figure flits at nightfall, like a moth . . .
>
> With every midnight the sweet contralto bells call the community who get up gaily to this difficult service. Of all the duties this one never grows easy or familiar, and therefore never habitual. It is something to have found but one act aloof from habit. It is not merely that the friars overcome the habit of sleep. The subtler point is that they can never acquire the habit of sacrificing sleep. What art, what literature, or what life but would gain a secret security by such a point of perpetual freshness and perpetual initiative? It is not possible to get up at midnight without a will that is new night by night. So should the writer's work be done, and, with an intention perpetually unique, the poet's.

After the Meynells had left Pantasaph, Francis Thompson, much improved in spirits, was hard at work, feeling a return of his poetical power. He wrote to them:

Dearest Wilfrid and Alice, – As you are together in my thoughts, so let me join you together in this note. I cannot express to you what deep happiness your visit gave me; how dear it was to see your faces again. I think 'the leaves fell from the day' indeed when your train went out of the station; and I never heard the birds with such sad voices.[13]

Later, when he had seen the article 'At Monastery Gates', Thompson wrote to Alice Meynell:

Madonna soavissima,

Just a line to say how delighted I have been with your Pall Mall article on Pantasaph. It is entirely in your old sensitive subtly perfumed style; which, to say truth, I have been half afraid you might be losing amidst the drudgery of *Autolycus* and such gear. How it touches me to hear the well-remembered unique voice once again, 'piercing sweet' as ever! What gratification it has given at the monastery perhaps another than I may tell you, or may have told you. I hope it is the prelude to a fresh welling-forth of the old waters.[14]

The meeting of Francis Thompson and Coventry Patmore had taken place in the Meynells' house, and Patmore gave his impressions in a letter to his wife. It is quoted in Derek Patmore's biography of his grandfather, but as no date is given to the letter there is nothing to tell us when it took place.

'Yesterday', Patmore wrote, 'was Mrs Meynell's day "at home" and there were several fine musicians and a good deal of music. Meynell's friends are, for the most part, tremendous radicals – *so* radical that I am amused, rather than angry, and they put up with my rabid Toryism with equal good humour.' He adds that he had seen Francis Thompson on the previous day, and had had some private talk with him. 'All I saw in him was pleasant and attractive – so I asked him to come for some Sunday to Lymington, which he joyfully promised to do.'

Probably this meeting – which must, of course, have occurred when Thompson was on a visit to London from Pantasaph – together with Patmore's praise for the other poet's work, helped to dispel the strong suspicion and dislike that Thompson had felt for Patmore. They became friends, and in October 1894 Patmore went to Pantasaph to visit Thompson. 'I have had a charming visit from Mr Patmore', he wrote to Alice Meynell. 'He bore himself towards me with a dignity and magnanimity which are not of this age's stature. By the way, he repeated to me two or three short poems addressed to yourself. I hope there may be a series of such songs. You would then have a triple tiara indeed – crowned by yourself, by me, and highest crowned by him.'[15]

In May 1895 Mrs Meynell was at Clevedon with four of the children. A few of her letters to her husband during that visit remain. One is concerned with family affairs, the happiness of the children, and her own longing to see Wilfrid again.

Dearest Love – I am just posting my *Album* and shall jog through my *Tablet* at the same leisurely rate. If I can think of a P.M.G. column I need not hurry about returning for I am more or less wanted here. Mary [the nurse] is very good but the two smaller children are wild. But for the occasional outbreak, they are exceedingly happy. They tumble down the bank and climb up again for something like ten steady hours a day and the rest of the time they are playing with the schoolchildren . . . Their appetites are noble. It is heavenly weather. If I stay, Darling, what would you think of coming down on Friday? It would be purely delightful with you. Try, my lad. Then you can bring us back. I should like you to see your lovely four on these daisies. I hope my poor little paragraphs will be in time to save you the last few hundred words. Heaven bless you my own little lad.[16]

At that time she was writing weekly articles for the *Pall Mall Gazette* (The Wares of Autolycus), the *Tablet*, and the *Album*, for which she was doing a series called 'Child Life'.

Another letter from Clevedon reported that she was recovering from one of the migraine headaches that afflicted her so often. 'I have been free from acute pain since the forenoon of today. In fact these are the merest retreating growls – so different from the advancing growls. I believe I shall sleep well.'[17]

The verdict in the final Oscar Wilde trial had just been made known, and she said of it: 'As *seclusion* two years are far too little. As punishment one wishes they might be made more tolerable. But while there is a weak omnibus horse at work or a hungry cat I am not going to spend feeling on Oscar.'

Another letter shows how troubled she was by the violent jealousies that Patmore was displaying; they were to become increasingly obsessive and eventually to end their friendship. 'I want to ask you this,' she wrote to her husband, 'never to be hurt by anything that C.P. may say or suggest until you have asked me. I hate to say it but he has real illusions and some of them seem ineradicable. On the point of Graham R.* he seems satisfied, but even there he does not seem fully to understand the plain things I said so I feared he might write to you. If he does, let me see the letter.'[18]

What exactly happened in the ending of the friendship between Mrs Meynell and Patmore we have never explicitly been told. The small number of her letters to him that remain all date from an earlier time, before there was any hint of trouble between them. After Patmore's death Mrs Meynell destroyed virtually all his letters to her; her son Francis, in his book *My Lives*, said that she had told him she felt they might be misunderstood. The chief scraps of information about the sad story are in the letters that passed between Patmore and Thompson, and in a few from Patmore to Wilfrid Meynell.

---

* Graham R., unidentified. Possibly Graham Robertson, the designer of the costumes for the banned production of Oscar Wilde's *Salome?*

On the subject of her feelings for Patmore Alice Meynell said nothing. We only know that she called this the greatest friendship of her life, and that in a letter written soon after his death she spoke of him as the friend 'who for four years had been much more than my second self'.[19] That there was admiration, tenderness, pity and deep affection for him is clear; and that it grieved her to make him unhappy. Plainly Patmore was not, in the end, content with the friendship which was all that she could offer him; and it seems that he believed that she loved him, and wanted her to acknowledge it. She, on her side, felt the whole edifice of her life threatened by the white heat of Patmore's passionate love for her, and understood that he had made their friendship impossible. Francis Meynell says in *My Lives* that she parted from Patmore 'at her husband's earnest wish'; and there is 'hearsay evidence' to corroborate this from one who relates that Wilfrid Meynell himself said, many years later, that he had asked her to end the friendship. This should not be taken to mean that he objected to the friendship in itself or felt it to be in any way a threat to his marriage. The evidence suggests that Alice Meynell was grieved by Patmore's violent and irrational jealousies and ridiculous accusations of unduly close friendships with other men, and that eventually his obsession (which was to become almost pathological) made life so difficult that Wilfrid, for her own sake, felt it better for her not to see him any more. That was probably in, or shortly before, July 1895, when Alice published anonymously in the *Pall Mall Gazette* a poem which was addressed (though not, of course, explicitly) to Coventry Patmore.

WHY WILT THOU CHIDE?

Why wilt thou chide,
Who hast attained to be denied?
   O learn, above
All price is my refusal, Love.
   My sacred Nay
Was never cheapened by the way.
Thy single sorrow crowns thee lord
Of an unpurchasable word.

   O strong, O pure!
As Yea makes happier loves secure,
   I vow thee this
Unique rejection of a kiss.
   I guard for thee
This jealous sad monopoly.
I seal this honour thine; none dare
Hope for a part in thy despair.

On 11th July Patmore wrote to Francis Thompson:

I need not tell you how much I value your good opinion of my little book.*
There is only one person living whose opinion would have been equally
valuable; but *she* has not deigned to say or write anything about it. I think she
treats us both very badly! You were right about the Preface being written *De
Profundis*. Though my physical health is pretty well restored, I go on with a
perpetual heartache. None can see God – or Goddess – and live.

I enclose a little poem, issued anonymously by our Friend, in the P.M.G. I
think you will agree that, though little, it is one of the finest poems ever
written by man or woman. Pray put it into an envelope, when you have copied
it, and return it to me.[20]

In a postscript to this letter Patmore says 'I have only seen our Friend
twice during the past ten months.'

On 29th July Patmore wrote again; the intermediate letter from
Thompson has disappeared.

My dear Thompson,

I am glad you think as I do about those 'wonderful' verses. I have quoted
your words in a letter I have written to our Friend. They will delight her
greatly. Her one abiding passion is for literary fame, and, though she would
like much to have 'popularity' thrown in, I think she values your praise and
mine more than she does that of the 'groundlings' – unless, indeed, the good
word of the latter should secure her, as that alone can, a tomb in Westminster
Abbey. This is her one real weakness – and her most exasperating charm.[21]

In September Thompson wrote to Patmore, sending him a poem
called 'A Captain of Song', which bore the inscription: 'On a Portrait of
Coventry Patmore by J. S. Sargent, R.A.' His affection and admiration
for one whom he had earlier called 'that man at Lymington' were now
great, and the friendship thrived upon their mutual preoccupation with
Mrs Meynell. 'I send you now', he wrote, 'a little thing which I think I
should flinch from A.M. seeing. She would be indignant at the
"mighty cruelties".** I think you will not. Like Cromwell, I take it, you
would disdain that your painter should omit a wart.'[22]

> Ye shall mark well
> The mighty cruelties which arise and mar
> That countenance of control,
> With minatory warnings of a soul
> That hath to its own selfhood been most fell,
> And is not weak to spare.

To this Patmore replied:

My dear Thompson, Your 'Captain of Song' is a very grand poem, and quite

---

*   *The Rod, the Root, and the Flower*

**   'mighty cruelties' refer to a facet of Coventry Patmore's character. The lines in the
poem read:

free, though colossal, from any partial violent emphasis. I am not, however, that Dantesque being which you and Sargent make me out to be; but that is no defect in the Poem or the Picture, *as* a Poem and a Picture.

I have taken the liberty to keep a copy, which, however, I will at once destroy if you object. I do not think that A.M. would disapprove. I have not hidden from her 'the mighty cruelties'. They have often drawn tears from her eyes . . .

A.M.'s Selection from my Poems will appear early in October, I believe. It is wholly her doing. I have not seen a page of the book, except the Preface, which, like your Poem, is 'colossal'.[23]

The selection from Patmore's poetry which Alice Meynell edited was published by Heinemann under the title *Poetry of Pathos and Delight*. She wanted to make his poetry known and loved by a wider public, and had therefore chosen such of his poems as she felt would 'give a world that was indifferent or estranged an easy approach to this unknown treasure as one might hope for any great good suddenly to befall mankind.'

In October Patmore again wrote to Thompson about 'A Captain of Song': 'A.M. thinks your poem about the portrait "exceedingly fine". As to her "silence", I confess I cannot understand it. There has been much, also, in her conduct to me which I cannot understand; but she is such a *woman* that one is compelled to worship her as much for what, in any other, would be called faults as for her other beauties.'[24]

In a postscript to this letter Patmore said: 'I have not seen A.M. since the beginning of May – and she does not seem to miss me.'

Patmore now wrote to the *Saturday Review*, which was edited by Frank Harris, suggesting the appointment of Mrs Meynell to the Laureateship, which had been vacant since the death of Tennyson three years before. Thompson wrote to him: 'I think your *Saturday* letter very felicitously put. But alas! small are the chances of any government acting on it.'[25] In this letter Francis Thompson said that ill health and depression had delayed his writing earlier:

A violent paroxysm of the A.M. – malady burst on me at the time I wrote 'A Captain of Song' (hence the tone of that poem); such as I have not known since the days, three years ago, when I put passion under my feet. It has only recently dropped from me, and left me feeling broken and much older. Indeed, one woman here told me that my beard was showing more white streaks, and my manner growing sterner. Your own experience, I think, will make you pardon my negligence . . .

I have not received the *Selections*. A.M. has only once in my life sent me any book of hers – *Essays* – and I expect it is the only one I ever shall receive from her. Women – and this sweet Lady and fine genius is 'no more but even a woman' – have a fatal ease in 'getting used' to devotion. It soon comes to seem no mighty merit on your part; since after all it is not your doing – you cannot help it. I should indeed like to see the book. The selections in themselves must possess a peculiar interest for me; and the Preface I am most eager to read.[26]

'Thank God', Patmore wrote in his reply to this letter, 'I never "get used" to any true good! I would rather hang for ever on the Cross of a lost felicity than that it should be consumed by the rust of "use".'[27]

In the *Pall Mall Gazette* of 23rd December, 1895 Alice Meynell reviewed George Meredith's *The Amazing Marriage*, calling it 'a masterpiece by a master hand. Mr Meredith is easily first of our living English authors, and among the highest of all time his rank is high. He stands towering above his contemporaries, distinguished by an especial power of delicate, intricate analysis; of a passionate energy of imagination; of a style that grips and holds the mind; of a subtle sense of humour; of a lightly-poising mockery; and of a romantic rare refinement of attitude towards the world that is his and ours alike, truly, but in how different and humbling a degree of possession!'

Obviously, this passage would not have been read with pleasure at Lymington.

CHAPTER 13

THROUGH THE AUTUMN AND WINTER Patmore continued to pour out, in his letters to Thompson, his bitterness and deep sense of injury. He was a sick man, sunk in self-pity, tortured by jealousy, waiting to die. It was a tragic ending to the life of a great man. In one of his most hysterical outbursts Vernon Blackburn was made the target of his obsessive jealousy. Blackburn was almost twenty years younger than Mrs Meynell, and it was quite absurd to imagine that there was anything romantic between them. He admired her greatly, and she had a fond maternal feeling for him. Two years earlier she had written to Wilfrid Meynell about him, after the healing of some slight misunderstanding. 'I had a nice Sunday with my dear Vernon whom I take back to a full measure of tenderness and confidence. He spoke to me freely of his life of real sacrifice for which he takes no merit. Everything I can do to make it happier I must certainly do and he well deserves to take pleasure in his little ambitions, seeing they are all he has. He told me he loves you most dearly. I always knew he did and now he has told me of his feeling.'[1]

Viola Meynell said that Vernon Blackburn was one of the 'dropping-in friends' at Palace Court. 'His chair in the drawing-room was the piano stool.' He was stout, and the children marvelled at the agility of his fat fingers on the keyboard. 'His sweet, weak, high voice, too, went oddly with his proportions. There was no question, however, of smiling at him; he was the first himself to find matter for smiling round about him. There can never have been anyone who laughed with more excellent pleasure.'[2]

Blackburn himself had expressed his feeling for Mrs Meynell in a letter written some time before. 'My own wild desires lead me to daily failure and to shocking shortcomings, but somewhere beyond, in my own heart, there is a place without law, for no law is necessary; without morality, for no desire is there to be checked; and there you stand, always virginal, always beloved.'[3]

Now Patmore wrote to Francis Thompson a letter to which the use of a dash for Mrs Meynell's name, and initials for Blackburn's, added an air of mystery, of malicious secrecy. 'I ought to tell you that, in a letter I have just received — tells me that V.B. has just engaged himself to be married. How this is reconcileable with his being every night at P[alace] C[ourt] and behaving otherwise to — as he does, I do not understand. What you tell me about the forgetfulness of the little Poem which conferred on — everlasting fame, is wonderful indeed!' He continued sadly:

'God bless you and help you to bear your crown of thorns, and to prosper in the great, though possibly obscure career He seems to have marked out for you! *My* work, such as it is, is done and I am now only waiting, somewhat impatiently, for death, and the fulfilment of the promises of God, which include all that we have ever desired here, in perfection beyond all hope.'[4]

Six weeks later Patmore wrote again in reply to a letter of Thompson's which is missing, still on the subject of Vernon Blackburn. Patmore said that he was surprised by the information that Thompson had sent him, and that if Blackburn ' "has come to grief" so suddenly, it is probably because he has presumed too far, and has found that permission to worship does not imply any reciprocity of adoration. I should much like to know more, if you can tell me more.'[5]

After some delay because he was unwell Thompson wrote back:

My meaning about V.B. was that he had come to grief *financially*, and, according to my information at that time, had disappeared from all his friends. Since then, I have heard of W.M. being in communication with him; but whether he now visits at Palace Court I have no means of knowing. In any case, surely the fact that, as you tell me, he had announced himself engaged before this crash came, prevents any occasion for uneasiness with regard to him. Surely no woman can believe in the constancy and exclusiveness of his devotion after that. And I am sorry to hear of your resolution to break off all communication with A.M., which I cannot think will make for your happiness; and I wish you might feel it possible to recede from it. It appears to me that what you saw at Palace Court, interpreted by what you mention of her demeanour, may bear another construction than what you put upon it. V.B. would be quite capable of adopting that demeanour out of personal and petty spite towards yourself, relying on her gentleness and timidity to prevent a public snubbing, which I do not think she is capable of administering to any man. And so she might well be embarrassed and frightened. It is impossible to believe that she has altered towards yourself, after that poem of hers, and what I saw and told you of her evident feeling about you in the last days of my own stay in London. I am sorry to think that the outpouring of my own bitter mood possibly stimulated yours; when I should rather do what I can to mitigate the darkness in your life.[6]

The reference in Patmore's earlier letter to 'the forgetfulness of the little Poem which conferred on — everlasting fame' arose from an unfortunate remark made by one of Francis Thompson's Franciscan friends, Father Anselm.* Talking one day of Mrs Meynell, Thompson said that when he last saw her he fancied her delicate health and hard work had made her grow absent-minded; and Father Anselm recalled

---

* Anselm Kenealy: for some time a member of the Capuchin community at Pantasaph; then Father Guardian of the friary at Crawley. He later became Archbishop of Simla.

that when he had quoted to her, at a recent meeting with her, two lines from one of Thompson's poems, she had said: 'I think I have heard them before; whose are they?' To the friar the lapse seemed pardonable enough, and he had not reckoned on the effect that the relating of the incident would have on Thompson. When, too late, he realised that the poet was bitterly offended, he wrote to Mrs Meynell to apologise. He had, it seems, received from her a postcard in answer to a letter of his, and as this was an unusual form of communication from her he had feared that it was a sign of her displeasure with him for his indiscretion.

My dear Mrs Meynell,

Your letter which I received this morning . . . is kindness and sweetness itself and I am grateful to you for the graciousness with which you have referred to our relations with each other. I should look upon myself as a consummate snob if I objected to a post card. And if I did so object to cards from all the world I never should from you. Your card is more precious than the letters of most women. But a post card was unlike you, so utterly unlike you that I gave it an interpretation and that interpretation was uttered by the small still voice of my guilty conscience.

He went on to relate the incident, and then described the aftermath.

Our conversation, still as a summer's evening and as sympathetic, was suddenly charged with the electricty of passion – I knew there must be a storm – What passed across the intervening spaces of Pantasaph and Lymington I know not precisely. But when I got your post card my conscience smote me and said 'See how the thunder has rolled.' Then he told me that in the uncontrolled emotion of the moment he had written to C.P. I did not know any more. I simply felt that you would naturally think I had not behaved well. My feeling of what I fancied you felt is well expressed by you in your last appreciated letter when you observe: 'I may have said it was a pity my temporary forgetfulness had been revealed to F.T.' It was the idea that you would feel this, and with so much reason, that caused me pain and made me think you would feel safer behind cards and silence.

And now I thank you once again for your charming indulgence.[7]

What had 'passed across the intervening spaces of Pantasaph and Lymington' was a bitter complaint from Francis Thompson which had added fuel to the flames of Patmore's jealousy, and he wrote to Meynell, commenting that his wife, presumably, was surfeited with praise and valued it no more. 'What fate', he asked rhetorically, 'must my poor verses to her expect if F.T.'s are so soon forgotten!'[8]

The busy mother of seven children – the youngest only five – and the busy journalist committed to meeting the deadline for her columns, constantly occupied with helping her husband in his editorial work, doing reviews and seeking bits of news that would make paragraphs, must often have been exasperated by the egotism and touchiness of these poets who behaved as though she had nothing to think of but pleasing them.

The correspondence went to and fro between Coventry Patmore and Francis Thompson. In February the older man wrote to Pantasaph:

My dear Thompson, Is it too great a favour to ask of you that you will come down here again for a night or two, this week or next? I live a very solitary and melancholy life. You dissipate my solitude and melancholy as no other, but one, can. We have both been made immortal by the same vision; and that, it seems to me, is such a ground of good fellowship as no other condition can supply.

> Yours ever,
> Coventry Patmore

I am restored to my normal state of health, and we can take walks. I have abandoned my intention of going to town soon. Give my kind regards to Mr and Mrs Meynell.[9]

The following month there was another and more mournful letter:

My dear Thompson,

I am very sorry to hear continued bad news of you. I cannot give much better of myself. In fact, I am literally dying of having seen God, and of the vision having been withdrawn. I have been continually ill – very ill – for some two years. Two eminent Doctors have asked me whether this long series of *acute* maladies was preceded by some long sorrow! My only comfort is that the end cannot be far off.[10]

Mrs Meynell and Patmore must have met again at about this time (if the dating is correct), for Mrs Belloc-Lowndes relates in her memoirs how they visited her together one afternoon at her house in London.

I heard a ring at my front door. As my maid was out, I ran down and opened it to see standing on the narrow pavement Alice Meynell with, by her side, a tall man I recognised as Coventry Patmore.

Alice cried gaily, 'We've come to pay you a wedding call!'* . . . They then followed me up to the drawing room . . .

Mr Patmore walked across the room and took up his stand in front of the fireplace. He did not speak, only stared before him with an angry expression on his face. I am not easily offended, but I remember feeling exceedingly offended at his behaviour, the more so that I could not but recollect the kind and affectionate way in which my mother always spoke of him. She had known him and his first wife, Emily Patmore, 'The Angel in the House', when he was an assistant librarian in the British Museum. They had met in the house of Mrs Procter, and she had been taken to his house by Rossetti. As was invariably her way when she came in touch with people who were anxious and care-laden, she had at once made friends with Mrs Patmore. This fact had been gratefully recalled by Coventry Patmore when my mother had called on him at Hastings

---

* Mrs Belloc-Lowndes was then newly married.

during my childhood. So I was astonished at his rude unkindness.

I sat by Mrs Meynell on my little sofa, and each of us would now and again say a few words which had for object that of bringing Mr Patmore into our conversation. But after saying 'yes' or 'no' in reply to a direct question, he remained silent. So soon she got up, and with a feeling of mingled relief and resentment, I saw them out of the house.

At the time Mr Patmore's behaviour appeared to me inexplicable, and years went by before I learnt what had caused him to put not only the daughter of a woman to whom he owed a measure of gratitude, but kind Alice Meynell also to so much discomfort. I now know that at the time of this, to me, memorable visit, Coventry Patmore, passionately jealous of Mrs Meynell's friendship with George Meredith, was exceedingly unhappy. He must have been bitterly incensed that his adored friend should choose to waste some of the time he must have felt to be precious – for they could never be really alone together when inside her house – paying a visit to a young married woman of whom he knew little. He died in the autumn of that year.

I had never liked him, partly because I thought him vain, and to quote an expressive word more in use then than now, 'touchy'. At the time of this enforced call on me, he was on the brink of old age, yet still a splendidly handsome man. He was tall, held himself erect, and his fine aquiline face was crowned by a mass of grey hair which he wore rather long. He had remarkable eyes – dark, piercing, and young in expression. His portrait by Sargent is exactly as I remember him.[11]

Plainly, the friendship was still in difficulties.

It is perhaps of interest to quote here what Mrs Belloc-Lowndes said about Alice Meynell:

Though I admired both her distinguished prose and her beautiful verse, what attracted me was her unusual personality, and her exceeding and unobtrusive kindness. She was also gifted with a quality which is rare and to me peculiarly attaching. This was her intuitive understanding of, and her sympathy with, the kind of problem which could never in any circumstances have touched her own life . . . Occasionally she talked to me in an intimate way of her life and of her feelings; even, now and again, of her verse . . .

She was pale, and in repose her face was grave, even sad; and she had peculiar, and most beautiful, dark eyes. The well-known drawing of Sargent reveals something of her gentle and delicate nature. The way she dressed gave me especial pleasure. Her gowns were simple and can have cost but little money, for when I knew them she and her husband were far from well off, and I think they had sunk what capital they possessed in building their house. But while her frocks and hats were sufficiently in the fashion to arouse no comment, at a time when women's clothes were often actually ugly everything worn by Alice Meynell, indoors and out-of-doors, was charming and distinguished.[12]

In June of that year – 1895 – Wilfrid Meynell went to Rome for a short visit, and Francis Thompson came to London and helped Alice Meynell in his own particular way which was sometimes helpful and sometimes not. She wrote to her husband shortly after his departure:

My dearest Lad,

I am sorry you laboured *quite* so hard. You should leave more to your industrious wife. It is early afternoon, Wednesday, and the paper is full and overset. I did a leaderette this morning after trotting to the *Pall Mall* with a tolly* proof which wanted much correcting and had not come the night before, having been sent to K[atherine] T[ynan] by mistake. F.T. has done a few books, being driven thereto at the point of the bayonet . . .

Was it quite dark when you passed all those historic cities between Turin and Genoa, and when you threaded that lovely coast from Genoa to Spezia which is particularly mine? I wish I knew the time of your arrival within sight of the dome . . .[13]

And on another day:

My Sweetheart, I follow you on your way all the time.

I am sure things will go well here. F.T. is doing his Catholic books but he discusses the theology with me the whole time, and exclaims with indignation at the various things he finds there. He is therefore in excellent spirits . . . I have left much of my life in the Churches near you – S. Andrea delle Fratte, the Gesù e Maria, Santa Maria del Popolo. Oh see *all* you can. Love from the darlings, Yours ever James[14]

In July, with Meynell home again, Alice went to Lymington on what was evidently meant to be a peace-making visit, accompanied by the five-year-old Francis. She wrote to Meynell: 'Everything here has gone, so far, much better than I thought. If you can get a proof of the photo send it – it will be something to talk about . . . Francis and Coventry get on very well and Mrs Patmore is exceedingly kind.'[15] The fact that she felt the need of something to help the conversation does not suggest an easy atmosphere, and if anything was accomplished by the visit the result was not lasting.

In June 1896 Patmore published in the *Saturday Review* an essay on Alice Meynell's work in which he disclosed the authorship of 'Why wilt thou Chide?', and said: 'Here is Mrs Meynell's "Belle Dame Sans Merci", which, I venture to prophesy, will some day rank not far below that of Keats. How incomparably noble, strong, passionate and pure are these words of consolation to the one lover who has been so near as to be denied.'

Patmore wrote intermittently to Wilfrid Meynell in the last year of his life. In January he had written:

I do not think that there is any prospect of my health improving. One cannot live long without delight. But I have done the best I can with such faculty as I

* The family name for her 'Wares of Autolycus' column.

had; I have always given my heart to that which is highest and 'I can wait to die' as Clough said.

Yours and hers as ever
Coventry Patmore[16]

Now, after the attempt at reconciliation, he wrote in answer to a request from Wilfrid Meynell that he should help in some undertaking:

It may seem absurd to you and herself, but my power of doing anything more in that matter or any other matter has been paralysed by my finding, from her own words and acts, that my primacy in her friendship has been superseded. I shall be as much pleased as I can be at anything by appearing in her new Anthology, and as I get no news from her now, I shall be very grateful for anything you can tell me about her.[17]

Four days later he wrote:

If you have not already put my last letter in the fire, will you kindly do so at once. It was a hasty expression of feeling which was more than useless.

Mr Pember was here yesterday and quite corroborated 'Tomorrow's' representation of the interest your wife's name is creating in London, especially in connection with her great new friendship.*

Give her my unalterable love, and believe me,

Ever your
C. Patmore[18]

But his praise for her work was never affected by his personal feelings. In another letter he told Meynell:

What Jeffrey said in the *Edinburgh Review* about Keats's poetry is exactly true of your wife's prose. J. said that K.'s poetry was the test of capacity in the reader for the understanding of what poetry was. It seems to me that the faculty of discerning the merit of prose is almost, if not quite, as rare. Your Wife's prose is the finest thing that was ever written, and none but kindred genius can see how great it is. I am glad to see that all the few competent judges are gradually coming to confirm all that I have ever said in her praise. If I were you, I should go mad with pride and joy.[19]

At the end of July, Patmore had written to Francis Thompson expressing anxiety about his health and offering to come at any time to Pantasaph to look after him if he were ill and had not sufficient attention.[20] In August, having had no reply to this touchingly generous, if perhaps impracticable offer, he wrote again.

My dear Thompson,

I feel anxious lest I should seriously have hurt or offended you by what I said to A.M. in the sincere intention of doing what I thought would please you; for I cannot account otherwise for your not having answered my offer to go to Pan-

---

* With George Meredith.

tasaph to wait on you, in case you required extra attendance. Now I have lost the great friendship of my life, I value yours above all others, and you may be sure that I could do nothing without a hearty desire to please you. A's new infatuation is so entire and absorbing that I have felt obliged explicitly again to withdraw from all intercourse, personal or by letter.

Yours C.P.

Have you read G[eorge] M[eredith]'s review? It is stolen from beginning to end from my last article, which, he has persuaded her, is calculated to injure her![21]

Meredith was now the principal object of his jealousy, and he was obsessed by the subject.

To the foregoing Thompson replied:

Dear Mr Patmore,

I am rather better today than I have been since my return, so I sit down to write to you. I have been very unwell, and often obliged to keep my bed the greater part of the day. My head has been the great trouble, threatening congestion or something of the kind; the blood rushing to it in an alarming way at night and keeping me awake far into the dawn. Then the next day it is stupified and will let me do nothing. However, I think I am coming round by degrees. Day has slipped day, with the hope each day that I might be better able to write the next until I am dismayed to discover the lapse of time. There was no offence at all in the matter you mention. You have been most generously kind to me; and I can truly say that I never yet fell from any friend who did not first fall from me. I thank you for the great honour you have done me by your offer to come up and look after me if I need nursing. Fortunately it has not come to that yet. I thought you would understand from my post card to Mrs Patmore that if I delayed writing it was owing to illness; but, as I say, I was not aware how time had drifted on since.

I am sincerely sorry to hear about your interruption of relations with A.M. Being entirely in ignorance of things, of course I cannot judge what cause she has given for it. I heard nothing until the beginning of the week, when I got a letter from Wilfrid, and discovered that he was away from home. I had written to her, forgetting that she would be at Meredith's (as I suppose from your letter is the case) and of course I have had no answer from her yet.

I have not seen Meredith's article – I am so completely cut off from the outside world . . . I should like to have been able to judge how far Meredith's article was taken from yours. It is an extraordinarily bold proceeding if it is.[22]

What Patmore had said to Mrs Meynell we do not know; neither do we know what he said in his next letter to Thompson, which has presumably been destroyed. But, whatever it was, Thompson was sufficiently disturbed to mention the matter to Wilfrid Meynell.

I have received [*he wrote*] an extraordinary letter from Coventry, to which I only refer in so far as it concerns myself. He asserts, as he did at Lymington, that Mrs Meynell is offended with me. And this time he gives a reason. I am not going to repeat it. Repeating of private letters or private talk only makes mischief, and does more harm than good. I recognise in it a wonderful distortion of a very simple thing. The distortion is his; but the thing must have come from someone – it passes my wits to think who. Only her assurance could make me believe it was Mrs Meynell; still less do I believe that it represents her feelings, so alien is it to her calm good sense. Therefore I simply set it aside; and only mention the matter to ask you both to treat anything coming from Coventry about myself as I treat anything about you – disregard it. It would take reams to discuss the misunderstandings which would otherwise sprout up. Not that he wilfully misrepresents things. But athwart the rolling clouds of his dark moods everything looms distorted and disproportioned. I have whirling moods enough to understand and sympathize with this; but I will not notice anything that comes to me through such a heated medium. A little common sense is the best remedy – and I at least mean to have it. If Mrs Meynell is really offended with me (and she has managed most successfully to disguise it) it must be for some better reason, or she will have to find one. I will not trouble to notice asserted 'offences' based apparently on simple and inoffensive things, in whatever grandiloquent language Coventry may trick them. I simply do not believe a word of it, or else there is a strange change in her nature. But it is nonsense, and with the warning to set aside any parallel things you may hear about me, I leave the matter.[23]

On the afternoon of 26th November, 1896, after three days of illness, Coventry Patmore received the last rites of the Catholic Church. That evening a telegram from his daughter was delivered at Palace Court. It said: 'Papa died at 4 this afternoon very peacefully.'[24] When she had read the message Alice Meynell left the light and warmth of the library, where her family was gathered, and went alone into the unlighted drawing room.[25]

A few days after his death Mrs Meynell received a letter from Patmore. Frederick Greenwood, former editor of the *Pall Mall Gazette*, and Patmore's executor, wrote to Wilfrid Meynell: 'I knew beforehand that Mrs Meynell had another shock to sustain when most of us were finding our way back to firmer ground. That letter, I found it in his strong box when I looked for his will, by which the letter lay. It was placed there before the sudden seizure of Tuesday week I think – even some time before; for of late, as of course you know, he expected that when his hour came, it would be with very little warning.'[26]

This was the letter:

My dear Lady,
 I am dying. Remember my last request. Let not your thoughts deny nor your heart forget the things your eyes have seen. Do not destroy the immortality of your truest visions by calling them moods. You are not disloyal to any lesser good in treasuring the higher. Our meeting again in Heaven depends on your fidelity to the highest things you have known.[27]

Whatever load of grief, remorse, pity, self-reproach Alice Meynell had now to bear – and it was a heavy load – she bore it alone; and, like all her griefs, in silence. She withdrew herself from those who tried to approach her in her sorrow as she had withdrawn herself into the dark drawing room. To a friend who wrote to offer condolences she answered: 'I am grateful for your very kind letter – sympathy is more than welcome, but mourners do not seek for comfort. We have just returned from Lymington.'[28]

CHAPTER 14

IN 1895 Alice Meynell began again to write poetry; she was to continue during the next few years – sporadically, it is true, but without any long and complete pause such as that now ended – and to work towards the torrent of creative activity that marked the last years of her life. She still said that she valued her prose more highly; but these later poems came nearer to satisfying her – and the distance from that goal was still great – than the early ones. If it be asked why, after the deliberate abstention of so many years, she began again, the only answer can be that the poet knows no better than the rest of the world why he is visited or why deserted by the power of poetry. Certain of the saints, she had said in *The Rhythm of Life*, were in complete subjection to the law of periodicity, enduring the vacant times and rejoicing in the 'beatitude of sweetness alighting in their heart. Like them are the poets whom, three times or ten times in the course of a long life, the Muse has approached, touched and forsaken. And yet hardly like them; not always so docile, nor so wholly prepared for the departure, the brevity, of the golden and irrevocable hour. Few poets have fully recognised the metrical absence of their Muse. For full recognition is expressed in one only way – silence.' Some great need forced her, at this time, to set aside her resolution to write no more poetry, the flood burst through the dam that she had so carefully built. She had never ceased to be a poet, for mere silence could not change her nature.

> No, I shall live a poet, waking, sleeping,
> And I shall die a poet unaware.[1]

In the *Pall Mall Gazette* that year appeared 'The Roaring Frost', 'The Fold', and 'The Shepherdess', a poem which was often to appear in anthologies in later years, though it is by no means one of her best. *Other Poems*, a small volume privately printed and paper-bound, appeared in 1896. It contained these three recent poems, with 'Why wilt thou Chide?' and six more. 'At Night' was addressed to Wilfrid Meynell.

AT NIGHT
To W.M.

> Home, home from the horizons far and clear,
> Hither the soft wings sweep;
> Flocks of the memories of the day draw near
> The dovecote doors of sleep.

Alice Meynell about 1895

Wilfrid Meynell about 1900

On the landing at Palace Court, about 1902. *From left*: Madeline, Everard, Viola, A.M., W.M., Olivia, Francis

> Oh, which are they that come through sweetest light
> Of all these homing birds?
> Which with the straightest and the swiftest flight?
> Your words to me, your words!

The little volume was dedicated to Agnes Tobin,* an American who had become a close friend of Alice Meynell's. Sending a copy, at the New Year, to Edmund Gosse, she wrote: 'I send you a mere New Year card of unpublished verses which were privately printed last year. They need no acknowledgement. I do not take my own verses so seriously as to call them what I know they are not – poetry.'[2]

Also in 1896 a book of essays drawn from her 'Wares of Autolycus' column was published by John Lane under the title *The Colour of Life*. It bore a dedication 'To Coventry Patmore', but he hardly lived to see it. In the first essay, from which the book took its name, she spoke of the common illusion that red is the colour of life.

But the true colour of life is not red. Red is the colour of violence, or of life broken open, edited, and published . . . Red is the secret of life, and not the manifestation thereof. It is one of the things the value of which is secrecy, one of the talents that are to be hidden in a napkin. The true colour of life is the colour of the body, the colour of the covered red, the implicit and not explicit red of the living heart and the pulses. It is the modest colour of the unpublished blood.

It is seen, she says, so rarely in London.

The little figure of the London boy it is that has restored to the landscape the human colour of life. He is allowed to come out of all his ignominies, and to take the late colour of the midsummer north-west evening, on the borders of the Serpentine. At the stroke of eight he sheds the slough of nameless colours – all allied to the hues of dust, soot and fog, which are the colours the world has chosen for its boys – and he makes, in his hundreds, a bright and delicate flush between the grey-blue water and the grey-blue sky.

'A Point of Biography' pleads for reticence about illness and death; 'The Honours of Mortality' claims that it is not only enduring work that is worth the artist's pains; and 'Donkey Races' takes the English stage to task for its slowness. There were essays on 'Cloud', 'Rushes and Reeds', 'Grass', and 'Winds of the World'. There was one on Eleanora Duse and one on the antiquity of childhood. In 'Eyes', the last of these essays, she said:

The colour of eyes seems to be significant of temperament, but as regards beauty there is little or nothing to choose among colours. It is not the eye, but

---

* Agnes Tobin, a Californian heiress, was a valued friend of the poet Arthur Symons, especially in the difficult years immediately following on the mental breakdown, in 1908, from which he never fully recovered.

the eyelid, that is important, beautiful, eloquent, full of secrets. The eye has nothing but its colour, and all the colours are fine within fine eyelids. The eyelid has all the form, all the drawing, all the breadth and length; the square of great eyes irregularly wide, the long corners of narrow eyes; the pathetic outward droop; the delicate contrary suggestion of an upward turn at the outer corner which Sir Joshua loved.

It is the blood that is eloquent, and there is no sign of blood in the eye; but in the eyelids the blood hides itself and shows its signs. All along its edges are the little muscles, living, that speak not only the obvious and emphatic things, but what reluctance, what perceptions, what ambiguities, what half-apprehensions, what doubts, what interceptions! The eyelids confess, and reject, and refuse to reject. They have expressed all things ever since man was man.

It is beautifully said, and for a moment it convinces; but this is one of the rare occasions when the originality of approach, and the singular freshness of thought that marked her writing, are overstrained. For those who would accuse her of preciousness it must be admitted that there is ammunition here.

In a long letter to Patmore, written as soon as he had read the volume, Francis Thompson said that there were 'some exquisite and entirely worthy things in it', but went on to protest excitedly against Mrs Meynell's attribution of the power of expression to the eyelid. 'A.M. [*he wrote*] has against her not only universal impression, but the *consensus* of the poets; behind her, deduction from "scientific knowledge". That is her weakness; she is proud of her "science" (because it is unusual in a woman), and accords it too unquestioning an homage. She would see better if she respected science less . . . She is to blame for sophisticating her poet's discernment of phenomena by *a priori* deductions from the basis of material science. "You only *think* you see it. It cannot be, because etc." When a poet begins to talk like that he is falsifying the precious gift of the natural eye which he has in common with the child. Many a bit of true seeing I have had to learn again, through science having sophisticated my eye, inward or outward. And many a bit I have preserved, to the avoidance of a world of trouble, by concerning myself no more than any child about the teachings of science.'[3]

The volume was enthusiastically reviewed in the press, and Mrs Meynell's dramatic criticism was hailed by the *Pall Mall Gazette* as the best of the age.

It was in the spring of 1896 that Alice Meynell first met George Meredith. He had long admired the Friday 'Wares of Autolycus' column, not knowing by whose hand it was written; and in the previous year, when he had met Harry Cust, editor of the *Gazette*, at the annual dinner of the Omar Khayyam Club, he had asked the identity of the writer. He had particularly mentioned the article on

Eleanora Duse, which was reprinted in *The Colour of Life*, saying that he considered that it reached the high-water mark of criticism in that age. Soon after he had learned that it was she who had written it he sent her a copy of *The Amazing Marriage*, inscribed 'In Homage'.[4]

The Meynells, on their side, held his work in high esteem, and their youngest son, Francis, had been given also the name Meredith, in token of their admiration.[5] Her pleasure, therefore can be imagined, when at the beginning of 1896 Clement Shorter* and Edward Clodd** called at Palace Court to tell her that Meredith said he had few wishes left and that one of them was to make her acquaintance. He invited her to come with her husband to visit him at Box Hill, in Surrey. When they accepted he wrote:

Dear Mrs Meynell,
 I would have you know that I am very sensible of your graciousness in consenting to come. I beg you will take assurance that you and Mr Meynell may count on my receiving you as among the most beloved of my friends. I can say it, for I have long been attached to you in the spirit, and am indebted past payment . . .
  I am, your most faithful
  George Meredith[6]

Meredith was at that time sixty-eight and was living alone at Box Hill, his second wife being dead. E. V. Lucas, in *Reading, Writing, and Remembering*, has described him as a handsome man, very vain about his appearance. 'He was Welsh and contemptuous and voluble and angry and enthusiastic.'[7]

Wilfrid Blunt speaks of him at about this time in a diary entry for 11th June, 1894: 'After luncheon drove to Box Hill to see George Meredith. Found him with his daughter, a pretty little bar maiden just engaged to Russell Sturgis, and another young lady. He is terribly deaf and is afflicted with creeping paralysis, so that he staggers from time to time while walking, and once today nearly fell. It does not, however, affect his mind, and he has a novel on hand at the present moment which keeps him writing six hours a day. He is a queer, voluble creature, with a play-acting voice, and his conversation like one dictating to a secretary, a constant search for epigrams.'[8]

---

* Clement King Shorter: 1857-1926: editor of the *Illustrated London News*, 1891-1900; founder and editor of *The Sketch*. Founded *The Sphere* 1900, and *The Tatler*, 1903. Writer of biographical and critical works, including several on the Brontës.

** Edward Clodd: 1840-1930: self-made business man, secretary to a bank. A rationalist, and writer of Darwinian studies. For his relationship with Thomas Hardy see Robert Gittings and Jo Manton, *The Second Mrs Hardy* (London, 1979). Clodd published his discreet *Memories* in 1916.

That visit to Box Hill in 1896 was the first of many that Alice Meynell was to pay – sometimes alone, sometimes with her husband or some of her family – and it began a friendship that occupied an important place in her life for the next few years. Her affection for Meredith as a human being was not, one feels, as great as her reverence for his intellect and his great reputation as a writer; but she prized his admiration, and she was always stimulated by talking with him of literature. He, from their first meeting, gave her his devotion, but it was distant, undemanding, tranquil devotion, and he accepted with contentment just as much of her company and her friendship as she cared to give him. In this he was different from Patmore, and she was grateful for it. 'I shall know', he told her, 'you have your good reasons if you cut at the fibres closing round you whenever you are near me.'[9] He wrote her long and frequent letters in his curiously involved and affected style, to which she replied – as she replied to all letters – hurriedly, in the midst of a dozen other occupations. 'I am in debate', Meredith wrote to her in the first year of their friendship, 'whether I would not barter the noble flourishes in your letter for just one line more. But the sage reflection tells me that the letter would not be yours without the flourishes, and such a verification makes me heartily content with my small allotment.'[10] And, recounting how someone had spoken to him of Mrs Meynell's 'beautiful *long* letters', he said: 'I repressed my start and moderated my stare.'[11] He delighted to send her things from his garden. White double violets were grown in a frame specially for her, and sent up to London, because she had said that they reminded her of Genoa; and his favourite flower, a pale blue iris with a golden centre, he renamed *Alicia Coerulea* after her.

With all her veneration for his great mind, she never hesitated to tell him when she thought him wrong in some literary judgement, and it was a joke between them that he made manful efforts to acquire a liking for those poets and writers that she appreciated and he did not. 'I swallow the spoonful of Cowley and Crashaw,' he wrote, after the publication of her anthology, *The Flower of the Mind*, 'and I hope I am the better for it.'[12] And when she wrote an article in the *Pall Mall Gazette* on Dickens, whom Meredith had never admired, he told her that it was 'a good Jack Horner study', since she had picked the plums out of Dickens's work to win approval for him. 'Portia as advocate', he wrote to her, 'is not to be withstood. When she cites her instances in defence of a slumbering Popular favourite, he awakens lively as ever; Shylocky critics are confounded, and she carries the Court – though growls are heard of her being a dealer in plums. But if she restores his Homer to the Cockney, what matters the means? I will confess that I am won by her. She hands me a plum, and I must own her client to be a lord outside cockaigne. It was very handsome pleading.'[13] The name thus bestowed remained, and Portia she was to him ever afterwards.

But he for whom she most desired to win Meredith's reverence was Patmore. Loving his poetry as she did, she could not bear that others should fail to see its beauty, and soon after their first meeting she persuaded Meredith to read her Patmore anthology. He wrote to her:

> I have read the Patmore extracts. I think there is nothing you would like that I should not esteem. As to the 'Angel' the beauty must be felt, but I have been impressed in the old days by the Dean, and the measure of the verse, correct as it is, with the occasional happy jerk, recalls his elastic portliness, as one of the superior police of the English middle class, for whom attendant seraphs in a visible far distance hold the ladder, not undeserved, when a cheerful digestion shall have ceased. I am afflicted, too, with the bleached transcendancy of the presiding Honoria.[14]

No doubt Meredith would have been less malicious about *The Angel in the House* had the author of it been anyone but Patmore. He could not resist the temptation to make him seem just slightly foolish in the eyes of Mrs Meynell. So, when Patmore's article appeared in the *Saturday Review*, speaking of 'Why wilt thou Chide?' as 'Mrs Meynell's "Belle Dame Sans Merci",' Meredith wrote to her: 'Coventry Patmore's article in the *Saturday*: good intention, and I like him for writing it. But why did he quote, of all things, *that*! Did he fancy himself addressing a circle of Provençal Princesses? And the mention of the poems of Keats, too, where there is no likeness except in the words "sans merci". The worst of it is, he stirs a demon imp in me.'[15]

And in a later letter he remarked when speaking of Patmore: 'There would seem to be great pretension in the whole blood of that family.'[16]

Meredith's praise, public and private, of Alice Meynell's work was liberal. On the publication of *Other Poems* he told her: 'Of your little collection all passes into my blood except "Parentage";'[17] and when he was at work on corrections for the final edition of his works he wrote: 'Much have I been reading you these days, and then I must away to correction of my books. And truth, it is as if from worship in a cathedral I were dragged away to a dancing booth.'[18] 'My sweet sister in the Muse shall soar higher than me without shaming me. My pride will be to keep the title of brother.'[19]

In August 1896 he wrote in the *National Review*: 'Her scorn, when it is roused, is lightly phrased, her wit glances, her irony is invisible, though it slays; and if she admires she witholds exclamations . . . She achieves the literary miracle of subordinating compressed choice language to grace of movement, an easy pleasant flow until her theme closes . . . In all her writing we read off a brain that has formed its untrammelled medium for utterance, with stores to deliver. Necessarily, where an intellect is at work, ours should be active, and we should know the roots of the words. She does not harp on a point; she pays her readers the compliment of assuming that they have intelligence. But she does not offer them puzzles. The writing is limpid in its depths.'

Of this article he wrote to Alice Meynell: 'It is inadequate – what could be adequate? I have curbed fervency as much as I could.'[20] And when she told him of the pleasure it gave her, he answered: 'You partly console me as to the article – but I failed in doing what I wanted to do, because of aiming with my heart and attempting to make it appear the head; so that neither of them had fair play. Writing as a stranger, I should have done more justice to my design and to you.'[21]

With the twenty guineas that he received from the *National Review* for the article he had Maltese Crosses made for Mrs Meynell and the four little girls.

Meredith looked forward to her visits with great eagerness. 'I wish it were today for your coming; we have the softest South-Wester to rock our daffodils and cowslips. May the Monday be as fair!'[22] 'Dearest of Friends,' he wrote another day, 'You will come tomorrow. I am not working, and, if I were, your presence the next day would inspirit me.'[23] 'When you come to me we will have talk of the art and aim of verse, and of sentiment, and the good thing it is when not pretending to be a kingdom of its own. I shall teach you nothing that can be new to such a mind as yours, but I shall be leaven to your deeper thoughts of Earth and Life.'[24]

Letters written by Alice Meynell to her husband from Box Hill tell of various visits there. 'It continues to be very sweet here. The Master and I are dearer friends than ever.'[25] 'The Master says he will write for me in future and laments the years before we met. I miss you, dear Sweetheart.'[26] And on a Thursday, which was the day of the week when the *Register* had to be got ready for the printer, she wrote:

> My dearest Willie, I trust this has not been a day too hard and rigorous. We have made the most of lovely weather, taking a long walk in the morning and a long drive in the afternoon – the latter with our host. Everything is looking lovely here. I am sorry to say that my recent writings are not in favour. It is certain that I must nourish my mind with new ideas if ever I am to add to the little that is really good that I have yet achieved.[27]

When a visit had to be postponed Meredith wrote: 'My day has lost its heart. I go about trying to think I was resigned beforehand and am not disappointed.'[28]

After Alice Meynell had been at Box Hill for a week with some of the children he sent her this poem:

> Shall I again have Lilac week?
> The coming days of sequence seven
> I view, and see an aspect bleak

Beside that flash of quiet heaven
Your presence gave; till I can think
An angel in one flitted wink
Was with me; and because I yearn
I needs must doubt, almost despair,
Of such kind season's chance return:-
'Tis but a moment's gasp for air.
A moment more and I behold
Your Lobby* in her bonnet white
Among the grasses' blue and gold
So sagely gathering; near in sight
Her tutelary Monica;
And near, their pencilling Mama:-
The mother with the ready smile,
Who wages warrior fight the while.[29]

---

* The family name for Olivia.

CHAPTER 15

THE FLOWER OF THE MIND, an anthology of poetry chosen by Alice Meynell, was published by Grant Richards in 1897. In her introduction she said: '. . . But my labour has been . . . to gather nothing that did not overpass a certain boundary-line of genius. Gray's "Elegy", for instance, would rightly be placed at the head of everything below that mark. It is, in fact, so near to the work of genius as to be most directly, closely, and immediately rebuked by genius; it meets genius at close quarters and almost deserves that Shakespeare himself should defeat it.'

The critics, startled by so unusual a judgement, fell upon her. A few applauded. Meredith declared the volume 'approved in its exclusions'. Her choice was one to provoke controversy in other respects besides the displacing of Gray, for she made known her dislike of the eighteenth century, which was sharpened by her love of what came before and after it. Some years later, in a *Daily Mail* article, she said: 'Light went out of English poetry as though a shutter had been closed to the west, before nightfall, when the noble seventeenth century came to an end with Crashaw, Vaughan and Lovelace; but a shutter to the east was opened after a hundred years by Coleridge and Blake and neither light nor stars, not natural night have been barred since then.'[1]

Soon after the volume's publication she was staying in the Constable's Tower at Dover Castle with her sister, whose husband, Colonel Butler, was stationed there. She wrote to Wilfrid Meynell:

My dearest Darling,

I am so delighted with my daily letters. I wish you said whether you slept better. I hope you will come. Tell my Monnie that it is for your dear health. The sea air would make you sleep and you would have *breakfasts* (Not to speak of luncheons and dinners). That will fetch her sympathy.

William the Conqueror built some of this, but the greater part underneath is Saxon – before the landing of St Augustine. All English history has passed through here. Geoffrey Plantagenet died here, and Mary Tudor built a Tower whence she looked across to Calais. Charles the First met Henrietta Maria on the steps close by.

This 'tower' makes a splendid house. There was a dinner party last night in the Judgment Hall, with the armour all round and the arms of the Constable and the Generals. I can tell you the General is a very big man in this place . . .

You won't find that military society knows much about *The Rhythm of Life*.[2]

While she was at Dover a review of her anthology appeared in *The Bookman*, and she wrote to her husband:

My own Darling . . . I saw the contents of *The Bookman* had 'Two Anthologies' by E. K. Chambers, so with some searching I got a copy here, and I think the notice excellent. How perfectly he understands what I said in my preface, which all other critics have mistaken or blundered over. E.K.C. says it better than I did. And his saying that Henley's choice is broad while mine is high, is good. Altogether there has been nothing so intelligible written about my work anywhere, nor ever will be.

The gale last night was without exaggeration terrific. It made one's heart beat.

I have been for a good walk today as usual. The fresh air makes my eyes so bright that you would not know them – real stars. I have done no work except the column so as to have the benefit of the holiday.

Expect me on Saturday. Try to be well. Poor lad, I think of you pent up with the *Register*.

Your loving Al[3]

She was always welcomed warmly both by her sister and her brother-in-law on these visits to them at Dover, and later at Devonport; she came to them tired from the pressure of her busy life, and her sister made her rest and fed her with nourishing things to strengthen her. 'They are all *too* kind', she wrote to Wilfrid when reporting her arrival on one such visit. 'William came into the room crying "Well, *dear* Alice". They would all like you to come so much. Costume does not matter – you need see no one, and they are really so simple – yet with every conceivable luxury toward. Mimi insisted on moving out of her room for me, because it has its own bathroom where I can have a boiling bath every hour if I want it, or late at night, which makes me sleep. Breakfast in my room, and perfect liberty I have also; and this morning, after the gale, bright sunshine.'[4]

In that same year John Lane published *The Children*, a book of Mrs Meynell's essays on childhood, most of which had already appeared in periodicals. These essays, with her later ones on the same subject, must stand among the best things that have ever been written about children. Alice Meynell achieved a perfect balance of tenderness and humour, and her light footsteps skirted unerringly the pitfall – so obvious and so hard to avoid – of sentimentality. She remembered, as so few adults can, exactly what it was like to be a child, and forgotten things from one's own childhood are thrown up to the mind's surface as one reads. She saw clearly the splendour and the limitations of a child's mind, and knew how it can startle by its visionary perception and exasperate by its imperception.

In 'Children in Midwinter' she said:

Children are so flower-like that it is always a fresh surprise to see them blooming in winter. Their tenderness, their down, their colour, their fulness – which is like that of a thick rose or of a tight grape – look out of season. Children in the withering wind are like the soft golden-pink roses that fill the barrows in Oxford Street, breathing a southern calm in the north wind. The child has something better than warmth in the cold, something more subtly out of place and more delicately contrary; and that is coolness. To be cool in the cold is the sign of a vitality quite exquisitely alien from the common conditions of the world. It is to have a naturally, and not an artificially, different and separate climate.

Memories of her own childhood and observations of her children's went into the essays. 'The Boy' was about Everard. 'The Child of Tumult' and 'The Child of Subsiding Tumult', both published in *Ceres Runaway*, described the slow taming of the wild rages of the young Francis.

He has absolutely no self-control and his passions find him without defence. They come upon him in the midst of his usual gaiety and cut short the frolic comedy of his fine spirits.

Then for a wild hour he is the enemy of the laws. If you imprison him, you may hear his resounding voice as he takes a running kick at the door, shouting his justification in unconquerable rage. 'I'm good now!' is made as emphatic as a shot by the blow of his heel upon the panel . . . When things are at this pass there is one way, and only one, to bring the child to an overwhelming change of mind; but it is a way that would be cruel, used more than twice or thrice in his whole career of tempest and defiance. This is to let him see that his mother is troubled. 'Oh, don't cry! Oh, don't be sad!' he roars, unable still to deal with his own passionate anger, which is still dealing with him. With his kicks of rage he suddenly mingles a dance of apprehension lest his mother should have tears in her eyes. Even while he is still explicitly impenitent and defiant he tries to pull her round to the light that he may see her face. It is but a moment before the other passion of remorse comes to make havoc of the helpless child, and the first passion of anger is quelled outright.

The book was as warmly praised by the critics as the former ones had been. Her popularity with the more discriminating of the reading public was reaching great heights. In the previous autumn Max Beerbohm had written in an article in *Tomorrow*:

A great crowd lines the pavement by the park, in the expectation of a rare sight. A loyal thrill and murmur pervade it, when, at length, a mounted policeman dashes down the road. All eyes dilate to the distance and discern already, through the trees, the moving glitter of cuirasses. The cavalcade comes! Comes a bevy of bright guardsmen, after whom is drawn a homely carriage with a lady in it; behind her, in the rumble, a brace of stalwart Highlanders; lastly, another bevy of bright guardsmen. Through cheers and genuflexions, waved hats and handkerchiefs, trots this cavalcade. Then the crowd 'passes along'.

This is not merely a description of a scene occasional in London. It is also a parable. The crowd is the reading public. The mounted policeman is Mr John Lane. The guardsmen are the literary critics. The lady is Mrs Meynell. The homely carriage is her new book. The Stalwart Highlanders are Mr Coventry Patmore and Mr George Meredith. Mrs Meynell had been lucky. Ever since her first book appeared she has not lacked splendid auspices. Between her and Mr Coventry Patmore the shuttlecock of praise has flashed incessantly from the battledores of their mutual admiration. And now, hark! The infrequent voice of Mr George Meredith is raised – in her honour.[5]

She was now invited to be President of the Society of Women Journalists. Lady Colin Campbell, writing to her, said: 'I suggested the self-evident idea that you were *the* fit and proper person to be our President.'[6] Meredith, who in the same year presided over the Society of Authors, addressed her in his letters 'Dear Fellow President' and 'Dear Chief of Journaliers'.

During 1897 she was writing in the *Pall Mall Gazette* a series of essays on London. In the following year these were published by Constable in a volume under the title *London Impressions*. A letter of hers to her husband, when he was away from home, relates her adventures in search of matter for these papers. 'This morning I took an omnibus drive through London to the farther end of Clapham, thinking to write about the London Sunday, but there was little to note. There was, however, the dreadful incident of a man's cutting his throat on the pavement in Shoreditch. I did not see the very act but I saw him lying. I took notes of London steeples and I went into a City church.'[7]

On a visit to Meredith she wrote to Wilfrid: 'It is sweet weather here and the country smells of everything including limes and hay. Mr Meredith is well and full of poetry. I fear he much dislikes my London articles, finding them thin and "frayed" which is not true. I have thought of your hard overwork with much compunction. All those columns and two leaders to do and no one to give you the help of a finger, my Dear.'[8] And during the same visit she mentioned her pleasure at a present that she had received. 'The lovely hat Agnes bought me is a real success and looks charming. I am sure you would like it. It gives the whole woman a lighter and smarter air.'[9]

She was about to start work on a short book on Ruskin for Blackwood's 'Modern Writers' series; when he heard of this, it gained Meredith's approval. 'The subject "Ruskin" should suit you', he wrote. 'No more anthologies or minute examinations of minor moths! I wish you could fix on a good biography. Otherwise an essay on the works of some known character, such as Mme de Sévigné.'[10]

In the spring of 1897, and again in 1898, Wilfrid Meynell went to Rome. The children and the weekly journalism meant that it was very rare for himself and Alice to be able to go away together. A letter to him during this absence speaks of the ever-present problem of finance. '*Without* anything for the *Children* and without some four pounds that are coming from America, my Bodley Head cheque is £48.11. which I fear may rather disappoint you. With the £25 sent before, it makes £73.11.0 for the Rhythm, The Colour and Poems from the end of July to the end of December.'[11]

Later, when Meynell was merely out of London for a few days, she wrote: 'Sweetheart, I am sorry to worry you with this notice, but I suppose you ought to have it. I wrote to the collector to say you were "abroad" (which means away from home) but that you would soon be back. I would willingly sell my diamond crescent if things are really pressing. I would take it to David Keys tomorrow if you will.'[12]

When he was in Rome in 1898 she wrote as follows:

Dear Love, I am still writing *in the hope* that you are to have a few more days of Rome in spring which is a peculiar life. I would work double as hard in order to enable you to have a rest you needed so much – and in those happy circumstances. I am quite proud of the *Register* I posted yesterday – quite. The children say I look it . . . The children are most sweet in every way – tender, charming and attentive. Monnie only a little too anxious about me . . . Now, my own love, farewell. I must turn again to adding up those 16,000 words. Once the *Pall Mall* is off my mind I can face the rest serenely. But before I find a subject for the Tolly I do feel uneasy.[13]

Later in the summer she went to the country, and it was Meynell who sat at the library table, editing the papers and doing accounts. 'I do not think without a pang, darling,' she wrote 'of this day of yours in town . . . The lists in my Cashbook are too intricate in sequence – being written in wherever there was a blank page – backwards and forwards – to be searched by any one except myself, I fear. Good luck to your hard work Sweetheart and good critic whom I thank.'[14]

In August 1897 Alice was at Pangbourne, and Wilfrid was briefly there with her. When he had left, she wrote: 'It was sweet to have you yesterday. I think we have not been anywhere alone since we went to Bruges in 1887.' Continuing, she said: 'This evening the sky is diviner than yesterday and the air even more balmy. I have done excellent work with my book. I have sent none of it to Lane, awaiting your orders, but I have asked him for the agreement and also for the accounts of the old books, and have sent him the title and contents.'[15]

In September she went with Agnes Tobin to the Three Choirs Festival at Hereford, and wrote from there:

Parsifal (Wagner) in the Cathedral was a great experience – one of the greatest of one's life. It was by far the best performed, too, for several things have been but so-so. I am delighted to have good accounts of you and the sweethearts.

The adorable Agnes and I are the best room companions that could be because we are both equally prudish – and on the whole we have managed well.[16]

Of Christmas at Palace Court in 1898 we have a glimpse in a letter written soon afterwards by Father Anselm, who, with another of the Capuchin friars, had been visiting the Meynells. 'I should be very dead indeed to all that is beautiful in life', he wrote to his host, 'if I failed to see how deliberately you set about making our stay at Palace Court the pleasure to us which you intended it to be . . . The tableaux and the dear Cross and Chalice and the unseen singer of the Gregorian notes of Christian dignity, the happy children, Alice's incomparable rendering of the Adeste, her dancing and leading me thro' the corybantic children, the Tivoli and – and – (a whisper comes deep from beneath the folds of Umbrian peasant's garb) Habana fragrance, the nectar of the gods – the birds of the forest – Ah! delicious memories all!'[17]

Guests were frequent in that hospitable household, and there were many – acquaintances as well as close friends – who had good cause to remember the kindness that they had met with there. Alice Meynell was not, perhaps, by conventional standards, a good hostess. Formal small-talk bored her, and those who knew her remember her silences. 'You write of your not being a talker', Meredith said in one of his letters to her. 'I can find the substance I want in your silences, and can converse with them.'[18] And Coventry Patmore, after a dinner party from which she had been absent, wrote that he had missed her silence. With laughter she was not much more prodigal than with speech. She did not care, in deference to a social convention, to laugh at what she did not find funny, for that seemed to her a betrayal of laughter. Her family, after many years, cherished the memory of a visit that W.B. Yeats paid to Palace Court, brought by Katherine Tynan, when his best story of the moment was met by a blank look from Mrs. Meynell and a remote 'Indeed!'[19]

'Surely', she once wrote in her 'Wares of Autolycus' column, 'a little of the Oriental idea of human dignity might not be amiss among a people like ourselves, containing whole classes who laugh without having anything to laugh at; audiences; a great many clergymen, who, perhaps, acquired the habit in the intention of proving that they were not gloomy, but an enormous number of laymen, also, who had not that excuse; and many women, from an uncertainty as to what was really funny and what was not.'

But when she perceived humour, none was more ready with her laughter than she. Katherine Tynan spoke of 'the sudden peal of laughter from Alice which one learned to wait for. When it came it was very good.'[20] Absurdity she enjoyed, and the simple often more than the sophisticated kind of humour. She repeated with delight a story of the Mother Superior of some French nuns in England who, desiring to tell the plumber that his bill for some work done in the convent greatly exceeded his estimate, said to the embarrassed man, 'You are much dearer since our engagement.'[21] She looked upon the high-spirited exploits of her large family, their pranks and practical jokes, with a benevolent and rather vague amusement. From Katherine Tynan, too, came a story of how, when a certain Father Angelo was staying in the house and was late for breakfast, Monica announced that she had tipped the water-jug over him to wake him up. Her mother remonstrated mildly: 'No, Monnie, no. *Not* a man with heart disease.'[22]

She was herself often the victim of her children's jokes, for they found her an easy prey; the readiness with which she laughed at herself afterwards, increased their enjoyment. The startling power of observation with which she perceived swiftly and in minutest detail the characteristics of a human face, the shape of a flower, the pattern of a bird's wing, was entirely absent when she looked upon her own possessions, from which she always remained curiously aloof and detached. On one occasion, when the children wished to test the limits of her unobservance, they dressed up a young man who was a frequent visitor at the house in their mother's clothes, and sent him in to see her. They talked gravely, and she noticed nothing strange.[23]

Francis Meynell records that 'To her children as they grew up, and always to her husband, my mother was someone to be protected – from household duties, from bores, from undertaking works of mercy beyond her strength. We had our jokes about her, untrue but plausible – for example, that she had spent an hour in a cabman's shelter in the belief that it was a slow-to-start tramcar.' 'I think now', [*he says*] 'that she was overprotected, even a little constrained by our care. Our view of her – the family view – was that she was complete: completely just, good and happy.'[24]

The household functioned somewhat haphazardly, its efficiency or otherwise depending largely on the domestics of the moment. To the need for dusting or darning socks Alice Meynell was oblivious, and if these things were not done by some other hand they were not done at all. The food was frugal and usually bad, for luxury in eating seemed to her not only unnecessary but wrong. When a newspaper sought her views on gastronomic matters, she replied that she deprecated that 'excess which not only puts our strength to ignoble uses, not only ministers to a sequestered and ungenerous pleasure, a pleasure locked, as it were, within our own teeth, not only encumbers the blood and embarrasses the spirits, and wastes the flame of life, but wrongs all our poor contemporaries on earth. It casts away the bread of the world.'[25] After a visit to some wealthy acquaintances she wrote to her husband: 'They have a park and water and conifers, and great lawns and a luncheon to match. Never, never, do I wish for luxury in food. Diamonds, yes; but not grouse and sweetbreads and creams.'[26]

All her guests did not share her disinclination for the pleasures of the table, and even Francis Thompson, who, poor man, had never had a chance to acquire the standards of a gourmet, remarked once to Meynell: 'Wilfrid, the Palace Court food is *shocking*.'[27]

Austerity prevailed in all the habits of Mrs Meynell's daily life, but it was not always as easy to her as it was in that matter of food. Clothes interested her, and she would have liked to have good dresses and pretty hats; but she was obliged largely to forego the pleasure; first by financial necessity and later by her conviction that the money was better spent on charity. Even in her work she permitted herself no luxury; she was known to desire, all her life, 'a desk that shuts up';[28] but she never had one. And yet, with that inconsistency which is a part of human nature, she, who was so dedicated to simplicity and economy, loved jewellery, and could speak with a faint longing of diamonds.

Some of the guests at Palace Court recalled in their reminiscences the visits that they paid there, and it is interesting to have the outsider's view of that family and household. Wilfrid Meynell was universally loved for his kindness and geniality, but it will be seen that, although she might be sparing with the talk, the laughter, and the food, it was Alice Meynell whose charm, goodness, intelligence, and unfailing generosity of heart engendered in so many men and women of diverse kinds a devotion that never faded.

'Never, surely,' wrote Richard Le Gallienne in *The Romantic '90's*, 'was a lady who carried her learning and wore the flower of her gentle humane sanctity with such quiet grace, with so gentle and understanding a smile. The touch of exquisite asceticism about her seemed but to accent the sensitive sympathy of her manner, the manner of one quite humanly and simply in this world, with all its varied interests, and yet not of it. There was the charm of a beautiful abbess about her, with the added *esprit* of intellectual sophistication. However quietly she sat in her drawing-room of an evening, with her family and friends about her, her presence radiated a peculiarly lovely serenity, like a twilight gay with stars. But there was nothing austere or withdrawn about her. In that very lively household of young people she was one with the general fun, which under the direction of her buoyant, genial husband used often to wax fast and furious and make dinner there a particularly exhilarating occasion. I give thanks here for the many joyous hours I have spent at the laughing board, and I have no other such picture of a full and harmonious home life to set by its side.'[29]

E. V. Lucas, in *Reading, Writing and Remembering*, described her as 'a priestess set in the midst of children, sharing their nonsense but thinking her own thoughts. One wants a new word to describe this aloofness; she was not apart because all their feelings she shared, and yet she carried her own sanctuary with her. But I must not give the impression that Mrs Meynell was alien to this world; her fun was instant and it was a house of laughter, remaining so until she died, while she herself was still, to the end . . . the most guarded and reverenced mother I have ever seen.'[30] And Major Fitzroy Gardner, in *More Reminiscences of an Old Bohemian*, wrote: 'I remember one Sunday evening, coming out of the house by chance with a woman of the world, more distinguished for her physical charm than for intellect. As we walked towards the Bayswater Road, talking about our hostess as if she had been some minor deity, my companion remarked: 'I feel somehow as if I must go to church and pray.'[31]

Let three brief extracts from Katherine Tynan's letters conclude this chapter. They convey the love and admiration which she, in common with so many others, felt for Alice Meynell, and the sadness of being always aware that, although she received in return love, kindness and abundant sympathy, there was so much of that heart that was locked away in an indestructible solitude and would never be given to anyone. It was a sadness that afflicted Mrs Meynell too, all her life: afflicted her with a sense of having failed those who loved her because she could never offer them her whole self.

'You will always fulfil one's highest ideal more than any other woman in the world could', Katherine Tynan wrote to her. 'There is no one like you – no one. You never fall below what one expects from you – you alone. I love you more than any woman in the world.'[32]

Later she wrote: 'I have always a kind of hurt about you that so many people are more to you than I am; but then I ought to be glad to be anything. Your affection for me came to me unsought, for I should never have thought of looking for it or for anything more than the most ordinary liking. I think hardly anybody is good enough for you to love.'[33]

And on another occasion: 'But you are somehow far away and seem as if you can do without people even if you can't. All the same, you are my ideal woman of all now living.'[34]

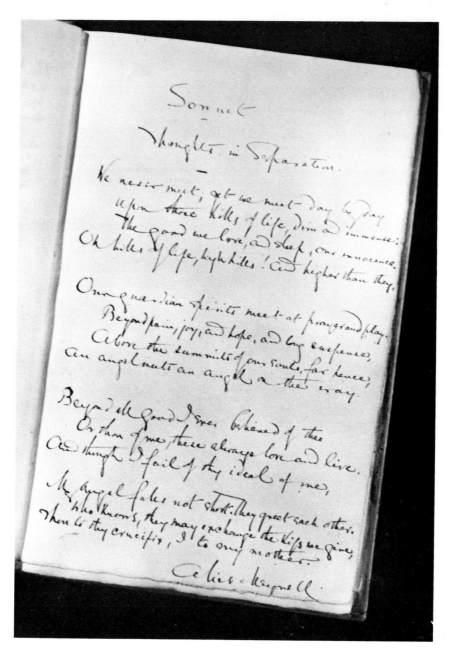

'Thoughts on Separation' written by A.M. into the autograph book of her
daughter, Olivia

Opposite: Francis Thompson,
drawing by The Hon.
Neville Lytton
Top left: George Meredith,
1896
Top right: Coventry Patmore

CHAPTER 16

A HURRIED VISIT to Le Portel, a little village near Boulogne, in the summer of 1898, gave to Olivia her first view of France, and to her mother the happiness of witnessing her excitement. Every holiday must serve the busy journalist by supplying material for a column, or more, and from this one was written a *Pall Mall Gazette* article, 'Au Portel'. The roughness of the road and the wildness of the omnibus from Boulogne were described in this article; so was the village wedding that they saw; and the little girl, 'brilliant with joy at her first crossing of the Channel', who was said to have 'the darkest and largest eyes in the coast'.

In October Wilfrid and Alice went down for a day to Wilfrid Blunt's house in Sussex, taking Francis Thompson with them in fulfilment of a long-standing promise to Blunt that he should make the poet's acquaintance. Thompson was untalkative, read the newspaper while their host drove them from the station through the beautiful Sussex countryside, and when taken for a walk in the woods pronounced an elm tree to be a maple. Luckily no one minded. In his diary Blunt said that the Meynells had declined his invitation to stay the night because of Francis Thompson's habit of setting his bed on fire. 'He is a little, weak-eyed, red-nosed young man of the degenerate London type,' Blunt wrote, 'with a complete absence of virility and a look of raptured dependence on Mrs Meynell which is most touching.'[1]

Wilfrid Blunt, poet and writer, great traveller, lover of the Arab world, was married to Byron's grand-daughter. He had a famous stud of Arab horses, and there was an annual sale of them at Crabbett Park, when great numbers of people were entertained to luncheon. To these luncheons the Meynells were always invited. Rather unexpectedly Alice Meynell enjoyed the talk of horses that went on round the table at these and other smaller gatherings at Crabbett. It is recorded of her that on one of their visits a hard-riding country squire was their fellow-guest, and that she was fascinated by the, to her, remarkable cut of his clothes and by his conversation with Lady Anne Blunt concerning a 'flea-bitten grey' that was suffering from 'sandy-toe'.[2]

That year saw the publication by John Lane of another book of essays: *The Spirit of Place*. The essay which gave its name to the collection attributed to its bells the essence of the spirit of a place:

Of all unfamiliar bells, those which seem to hold the memory most surely after but one hearing are bells of an unseen cathedral in France when one has arrived by night; they are no more to be forgotten than the bells in 'Parsifal'.

They mingle with the sound of feet in unknown streets, they are the voices of an unknown tower; they are loud in their own language. The spirit of place, which is to be seen in the shapes of the fields and the manner of the crops, to be felt in a prevalent wind, breathed in the breath of the earth, over-heard in a far street-cry or in the tinkle of some blacksmith, calls out and peals in the cathedral bells. It speaks its local tongue remotely, steadfastly, largely, clamourously, loudly and greatly by these voices; you hear the sound in its dignity, and you know how familiar, how childlike, how lifelong it is in the ears of the people. The bells are strange, and you know how homely they must be. Their utterances are, as it were, the classics of a dialect.

'Rain' speaks of the swiftness of Nature which is too great for human eye:

Not excepting the falling stars – for they are far less sudden – there is nothing in nature that so outstrips our unready eyes as the familiar rain. The rods that thinly stripe our landscape, long shafts from the clouds, if we had but agility to make the arrowy downward journey with them by the glancing of our eyes, would be infinitely separate, units, an innumerable flight of single things, and the simple movement of intricate points.

And in 'Shadows' Mrs Meynell thus described the dual flight of a bird:

There are two separated flights for the fancy to follow, the flight of the bird in the air, and the flight of its shadow on the earth. This goes across the window blind, across the wood, where it is astray for a while in the shades; it dips into the valley, growing vaguer and larger, runs, quicker than the wind, uphill, smaller and darker on the soft and dry grass, rushes to meet its bird when the bird swoops to a branch and clings.

There was the exquisite 'Solitude', already quoted from, in which, writing of a woman alone with her newly born baby, Mrs Meynell says the one right and true thing, uses the one felicitous image, as she so often did: 'There is no innocent sleep so innocent as sleep shared between a woman and a child, the little breath hurrying beside the longer, as a child's foot runs.'

And there was an essay on Marceline Valmore,* and one on Mrs Dingley which she called 'a paper of reparation' because all Swift's love had been commonly thought to belong to Stella, and Mrs Dingley had been 'defrauded of her honours'.

Shortly afterwards came the book on John Ruskin. It was necessarily very different from any other book that Alice Meynell had produced, and showed her to be capable of grasping thoroughly and expounding clearly the political and economic Ruskin as well as the author of *The Stones of Venice*. She found it hard to write, and she worked on it with difficulty and with strain. Viola Meynell says of it: 'The children

* French poet 1787-1859

visiting now their mother's bedside – invading even her last retreat from them – realised that the books and sheets of manuscript they saw there represented an unusual strain. Common as it was for that bedside to be visited by wandering children and found to be given over to work, the Ruskin time created for them a new standard in bedside silence, the spectacle of interminable hour-after-hour work, a new pitch of headache in their mother. Requiring the kind of trained thinking along fixed lines that she never found easy, her wrestle with her greatly-loved Ruskin left her tired and depleted.'[3] But she was rewarded by the good reception that was given to the book. The *Times's* reviewer said: 'Speaking after reflection, we fancy that few people in England could have written a better book.' And Wilfrid Whitten, writing in the *Academy* said: 'It expounds a known mind by its effect on a known mind, and we watch the impact. It is impossible to read her acute exposition and not be thinking almost as much about the author of *The Rhythm of Life* as about the author of *Modern Painters*. This is not to diminish the expository value, but to describe it.'[4]

One thing in *John Ruskin*, however, caused an uproar. This was her indictment of Gibbon, placed in parenthesis: '(Ruskin, at this time and ever after, used "which" where "that" would be both more correct and less inelegant. He probably had the habit from him who did more than any other to disorganise the English language – that is, Gibbon.)' Her complaint had been more fully stated elsewhere, for she had devoted a *Pall Mall Gazette* article to Gibbon's iniquities some time before, and had said in it: 'The dregs of his style have encumbered the nation. It is not his fault that posterity divided this property so lavishly among themselves.' There had not, on that occasion, been any particular outcry against her expressed opinion, and it seemed reasonable enough to reiterate it in a sentence to explain Ruskin's grammatical fault; but the critics held it to be an unpardonable slighting of a great writer.

In his article in the *Academy*, part of which has already been quoted, Wilfrid Whitten said that 'Mrs Meynell's *ukase* method of criticism' was to be regretted. 'Page after page passes, and the criticism is gracious, experimental, or proven; then comes a *ukase*, an emanation of opinion, decisive in inverse proportion to its needlessness. These *ukases* are in your hands before you recover speech. You would explain, you would summon assistance, but Mrs Meynell passes on in the gentle, deaf autocracy of her mood . . .' After quoting the offending passage, Whitten went on: 'That is the perfect *ukase*. Note the intensification of authority by the with-holding of Gibbon's name until the air has been darkened with his sin. But is it fair, or quite in the scheme of things, thus to ban Gibbon in a casual breath; to flout, *en passant*, the reader's probable cherished opinion of Gibbon, as if it were nothing? We picture Gibbon's own astonishment, when this judgement is

whispered along "the line of the Elysian shades". He may have
expected it, may have humbled himself for its coming; but the manner
of its coming he could not have foreseen. "In parenthesis" we hear him
gasp, as he sinks back on his couch of asphodel.'

Even the admiring Meredith protested. ' "A.M." in the "Pall Mall"
is good to see', he wrote to her; 'and she may lash her Gibbon in those
columns; but when she darts a sneer at him in parenthesis out of a
book, she seems under the public eye to betray sentiment deeper than
the disapprobation of style; and this is inartistic on her part.'[5]

The 'Wares of Autolycus' column came to an end at the end of
1899; but there was plenty of other work to be done. Grant Richards
asked her to write an introduction for his edition of the *Confessions* of
St Augustine; there were art criticisms and book reviews to be done for
the *Pall Mall Gazette* and other papers. In addition, during these last
years of the old century and first years of the new she wrote critical
introductions to Elizabeth Barrett Browning's *Prometheus Bound*
and to selections from Wordsworth, Tennyson, and Shelley for
Blackie's 'Red Letter Library'; for the same series she wrote also introductions to a seventeenth century anthology, and to poems by
Browning, as well as to a selection from his wife's poetry. In an unpublished note on *Sonnets from the Portuguese* Mrs Meynell wrote:
'Elizabeth Barrett Browning's abundant genius is so much at its best in
the series of lovely sonnets which she sought to disguise by their fan-
tastic title, that we must acknowledge some directing, some guiding,
some restraining influence in the motive of those sonnets. Love was
evidently for her a great training, and so was solitude. She had actually
lived long alone, but there is something unexpectedly public in the
writings of her secluded sickroom, something of Rosalind's "swashing
and martial attitude", and in the work of later days – in "Aurora
Leigh" also – this amazon attitude appears.'[6]

In 1900 Basil Champneys' *Life of Patmore* was published, and Alice
Meynell reviewed it anonymously in the *Athenaeum*.[7] Champneys
wrote to the editor: 'I must thank you . . . for having put it into the
hands of so exceptionally and conspicuously competent a critic.' He
enclosed a letter to be sent to the reviewer, of whose identity he had no
suspicion. In this letter he said: 'I have to thank you for your very cor-
dial notice of my book and still more for the deep insight and thorough
appreciation of the subject which it shows. The article is in all respects
such as I hoped I might be fortunate enough to give occasion for . . .'[8]

But among all these other occupations, Mrs Meynell's own poetry
was not neglected. 'The Modern Mother', written in this year, was
sent to George Meredith, who had some criticisms to make.

Dearest Portia,
    The last line of the first verse cannot stand. It reads as if purposely dark for

ushering in a portentous rhyme – a very beadle instead of the Lord Mayor. Nor do I like 'musing steps to fold . . . an answer'. Again, the last line of the last verse is iteration masking a weakness under an appeal to the sympathetic. But as you please in that respect. Always apply to me if you think I can be of use . . .[9]

The poem was altered in accordance with his judgement.

There is a letter written at about this time by Mrs Charles Hunter, sister of the composer Ethel Smyth, who had become a friend of Mrs Meynell's, which seems to suggest an occasion on which some of her poetry was set to music. There is no clue as to what this occasion might have been, but the letter is worth quoting since it shows yet again the extraordinary power that Alice Meynell had of arousing devotion in those who knew her.

I must try to tell you what pleasure you gave me today and what light you have brought into my life . . . I looked out of the Hansom and wondered if you could know what you do – You walked along so unconsciously, not the least uplifted by the homage – and then I wondered if the music had completely satisfied *you*. I *felt* it did, but afterwards I began to think it must be impossible for anyone outside your own mind to know *all* you meant.

It satisfied me. I loved the Restraint and the Purity and the Passion – the Conquering Spirit of the Music exactly in tune with the Self Mastery of your words.

Thank you, thank you, today more than any other day, perhaps, as I had a rare fit of Despair.[10]

Meredith's health continued to fail. 'It is my natural process', he wrote, 'that I am rather more crippled. I could rejoice to see you, and at the same time hate to be seen.'[11]

At the outbreak of the Boer War he wrote saying: 'I need patience even to speak of this Boer War, and the Outlander and the Suzerainty. Most of my friends are against me . . . My only feeling for the Boers is that for brave men. Notwithstanding their intimacy with the Almighty they are hard to deal with. But it might have been done.'[12]

The Meynells, too, believed this war to be unjust, and Alice's brother-in-law, who had by then attained the rank of General, resigned his command of British troops at the Cape and came home.

Wildfrid Meynell had sold the *Weekly Register* in 1899 for £800; but he now added to his many other employments that of literary adviser to the publishing firm of Burns and Oates, and this necessitated constant attendance at their office. In the early summer of 1900, however, he managed to take a month's holiday, and he and his wife made their first journey together to Italy. It was also the first time that Mrs Meynell had returned there since her marriage, and in a sense it was a homecoming; for Italy, more than England, was the land of her childhood, and twenty years' absence could neither dim her love for it nor cut the ties of memory and affection that bound her to the Ligurian earth. She had grown up among the Italian peasants, and their speech, their customs, their humour, their way of life, seemed always to her more natural, more comprehensible, than those of the English populace which she never really understood. Although she loved the fields and woods and gardens of England, its greenness was something she never really appreciated, preferring always to see the colour of cultivation, of what she called 'the signs of man, the traces of his brown hand'. It was the Italian landscape that had her most firmly by the heart. Its secret, she declared, was to be found in Thomas à Kempis's counsel of perfection: 'Seek to have less rather than more.'

The legend of Italy is to be gorgeous . . . But Italy is slim and all articulate; her most characteristic trees are those that are distinct and distinguished, with lines that suggest the etching-point rather than a brush loaded with paint. Cypresses shaped like flames, tall pines with the abrupt flatness of their tops, thin canes in the brakes, sharp aloes by the road-side, and olives with the delicate acuteness of the leaf – these make keen lines of slender vegetation. And they own the seasons by a gentle confession.[13]

They went first to Milan, and from there Alice wrote to Sebastian, describing their journey:

We find Milan so splendid – against all anticipations – that we are probably staying here for a second day. It was bitter and wintery with us at Calais and along the dreary country of France, and we could hardly make up our minds whether it would be more miserable to stay in the train or to get out in the drizzle. We . . . resolved that it would be more desolate to go to an hotel shivering. So we sate where we were for the night, although we had brought no wraps! We unpacked our things and put on underclothing round our necks and skirts over our knees. But we could not sleep and we were black and sad objects in the morning when we crossed the Swiss frontier and breakfasted (feeling bilious) at Basle. It was raining so we saw nothing of the place or the young Rhine. It went on raining steadily as we steamed off along the Swiss valleys. One of them was full of factories, but the other, which took us hours to go through, was wonderfully beautiful. Great mountains rose on each side and between lay orchards sprinkled with a million apple trees in flower. The radiant green and the buttercups and white flowers took the place of sunshine and in spite of rain the country was brilliant. Yet it was cold, and sulky clouds floated halfway up the mountains. We had little hope of the weather; but when we came to the higher ranges some gleams of soft sunshine lighted the snow and it was very beautiful. The Saint Gotthard pass, through which we came, is the most splendid of all. We could see our line high up above our heads on an opposite mountain. It was curious to think that we should soon be there by zig-zag.

We lunched at the entrance to the long tunnel, and when we came through the sun began and the climate changed. It was too wonderful, mountain beyond mountain, and the waterfalls that came from the summits to the valleys. And as we came out of the last tunnel and round the last winding and saw the Italian plain at our feet in a flood of sunshine with a lake at the far end, it was a vision. Through villages, all with their ancient Lombard church towers, and along the lovely lakes of Como and Lugano we came to this great and beautiful city, arriving on Saturday night. We find the Cathedral, which is enormous, a mere gimcrack in architecture – except that the columns of the interior have a grandeur. It is the largest, except St Peter's and the Seville Cathedral, of all churches in Europe.[14]

Later they stayed at the Castello di Pavone, Cavanese, at the mouth of the Val d'Aosta, where lived the daughter and son-in-law of Alice Meynell's half-sister Fanny. She described it in a *Pall Mall* article:

. . . The Piedmontese castello rises on Roman foundations whereto the village clings, locked into the rock. From the Machicolations – the swallow-tail battlements of tower and long enclosing wall – and from the windows with their thick internal shutters of timber, the dwellers in the castle . . . look down the steep rock into the climbing streets of stone, into the courtyards netted in and out with vine, down a score of open stairways, and down the rolling course of the falling stream. Terrace under terrace of grey stone they see, roof under roof of dark red tile roughly curved, walled vineyard under vineyard, and not far from the level of the castle gateway, the top of the clamourous belfry tower.

Nothing is hidden except extreme sickness, birth and death by those broad roofs; the villagers live outside their narrow doors, and their illnesses are brief. You cannot persuade them to keep their beds until the eve of death.

Three churches are in the village, and one of these – needless to say, in the late Renaissance taste, large enough for a town, was built by the unpaid volunteer labour of the villagers. Within those walls they spend half an hour before the hard work of every day, and the greater part of every Sunday. Moreover, from these belfries the loud bells peal in the middle of the night or in the dark of the dawn whenever thunder and lightning and the downpour of Alpine rains threaten the fields. There is no sleeping through the bells; they are not swung so as to spare the slumbers of the tired. No one lies far from the sound of that summons to prayer and to the bitter vigil of the farmer in the floods.

The June of my visit was a time of floods. The days were Italy's, open to the sun and the luminous plain, but the nights were the mountains! Few were the fields that lifted themselves again after those loud rains that roared against the bells . . .

Now and then a night came in June when there was no storm. Clear of thunder, rain, and the bells, those nights were audible under the moon. The ear of man was barely able to catch their thrilling voice. Tree-frogs, it seems, make this subtle and universal trill, softer but nearly as fine as the bats' cry, sweeter than the crickets', and so slight a sound that the long song of the nightingales was as clear against the scattered whisper as a strong star shows distinct upon the Milky way; the sound shook the night air as though a finger touched a string in tune . . .

Not a child's voice stirred in the village; and never – albeit even the murmurs of that short sleep seemed to enter at the castle windows in the night – was there any sound of oppression of women or children, of violence, imprecation, or derision. The people love their children throughout this country. The image of a young father, with his young child on his shoulder, seems to be the most familiar of all remembrances of a Piedmontese, or Venetian or Lombard holiday. The child holds on to its father's hair, in church or in the street, and steers the way of the man, and seems generally to direct the spending of their days together. Of unkindness or neglect you see no sign, for the children of the poorest are delicately kept and sweetly cherished . . .[15]

A letter from Meredith hailed the appearance of this article in print.

Dearest Portia,

Your column in the P.M.G. on the Piedmontese chateau at the mouth of the Val d' Aosta is rich with North Italy, such as only poet could have written, and enough that is your prose. Be inspired to give us more. Your observation is minute, and here the feeling goes with it. A collection of your Pictures of Italy would honour us.

> Ever with gratitude
> George Meredith[16]

They went on to Venice, and from there Alice Meynell wrote to Viola. Their lodgings had 'exquisite old pink marble stairs, worn quite smooth . . . We are very comfortable there except for the noise. The Venetians seem never to go to bed or to stop working, singing, talking and strolling. Strange is the noise of the city where there are no wheels or horses, but it is noisy.'[17]

CHAPTER 17

IN THE AUTUMN OF 1901 Alice Meynell was invited by her friend Agnes Tobin to go to America as her guest, and, with her, see something of the United States in a stay of about three months. The sadness with which she contemplated a separation from her husband and children made the decision a hard one; but she had long desired to see America, and to see it in the company of this beautiful, intelligent, and dearly loved friend was a happy prospect. Added to this, the suggestion that she should give some lectures during her stay indicated a way in which, though absent, she could help her husband. Some years before she had written to Patmore: 'Do you know the Americans are very much interested in me? They are the only enthusiasts who write to me for autographs. An editor in Illinois has just written to me peremptorily for a photograph and . . . a New England newspaper seriously proposed me for the Laureateship.'[1] She could, therefore, contemplate a lecture tour with reasonable confidence; besides the money she could make by it, it would enlarge her reading public in the United States.

So the decision was taken. On hearing of it Meredith wrote to her:

My dearest Portia,

What magnanimity in the husband! – And I who am always throwing myself into other person's minds and hate to be outdone in this particular, have to confess that it would be ruefully, grimly, and upon supplication, in sight of a pained and reproachful countenance, that I, a spout of doleful forecasts, could be brought to yield the releasing word. But outside the husband's view, there is the glorious news for you, a splendid Aurora, a fresh spring; and though I shall be glad when it is over and you home again, my sympathy will be running with you during the course and for as long so long as you keep out of accidents. Otherwise I shall find a tongue to have told you so. But no, you will be careful and propitiate Fortune, who has, in spite of the poet, a divinity for travellers.

Give my love to all at home, and take the remainder of an inexhaustible heart.

George Meredith[2]

She sailed from Southampton in the *Saint Paul* on 7th September. Agnes Tobin was already in California, and Mrs Meynell travelled with Agnes's brother and sister, Edward and Celia Tobin, who were bound for San Francisco. 'Darling, darling,' she wrote to Wilfrid Meynell, as the ship steamed out of Southampton Water, 'this *is* part of the romance of my romantic life, isn't it?'[3]

They arrived at New York a week later, at sunrise on 14th

September, and on the last night Mrs Meynell did not go to bed, so that she could 'see the dawn and the new Hemisphere together'. She was not a good sailor, and the voyage had not been pure pleasure: 'That "St Paul" is a pitcher and a tosser, and a roller, and, long as she looks, she contrived to do all these in the brief length of my poor bunk.' On arrival the passengers heard the news of President McKinley's assassination.[4]

From the Murray Hill Hotel in New York she wrote to Wilfrid:

. . . Nor will I let it be tragic to think of the solemn ocean – no one can guess how solemn without seeing it – between me and all I love. The sun comes up three hours late from Palace Court to me. I must say it looks upon an anomalous city, with Italian clearness of air, but nothing Italian to shine on, except ragged harness in strings, high collars on the skeleton horses (which indeed remind me sadly of the Italian horses of my youth – they look better now) and a considerable number of young Italian men at work. As for the noise, never have I heard such a rattling racket. The traffic is quite unregulated and everything dashes, strains and struggles.[5]

Two days later she reported:

It is tropically hot and steaming. Yesterday, Sunday, I lay up, for I could not get the continent of America to stop rocking under me. Even today it swings, but I can keep my feet! I am in the lap of luxury and the town looks bright in the sun . . . Darling Wilfrid, you have the children and they have you, but what have I![6]

They stayed for ten days in New York and met a number of people, visited the Metropolitan Gallery, lunched at the Waldorf Astoria, 'in that kaleidoscope of moving and feeding people amid their palms and marble', went to the theatre and the music-hall, and dined at Sherry's. American cooking she declared to be better than anything in Paris, and their food altogether exquisite. 'All my gloves, shoes, veils, ties are nice', she told Wilfrid, 'which retrieves my somewhat under-dressed appearance.' She longed for letters from home but could expect none until Agnes Tobin met them east of the Sierras on their way to San Francisco.

'Celia and Edward are too kind; but the talk at luncheon and dinner bores me. It is all about persons and *never* about things or thoughts; and about the paltriest parts of personality.' She had waves of homesickness: 'Oh, my own Love,' she ended one letter, 'how much I think of you! Oh, my beloved sons and daughters! Your Johnson.'[7]

From New York they travelled westward right across the States, breaking the journey at Denver, Colorado, and then going on by way of Great Salt Lake. On the journey she wrote to Viola:

In the train, early morning, just through the Rocky Mountains and crossing a dreary desert.

My own darling Viola, This ought to reach you exactly on your birthday
morning. I do hope it will. I shall post it in Salt Lake City, the Mormon town
which you may have heard of, to which emigrants used to travel through terrible perils from the Indians. I think of you, my darling girl, in this strange and
distant land, and wish you so much happiness, health and goodness that I can
never speak it all. May you be blessed on this beautiful sixteenth birthday, a
blooming and blessed girl. (I think my literary style is queer this morning. I
cannot sleep much in the 'cars' and the constant movement makes me
somewhat giddy, though you can see from my writing that the train is fairly
steady.)

Last evening we came through the tremendous canyon. It is terrific but not
beautiful. There is exceedingly little beauty on this continent – at least on this
side of the Pacific slope. But the distant view of the great mountains was
magnificent – one of the sights of the world . . .

The sunshine is perpetual and dazzling, the sky a high, unchanging *pale*
blue. The light is not rich but intense. There is no gold.[8]

And to her husband:

My darling Wilfrid, – I dream, in the strange nights of these trains, of meeting
you, on the mountains, in the canyons, on the plains, and you are
paragraphing there. I wish I had some pars for you, but though I have *plenty* of
Pall Mall matter, it does not take the shape of pars on the actual journey . . .
The country we are now going through is made of mud that dried in the beginning of the world.[9]

Agnes Tobin met them at Reno and accompanied them to San Francisco, whence, after six or seven days, she and Mrs Meynell set out for
the Yosemite Valley.

Oh, Wilfrid, [*the traveller wrote ecstatically*], California is the earthly
paradise. All the strange drought and whiteness of light of the plains disappears
and you are restored to sweetness, richness, and gold of sunshine. The mountains are like the Alps, the valleys are heavy with fruit. Little hills rise with
cypress and orange trees dark in the sun. But the absence of the church belfry
at once prevents it from looking like Italy. Otherwise it would.[10]

In an article which was subsequently published in the *Pall Mall
Gazette*, called 'Across the Sierra Nevada', she described San Francisco
and the country inland.

This is the Sacramento Valley – appropriately the valley of wheat and
vineyard, fertile enough to fill a nation with bread and wine – which lies, with a
narrowed river in the midst, for many and many a league on the way to the bay
of the Golden Gate. With the corn and the vine are closes filled with fruit, and,
at the season between the rains, beautiful tracts of land lying in a rest of
drought, bleached to the soft, gloomy silver colour to which grass burns under
the Californian sun.

San Francisco, which has no slums, has clean, scattered, small and streetless
suburbs. In the bright evening, after sunset, as you drive home from the ocean

sands, you have wide views of the neat, sharp outskirts of the city among the great company of hills. The small houses of wood . . . are gabled and painted a clear white. There are no rows of Houses. And the eucalyptus stands, exceedingly deep and dark in the large shadowless light, in squares and blocks of sombre green, while between and beyond house and tree is the soft silver-brown bloom of the grass long dry.

From the Yosemite Valley on 9th October she wrote to Wilfrid:

My Darling, – Here we are for a week or a fortnight, Agnes and I, in the most overwhelming scenery. We took train on Monday afternoon and reached the end of railways on Tuesday, after which we drove four in hand in a rough wagon fifty miles one day and twenty the next up those magnificent mountains, under a more than Italian sun. Such roads, or rather tracks! I am enjoying it greatly.[11]

Out of that journey she made an amusing 'par' for the *Daily Chronicle*:

On the long coach-drive to the Yosemite Valley there is a turn of the road that suddenly reveals those tremendous rocks, of the height of mountains, with the narrow space between, and its crystal river; and this halting-place is called 'Oh My! Point'. It is a dreadful name and might persuade me to use the little contracted 'my' for ever after.[12]

The blueness of the sky and the dramatic quality of the scenery there among the mountains enthralled her, and she was eager to see all she could during their brief stay.

Agnes and I went up one of the heights by an Indian 'trail', which is a track imperiously placed on ledges and landing places up from the valley to the summit. We went up on Californian horses which climbed like cats. In some places the trail was a stair cut in the rock or made with stones. The horses did it all with the utmost cleverness. The guide rode first, then I, then Agnes. I need not say we had to ride like men or we could not have kept on our saddles – Mexican saddles with carvings and silver and a high pummel for the lasso. You would never say I had a weak head if you saw that trail. We were six hours in the saddle.[13]

Mrs Meynell had just passed her fifty-fourth birthday, and although, by their father's special wish, she and her sister had been well trained as horsewomen in their girlhood, she could not have been on a horse for many years. To be for six hours in the saddle after so long an interval, to ride astride, which she was not accustomed to do, and to climb, mounted on a strange horse, that pathway where one false step would have meant death, was a considerable test of physical endurance. Many people who knew her spoke of her as 'frail'; but in fact, one learns from this, from her long journeys sitting upright in crowded railway-carriages, her seven-mile walks, and her days of gruelling work, that she had a remarkable physical toughness that enabled her to survive these ordeals without even thinking it surprising that she should.

It was while they were in the Yosemite Valley that Agnes Tobin told Mrs Meynell that she could not travel with her to England in December as she had planned, since, in consequence of poor health and a persistent cough, she was not fit for the journey nor for the rigours of an English winter. She implored her friend to stay with her in California through the winter, and to look after her on the journey to England in March.

Alice wrote to her husband in great distress: 'I have noticed how weak she is . . . I see too well that she ought not to go until the Spring. It is with tears that I think of staying longer away from you. How can I? Oh, Wilfrid, I do feel about the separation all that you do, with the poignant pain of absence from the children added. Write and tell me what to do . . . Your poor Johnson'[14]

On the same day Agnes wrote to Wilfrid to tell him of the proposal she had made to his wife: 'She is simply overpowered by the mere suggestion – and is sitting in the next room now, not knowing what or how to write to you. So I thought I would dash off a few lines to let you share our perplexity.' At the end of her letter she said, 'I hear Alice weeping in the next room.'[15]

They returned to San Francisco with the question unsettled, and at the end of October Mrs Meynell gave her first lecture in America. The subject was 'The Great Transition in English Poetry from the Seventeenth to the Eighteenth Century', and she looked forward to it with a good deal of anxiety, fearful that no one would come to hear her in spite of the efforts of Miss Tobin to advertise the lecture and to sell tickets. However, she had a good audience, and the lecture was well received. She wrote to Viola:

> I am sending you the only notice I have yet seen of my lecture. I am quite grieved that the man says I have a weak voice. I seemed to myself to be roaring at the people. But it is too true that I saw a priest in the distance with his hand up to his ear the whole time! I looked at him reproachfully.[16]

A fortnight later she followed this lecture with 'Dickens as a Man of Letters', from which she made a profit of £20.

All through November she was anxious about her plans, and uncertain of what she should do. She longed to see her husband and children and yet felt that she could not refuse to help Agnes, who had been kind to her and was a much loved friend. 'Agnes said to me yesterday', she wrote to Wilfrid, 'that she had no chance at all but in my staying. It is almost as though she asked me for her life.'[17]

To Everard she wrote:

My dearest Everard,

In case I have to stay – and I cannot yet tell how it will be – till March, I want you to undertake this for me – to send me word how your father is *really*. I mean as to spirits, fatigue, overwork and everything. I have heard nothing of him except that he had a sore toe. Was this gout? Tell me whether he enjoys things, whether he sees people who amuse him, whether he still pats (!) Brin* on the back, whether he plays with the children. If he seems cast down, I ought to know it.

One other thing; I trust you to send me one word by cable, 'Return', if you think there is any urgent reason of any kind – if one of you was ill, for instance. For that would of course over-rule any obligation I have here, including lectures.[18]

And to Viola she wrote:

Sweet Viola, you ought to learn the lines

> Love has this difference from gold or clay,
> That to divide is not to take away.

Therefore I love each of you as much as you can possibly love the single *me*. I have seven loves, each one of which is as great as though I had but one love for one child.

Heaven bless you ever, my darling.[19]

And in another letter: 'I think your father would be comforted for my staying if he knew that I never have cold feet. But it does not comfort me.'[20]

'To stay three months more', she wrote to her husband, 'would be, for me, a sacrifice I need not dwell upon. It would be a sacrifice for you, too, my Dearest, and for my Babes. If I must stay it shall not be with an aching heart, and I shall ask you, for love of me, not to let your heart ache. I could not bear that.'[21]

On 29th November she wrote: 'Yes, it is settled at last that I stay . . . One can compel oneself to most things, and once the decision is taken the sacrifice seems easier.'[22]

Agnes Tobin wrote to Wilfrid: 'The complete change of a Christmas here – and also the trip to Mexico we hope for next month – will do her worlds of good. But naturally she feels being away from you all very much, and at the least suggestion that you are not well or are depressed, she has headaches!!! Your letters are the *foundation* of all the good the change can do her – so I want to urge you to keep them as bright and encouraging as possible.'[23]

Mrs Meynell determined to turn her enforced stay to good account by giving as many lectures as possible, and she immediately wrote to an agent whose name John Lane had given her, asking him to arrange a

---

* Bernard Whelan, architect; an old friend of Wilfrid Meynell's; at that time engaged in restoring St Etheldreda's, Ely Place.

tour for her. To her disappointment, he replied that this was not possible except on a small scale unless he had six months' notice; but she
received invitations to lecture in New York and Chicago, and
arrangements were also made for Santa Barbara, Los Angeles,
Indianapolis, and Boston.

She was everywhere received with enthusiasm. The American passion for lecture tours was then at its height, and the personal
appearance of an author on the platform was almost certain to be
greeted with demonstrations of an embarrassing fervour. The familiar-
ity with her work which her audiences showed was undoubtedly to a
great extent genuine; but it was also, perhaps, in some degree due to
the fact that the announcement of her coming had set the whole town
to reading her in preparation. After a day when she had been the guest
of the Century Club in San Francisco, she wrote: 'What is remarkable is
the wish of everybody to exaggerate in one's favour. It is the old lioniz-
ing passion still surviving. They *want* to believe you are the most
remarkable woman in the world. I have never seen quite that kind of
spirit before.'[24]

Another lecture, 'The Treble Note', a study of Charlotte Brontë,
was given in San Francisco early in December. She had a heavy cold,
and was doubtful beforehand whether she would be able to speak; but,
she wrote afterwards, 'By I know not what force my voice was preserved clear and strong during an hour and a half's lecture . . . and as
soon as it was over I could not make a sound. It needed courage.'[25]

The approach of a Christmas which she must spend away from her
children sharpened her longing for them, and her thoughts turned
homeward in constant anxiety, in dread of illness or accident or some
nameless harm that might befall them.

'When I go to ten o'clock Mass', she wrote to Everard, 'I think of
you just beginning to have tea in the drawing-room with a fog outside.
When I am going to sleep, the post is just about arriving at Palace
Court and you have already a different date from mine.'[26]

To Francis, her youngest child, she wrote: 'My longing to see you is
sometimes too keen. Heaven keep us all well until the happy day of my
return.'[27]

A letter from Wilfrid brought news that Viola was in bed with a
chill. This, being followed by several days of silence, alarmed her
greatly. The tremendous distance and the time that letters took added
to her feeling of helplessness; begging for news, she said: 'It is vain to
write this now for you to read a fortnight hence. Your last letter was
dated eighteen days ago.'[28] Even though she realised how useless delay
rendered such advice, it comforted her to tell the children of little
remedies for their ailments – rosewater and zinc for a bad eye, which

must surely be better before the four weeks had passed that would carry the news to her and bring back her prescription.

Early in December she heard from Wilfrid that their oldest son, Sebastian, who was now twenty-three, might be going to Canada. Writing to him she said:

My dearest boy, It is a very serious thing to send you alone so far from home. May everything good attend you. I beg you to take with you the Testament I gave you and to keep true to the Catholic Church and to your duties. That is the only safeguard from dangers and errors which lead to eternal regret and grief. I don't want to preach too long a sermon, but I beg you to take these words really to heart.[29]

And to Viola, at the end of a letter in which she described Thanksgiving Day in San Francisco, she said: 'I don't forget your dear, dear face hidden behind the carriage door when I left because you were weeping, my love.'[30]

On Christmas Day letters arrived telling of Viola's illness, and her mother wrote to her:

My darling Viola, – How ill you have been! I was wondering what sort of a chill but never thought of an abscess – the most painful thing one can have. That is all happily over. I was much pleased with your verses, especially the first one. You have something to say in them – a little thing but still a real thing – and that is the important matter in writing. It seems obvious that no one should write without something real to say, and yet that is the point most generally ignored . . .

You are a darling to give me a sermon on humility. But if you knew how little temptation there is to care about the praises of San Franciscans! I do not take anything seriously here. Agnes, of course, I wish to please, and Mrs Crocker who is clever, and I rather like to please Mr Lapsley, a young professor at the university, but that is *quite* all.[31]

Soon after Christmas Mrs Meynell and Miss Tobin left San Francisco and travelled south to Monterey.

If you have *Across the Plains*,* read 'The Old Pacific Capital' again [*Alice Meynell wrote to her husband*]. That is where we are, lodged in the huge and magnificent hotel which R.L.S. speaks of at the close . . .

What a place this is, what a place! No. Nothing in the astonishing Yosemite was so beautiful. Here is something of the past which was not there. For the Ancient Indians who had lived always in that valley and live there still bring nothing of the past to us. Time is change, and the Indians do not change, except by coming, as they have done here, under an energetic, benign influence, such as the Jesuits'. We have something of the seventeenth century in the pathetic signs of the despoiled and destroyed Catholic missions here, the only trace of good – not predatory – dealing with the natives. And yet our

*   by Robert Louis Stevenson

histories tell of nothing but Spanish 'Cruelties'. The Spaniards alone dealt with the Indian for his sake and not for their own. South California is sprinkled not only with churches but with hospitals and schools, all built for the Indians, and now either destroyed or turned into barracks, hotels and restaurants. The revolutions at the beginning of the nineteenth century – late and last reverberations of the thunder-storm in France – did all the destroying and secularizing before American acquisition.[32]

In San Francisco Mrs Meynell had met Stevenson's widow, and here at Monterey she had lunch with Mrs Lloyd Osborne, wife of his stepson, at a little restaurant where R.L.S. used regularly to dine. She had a great admiration for his work, and being with his family in a place that he had loved and written about made her think much of the tragic story of his life. She spoke of it in her letters to her husband; particularly of Henley's cruelty to him after the break in their friendship. 'The only thing [*Mrs Stevenson*] said about Henley was that he must have been drunk when he wrote the article on Stevenson. She was naturally indignant, – but that article is not the work of a drunken man.'[33] And in another letter she exclaimed: 'Oh, Wilfrid, to think that the "word of three letters" in the assassin article of Henley's was "cad". That is really worse than anything else.'*[34]

On the journey to Los Angeles she wrote to Olivia:

My Darling Olivia,

Agnes and I are spending three mortal hours at a wayside junction on our way south from Monterey. An American country waiting room is something drearier than an English, even. Here there is nothing but a scanty sandy country to look out on. We have spent the last fortnight in a great hotel in the heart of an old forest of live oak and pine turned into a most magnificent garden, without spoiling the trees. The hotel was, of course, wood, but immense, with a dining room you could hardly see the end of. Hotel life is about the idlest thing in the world, and I didn't like to see people leading it. There was no one, except a single Englishwoman and me, who was not enormously fat after a certain age. And this is true of America generally.

I went yesterday to say goodbye to Simoneau and his squaw and his intensely Yankee daughter. The inscription in the copy of *The Strange Case of Dr Jekyll and Mr Hyde* which Stevenson sent him is: 'But the case of Robert Louis Stevenson and Jules Simoneau, if one could forget the other, would be stranger still.' In 1880 Stevenson was staying here, very poor, and dining every day at Simoneau's restaurant. When he did not appear for several days, Simoneau went to his little lodgings and threw some gravel up at the window, and Stevenson showed himself and confessed that he had no money. Then Simoneau told him to come and dine all the same; and that was the beginning of their friendship.

---

* On the appearance in 1901 of Stevenson's biography by Graham Balfour, Henley, who had been R.L.S.'s closest friend, wrote a disparaging article on the dead writer, which appeared in the *Pall Mall Gazette* (December 1901).

I was so glad to get a good batch of letters last night . . . Your father's little letter of the 8th was there, a *lovely* long one from Monnie, a little less long but still long and delightful one from Viola and a briefer one from my Dimpling. And so the hair is really up! what an altered Dimpling I shall see![35]

A preliminary warning of her adoption of a grown-up hair style had been given my Madeline in the letter in which she described their Christmas at Palace Court:

On Xmas night the Kocks came to dinner, also Mrs Russell, Bryn and Francis Thompson. We had a very jolly dinner . . . After dinner we acted a little play, written by Father, called 'A Christmas Tragedy'. It was about your being away – it was awfully funny. Prue was you and she did it awfully well – she copied your voice and walk exactly. Evie was Father and also Major Pond in another scene – he was excellent. Bastian was Father O'Keif and I was Agnes. It was a great success. When that was over we went downstairs to the dining room and played ping-pong. We made Bryn and F.T. have a match together it was really too funny for anything – we all screamed with laughter. Francis was awfully excited about it and when he was going he asked Father if he might come again the next night to play and he came and got really quite good at it . . .

I am housekeeper now, you know, and so I must go and do my shopping. I have forgotten to tell you a piece of news – I am going to put my hair up for New Year's Day. I am 17½ years old so I suppose I ought . . .[36]

In another letter Madeline confided to her mother: 'I do love going to the theatre. The dream of my heart is to be a *great* actress. I always think about it before I go to sleep at night and when I wake in the morning.'[37]

And from the twelve-year-old Olivia came a letter full of longing for her mother:

Oh, my darling mother do write to me soon. School *is* a nasty place. But mother dear, come home, but on no account if the crossing will be bad. I would like to just be able to bring you home, to look after your most precious welfare. For you are the most precious thing in existence to so many people. Mother, every morsel of you is precious – A little scratch, if I see one, makes me un-happy. For you are my mother and a mother must be more precious than anything except, perhaps a daughter . . .

Your ever most devoted daughter,
Olivia

I want to be such a mother as you.[38]

Another letter from Olivia reported:

Caleb Saleeby (a relation of Father's*) just came and is coming tomorrow

---

* Caleb Saleeby's maternal grandfather, Dr Caleb Williams, was Wilfrid Meynell's uncle.

with us to skate at Regents Park. He is very handsome, very tall, very dark, and very nice. He is staying with Mrs Leech and Father met him there the other night.[39]

This was the man who was one day to marry her sister Monica. He was the son of the head of the Mount Lebanon schools, and was descended from a Venetian crusader who had settled in the Holy Land. He had at this time just qualified as a doctor at Edinburgh University.

From Monterey the travellers went on to Los Angeles, where Mrs Meynell gave her lecture 'The Seventeenth Century' in a large hall to an audience of three or four hundred people. 'I confess', she wrote, 'I find it a moving experience to be treated as I was this morning after my lecture . . . What an intelligent audience, and what attention! They came up to the platform, some even weeping.'[40] When she was able to send some money to Wilfrid after a lecture her joy was great. 'I am sending you an absurd £15 to help the budget of one week, my dear, dear worker.'[41] In all her journeyings she was on the look-out for material that would make *Pall Mall Gazette* articles or *Daily Chronicle* paragraphs, so that in that way, too, she could continue, despite her absence, to help her husband in his wage-earning.

From Los Angeles on 27th February she wrote: 'Yesterday I was taken to a concert where an excessively Yankee Reverend Mother proved to be a great Francis Thompsonian and Patmorean. She knew all about everything and had kept a portrait of me for five years, both for the sake of my work and for love of F.T. That remarkable Reverend Mother sends messages of sympathy and admiration, spoken through her pretty nose, to him.'[42]

At Santa Barbara, whither they travelled early in February, they stayed first with a Dr and Mrs Whitehead, in a beautiful country house that reminded Alice Meynell of Castagnolo. Next they visited Dr and Mrs Blair Thaw, with whom she established a lasting friendship. 'How strange and beautiful was the experience of meeting them!', she wrote. 'Intellect and a passion for literature and such conversation as one seldom hears make a wonderful household.'[43]

Mrs Thaw gave a reception for her in their house which was called, for love of Shelley, Field Place; and the hostess stood up and recited to the guests 'The Shepherdess' and 'The Garden', and then read 'Domus Angusta' and 'The Rhythm of Life'. An Englishman present was vexed and said these should be read in silence; '. . . but', Mrs Meynell wrote to her husband, 'you should have seen how sweetly Mrs Thaw did it all.'[44]

The last of their visits in Santa Barbara was to Mr and Mrs Rogers, and in their house near the Spanish mission church Alice Meynell gave a lecture.

Oh, my Viola, [*she wrote to her daughter*] what a successful lecture I have
given today in the hall of this lovely house. I have made about £23 in the most
placid and delightful way. As to the kindness of Mr and Mrs Thaw and Mr and
Mrs Rogers – no, I cannot describe it. They have been driving about selling
tickets, they have bossed the whole show, overwhelmed me in orange blossoms
and violets, and taken me in their arms and kissed me. . . Don't you really
think, my Viola, the little money I shall make is worth while? It is some small
help to your darling father who is overworking himself so.[45]

To Olivia she wrote:

What a sweet letter you wrote me, my own Lobbie. I know you want me to
have a chance of a decent passage, and that will reconcile you to my coming
across in April instead of March, but I am staying for the sake of the lectures.
My own daughter and darling, a little while and I shall have you in my arms,
by God's blessing. We have all to keep a quiet heart.[46]

A few days later she told Wilfrid:

I think you would have been pleased with the lecture last Friday. Each time
it goes better, and I have now no nervousness . . . The welcomings and
enthusiasms of San Francisco always seemed to me rather a joke. But here it is
quite another matter. There is no one in England (after you and Meredith and
a few more) for whose opinions I have a more serious respect. They read more
than anyone I know in England, have libraries filled with the English classics,
and all such things as the Constable edition of Meredith and the Edinburgh
Stevenson, as a matter of course. And as to art: in San Francisco, with the
single exception of Mrs Crocker's daughter (she has Corot, Rousseau, Millet,
Degas, Luca della Robbia, Monet and everybody in her splendid house) the
pictures on the walls were so utterly below all possible marks as to make one
wonder.[47]

Towards the end of February Agnes Tobin received news that her
sister was seriously ill in Paris, and she left Santa Barbara hurriedly to
go to her. Thus her plan of their travelling together to England, for
which Alice Meynell had made so great a sacrifice, was defeated; but it
was no doubt due to the care she had received in the mild Californian
winter that Miss Tobin was well enough now to answer the urgent
summons to Paris; and her friend's sacrifice had not been in vain. Mrs
Meynell's departure for England could not be hastened, for a series of
lectures had been arranged for her on her journey eastward across
America. From Santa Barbara she wrote:

I can hardly wait now the time is drawing so near. I think the hardest time is
now, in the leisure of this visit, with Agnes gone. Oh, may all prosper in these
weeks still to be lived through! May you all be well; may God protect you.
May my journey go well![48]

On 10th March she gave her lecture on Dickens, her farewell to
Santa Barbara, since she left the next day for Los Angeles, on the first

stage of her long journey. The lecture brought in £15, and she wrote to Viola: 'It really did go off well . . . People thronged up to me. It is partly their amiability, but partly also a real interest in a fresh lecture on so old a subject.' In the evening Mrs Cameron Rogers gave a farewell party for her. 'They made speeches and drank my health and happy journey, and I can never tell you their kindness. What darling people!'[49]

From Los Angeles she travelled to Indianapolis, where she gave a lecture.

My first lecture in the Middle West (that is what we call ourselves) went very well last night . . . There was a large and attentive audience. The only contretemps was that the much vaunted American system of checking baggage played me false and my things were left on the way, so that I had to lecture in my travelling dress (with the 8/6 grey blouse I got in Pontings) to a great gathering of people in evening dress. It was rather painful but they congratulated me on the fact that my skirt was not really short. That just saved a remnant of dignity. So you see there is a little occasional use in a longish skirt. Mrs Elder in introducing me very cleverly said that though I liked America I had no reason to admire the checking situation. She said everybody would understand it as an explanation of my dress . . . After the lecture, the Elders gave a splendid supper to which the most literary Indianapolites were invited. It was exceedingly pleasant. The knowledge of literature struck me as ever – the interest in Coventry Patmore, for instance.

At the end of her letter she said: 'How lonely I am on this hemisphere.'[50]

Another night's journey – 'rather wretched, through lack of air and snoring men' – took her to Chicago, where she arrived in the early morning. There she retrieved the trunk whose temporary loss had inconvenienced her at Indianapolis, went on to Beloit, hurriedly changed and attended a large luncheon party, followed by a reading. In the evening there was a dinner party for her, attended by numerous professors, after which she lectured in the church, and then attended a reception at the College, where all the students were presented to her. The next day back to Chicago in time to give her Charlotte Brontë lecture to the Fortnightly Club. 'There is a law that this club does not applaud,' she wrote to her husband, 'but you should have heard them!'

The next night she gave the Seventeenth Century lecture, that being her third consecutive day of lecturing, at the end of her tremendous journey across America. 'I had a splendid second lecture at Chicago. What enthusiasm, what friendliness! And *not* humbug. When I recited "The Shepherdess" with one word wrong ("walk" instead of "roam") my hearers came one after another to reproach me. They simply know my work by heart.'[51]

On to Boston. There she gave a lecture in the town, one at a college club, one at Wellesley College, and one at Harvard. She stayed with Mrs Fields, who, like the Thaws, was a friend for ever after.

New York saw her final lectures and her farewell to the great country that had made her so welcome. 'In fifteen days', she wrote exultantly to Viola, 'I may have you in my arms, beloved.'[52] She sailed for England early in April, in the *Lucania*. Wilfrid met her at Liverpool, and when their train drew in to Euston her children were on the platform, dancing with excitement.

Meredith wrote to her on 10th May.

My dearest Portia,

The day before your letter came I read of the glad return, and saw the children crowd and leap about you, the husband beam like a ripe grape on the burst between thumb and finger; you feeling at rest, astonished, repentant, and with a side eye on your gathered riches. I shall rejoice when it is my turn to see you. I would propose to come, but age is telling horribly on my legs and I go nowhere. I need an arm when I walk, and enliven conversation with the frequent Eh! You will be charitable, I know. Meanwhile I am part of you and the family in the happiness of your being together again.

Ever most warmly
George Meredith[53]

CHAPTER 18

IN 1901, during Mrs Meynell's absence in America, her *Later Poems* was published by John Lane. The volume consisted of nineteen poems, ten of which had already appeared in the privately printed *Other Poems* in 1896. Among the more recent ones were 'November Blue', 'The Two Poets', 'West Wind in Winter', and 'A Poet's Wife'. In 'Chimes' she used again, with beautiful effect, the image of the dovecote. It was so dear to her that one can believe that she had lived beside an actual dovecote in one of the many homes of her childhood, and had retained clearly in her memory the picture of the doves returning at evening and of the great controlled explosion of feathered bodies as they left the cote in the morning. In 'At Night' she had written:

> Flocks of the memories of the day draw near
> The dovecote doors of sleep

and in 'The Spirit of Place' she had spoken of the chiming hours which 'await their appointed time to fly – wild prisoners – by twos or threes, or in greater companies. Fugitives – one or twelve taking wing – they are sudden, they are brief, they are gone; they are delivered from the close hands of this actual present. Not in vain is the sudden upper door opened against the sky; they are away, hours of the past.'

Now she returned to the same thought:

> Brief, on a flying night,
>   From the shaken tower
> A flock of bells take flight,
>   And go with the hour.
>
> Like birds from the cote to the gales,
>   Abrupt – oh, hark!
> A fleet of bells set sails,
>   And go to the dark.
>
> Sudden the cold airs swing.
>   Alone, aloud,
> A verse of bells takes wing
>   And flies with the cloud.[1]

In 'Unto us a Son is given' she wrote of the Nativity:

> Given, not lent,
> And not withdrawn – once sent,

This Infant of mankind, this One,
Is still the little welcome Son.

New every year,
New born and newly dear,
He comes with tidings and a song,
The ages long, the ages long;

Even as the cold
Keen winter grows not old,
As childhood is so fresh, foreseen,
And spring in the familiar green –

Sudden as sweet
Come the expected feet.
All joy is young, and new all art,
And He, too, Whom we have by heart.

The critics praised the little volume, but all remarked upon the smallness of Mrs Meynell's output of poetry. 'But she has accustomed us', the *Pall Mall Gazette* reviewer wrote, 'to look for quality rather than quantity and we are not disappointed. The rarity of her verses, measured by the gross test of counting pages and lines, is paralleled by the uncommon beauty of the poetry they embody, and the distinction wherewith it is expressed.'

After her return from America Alice Meynell resumed the work of art criticism for the *Pall Mall* which she had undertaken the year before, and which had been done in her absence by her husband and Everard, then an art student. The *Daily Chronicle* paragraphs, printed under the heading 'The Office Window' and filling two columns every day, were written constantly by both the Meynells, upon a diversity of subjects. Mrs Meynell's account for the month of August 1906 shows that thirty-one of her paragraphs were printed on fifteen days during that month, and that she received for them a payment of £4.7s.0d. Viola Meynell has written: 'My father's paragraphs were trusted to the extent of being passed on to the printer unread by the editor, while my mother's, in common with other contributors', were judged and perhaps rejected. She also received the common rate of pay, while special terms had been offered to him . . . The paragraphs are indeed the closest thing there is to a record of her conversation; the daily, hourly, incident or reflection, the things that form conversation, formed also them.'[2]

Her personal opinions were often expressed in these paragraphs – her dislike of sloppy grammar, her thoughts on fashion, her love of cultivation in the landscape rather than pasturage. 'Dull is any landscape in any part of the Globe – from California to Constantinople and back the other way – without sign of the hand of man; of the country man, that is, not the factory man. Whether in white wall or red, belfry or barn, or merely tillage and orchard, man must have laid his brown hand upon the view before it can be really beloved and lovely.'

Her sense of humour looks out, often, between the lines of small print; she was amusing in a delicate, slanting, uninsistent way. In her humour, as in her wisdom, she never stayed to labour a point, but touched swiftly, lightly, not upon the edge but upon the very core of the matter, and was away again.

When Professor Rutherford tells us that radium has been found in activity in fango, and that fango is 'a fine mud obtained from hot springs in Battaglia, North Italy', he specialises unduly. Fango 'may be obtained' from any street or road or swamp. It is merely the Italian for mud . . .

Anthony Trollope [*another paragraph declares*] (whose novels some of us still read, say, about the second week of a serious convalescence) had virtually but one subject – the lady between two lovers, the lover between two ladies. They seem to alternate, if one looks at the dates of his books, but whatever the sex of the doubter, it is always, if one may be permitted the phrase, one donkey and two bundles of hay . . .

And in a paragraph on Elizabeth Barrett Browning she spoke of a little vanity she shared with her. 'It is certain that her husband did not know her precise age until long after her death. With creditable feminine weakness she did not tell it, and with creditable masculine delicacy he did not ask it. He would have loved her as much had she been sixteen years instead of six years his senior.'

Alice Meynell, too, kept the secret of her age, though she did not go so far as to hide it from her husband. Editors of anthologies and books of reference were obliged to guess at it, and their guesses annoyed her. 'I like that article on me in that magazine', she wrote to her husband in 1916. 'But why will they announce fancy dates for my birth in the calm tone of facts?'[3]

In the November after her return from America she paid a visit to the Butlers at Devonport, leaving Everard to visit a Watercolour Exhibition in her stead and write a *Pall Mall* column on it. 'If he is diligent in this, as I know he will be,' she wrote to Meynell, 'I shall stay a fortnight and finish Emerson, Holmes and Keats.'[4]

The work on Keats was a selection of his poems with a critical intro-duction which she was doing for Blackie's 'Red Letter Library'. Over the course of the next eight or nine years she selected and introduced for this series the poems of Coleridge, Cowper, Herrick, Matthew

Arnold, Christina Rossetti, Blake, and Jean Ingelow. This year saw the publication of Agnes Tobin's sonnets, *Love's Crucifix*, with an introduction by Mrs Meynell; and an essay of hers had also introduced *The Madonna*, a collection, published in the preceding year, of reproductions of the great paintings and sculptures of the Virgin, with text translated from the Italian of Adolfo Venturi.

To the task of literary criticism, in this more permanent form as well as in her journalism, Alice Meynell brought a fine perception, a judgement that was clear, steadfast, and above the changing fashions of contemporary taste; she was generous, but where she detected falseness, slovenliness, or the cheap jibe, she attacked without mercy. Of prejudice she might have been accused only twice in her long career of literary criticism, and it is by no means certain that she can be found guilty. Gibbon she could not forgive for what she believed his grave disservice to the English language, and Swinburne she accused of a 'little intellect, and paltry degree of sincerity, and rachitic passion, and tumid fancy'.[5] Her contempt and dislike for the author of *Atalanta* sprang, one suspects, from *his* contempt and dislike for God. She could answer with coolness and calm an attack on anything she held dear except that one thing: the Christian faith; and in answering *that* challenge her anger sometimes spoiled her logic. Yet she could hand due praise to Swinburne too: 'Swinburne is a complete master of the rhythm and rhyme, the time and accent, the pause, the balance, the flow of vowel and clash of consonant, that makes the "music" for which verse is popular and prized.'[6]

An introductory note to a volume of a different kind was written in 1903, when Heinemann published a collection of reproductions of Sargent's pictures. It was by the artist's own request that Mrs Meynell wrote this brief study of his work, and in October 1903 he wrote to her: 'I have just read your introductory note with great pleasure and a feeling of gratitude that dates from the time when you consented to do it, and that is now doubled, for you have done it so well. I am glad of the slight reserves and distinctions and oppositions which give your essay the character of a study in spite of its very high praise – and am honoured that such praise should come from you, "wonderful you" as Henry James says . . .'[7]

In that year she also wrote the text for *Children of the Old Masters*, an art book published by Duckworth.

Of poetry there was little at that time. 'Veneration of Images' appeared in the *Pall Mall Gazette* in January 1902, and in September 1903 the same journal published 'A Restless Season', which was subsequently printed, with some amendments, in the *Collected Poems* under the title 'The Rainy Summer'. Of these poems, so rare in a double sense, the *Pall Mall* editor, Harry Cust, wrote to Mrs Meynell: 'I worship your verses, the best of the Occs [Occasional Verses] and pray for your nearer friendship.'[8]

Besides these many literary occupations that filled her days, Alice Meynell had always a busy social life, with engagements that ranged from the guests entertained at a noisy, cheerful Sunday night supper to the formal luncheon party of literary celebrities. The children, growing up, brought their friends to Palace Court, and in that hospitable house there was often to be found the casual caller, the friend who brought a problem, the writer who wanted to discuss his work, for each of whom time must be found. And, of course, the wraith-like figure of Francis Thompson was never for very long absent from the Palace Court library. There were, too, entertainments on a larger scale in the world outside to which the Meynells sometimes went. The Duchess of Sutherland* had become a friend of Mrs Meynell as a result of writing to express her admiration of a poem; her great receptions at Stafford House were the most magnificent of the parties they attended.

To her mother, who enjoyed reading of these occasions, Mrs Meynell wrote of one of them in 1904: 'It was one of the greatest and most brilliant parties of the whole season and I have never seen anything like it. The great staircase, open to the high roof of Stafford House, has two great arms, at the top of which stood that beautiful creature in her diamonds with a stream of the whole of the great London society passing up – the Duke and Duchess of Connaught representing royalty, and every peer and peeress in London.'[9]

A little later the Duchess began to hold 'intellectual' Friday evenings to which the Meynells were invited, and an account of one of these in a letter to an absent daughter lists some of the guests. 'The Duke of Argyll (who has literary ambitions) was there, the Duchess of Rutland, Winston Churchill, Lord Ribblesdale, Mrs Hunter, Andrew Lang, Herbert Trench, the Beerbohm Trees, Laurence Binyon, Oliver Lodge, who said he had read all I have written, Mr Birrell – I cannot remember any more; the gathering was small.'[10]

It was with difficulty that the grown-up daughters could be persuaded to accept these invitations into London society. 'Madeline and Viola', Mrs Meynell told her mother, 'don't care for the world. They enjoy cricket at Wormwood Scrubs in short petticoats, and hockey in Battersea Park, much better.'[11]

Mrs Charles Hunter, mentioned among the Stafford House guests, often sought Alice Meynell's company during these years. From her house near Middleton-on-Tees presents of game were sometimes dispatched to the Meynells; and both there and at Hill Hall, near

---

* Millicent Fanny, wife of the fourth Duke, and daughter of the fourth Earl of Rosslyn.

Epping, she was on many occasions a welcoming hostess to Mrs Meynell. Staying with her in 1905, Alice wrote to her mother: 'We are motoring every day among the Westmoreland lakes and the Cumberland hills and Yorkshire moors, careering along the high country at fifty miles an hour. It is exciting. I think there is no pleasure like it. I wear goggles and three overcoats. Fast as we go, our hearts go ahead.'[12]

Fifty miles an hour was then a speed so unattainable as to be a figure of speech; but that she was able during her lifetime to travel in motor cars that really did attain it must have been a great pleasure to her. She loved speed, both for itself and for the taste of danger that was in it, and was fascinated by the mechanical world and the jargon of those who belonged to it. An enthusiastic letter of the early days of motoring speaks of a car, most correctly, by the feminine pronoun.

Her enjoyment of danger is demonstrated by her account of an incident when she was being driven not in a motor car but behind horses. 'Is it something rash in the feminine character that made the moment of "What next?" a pure joy to me the only time that I underwent it? It was when motor cars were rarer than they are now; and the appearance of one at the top of a short hill caused the two young horses a friend at my side was driving to bolt and hurl us down a bank. If life contained many such moments it would indeed be a gift beyond price. Not only was that one moment "stretched" (as George Eliot says) with delight and wonder, but there was full energetic presence of mind to enjoy it in detail. It has served to comfort me, in hearing of danger or distress, with the thought of secret pleasures; and I have heard of such, not only in peril, but in pain.'[13]

In 1905 the Meynells left Palace Court. The disused top floor of Burns and Oates's premises at the corner of Orchard Street and Granville Place, off Oxford Street, was converted under Wilfrid Meynell's own supervision into a flat for them, containing drawing-room, dining-room, five bedrooms, and a dressing-room. For Wilfrid, who had to spend a lot of time in the offices downstairs, the advantage was obvious; and the letting of Palace Court would bring in a little money. Monica, the eldest daughter, had married Caleb Saleeby in 1903, and the grown-up members of the family were no longer all at home; so a lesser dwelling than Palace Court was now adequate. The *dis*advantage was that more than seventy stone steps must be climbed before reaching the flat, which, with its long, narrow, white passages, resembled, Viola Meynell tells us, a ship; but later, when Alice Meynell's health began to fail, a lift was put in. Here, as at Palace Court, the Sunday evening suppers were always open to visitors; the children's friends came, and those of the parents, as well as literary acquaintances. Francis Thompson, of course, still wandered in and out from his lodgings, often failing to come when expected or arriving at some strange hour. A letter from Alice to her husband, who was away from home, describes a visit of the latter variety. 'He came the night before last when we were all in bed and, being told so by the (new) maid, went away; then came back and pushed past her into the drawing room asking for paper and envelopes. She was dreadfully frightened and staggered, livid, into Dimpling's room, saying, "He is mad or a robber." '[14]

In the summers of 1904 and 1905 Wilfrid Blunt lent the Meynells the group of small wooden bungalows which he had designed himself and built in a clearing in the woods near Beaulieu, in Hampshire; Alice Meynell made long visits there with the younger members of the family.

Towards the end of the summer of 1905 a plan was made to take the young Meynells to Italy. Mrs Meynell set off in August and travelled to Munich with a party of friends headed by Agnes Tobin's brother Dick, who was later to become United States Ambassador to the Netherlands. In Munich they were to hear opera, and go to the Passion Play at Oberammergau; and then she was to travel on alone to meet her husband and the family at Verona.

On the way to Munich they stopped in Paris, where they went to the theatre and spent a day at Versailles, which Mrs Meynell found exceeded all the descriptions she had heard of it. 'I saw Horace Walpole everywhere', she wrote.[15]

The death of a Bavarian princess caused the opera in Munich to be put off for two nights, but there was much to do and see. 'We have spent the two days in seeing Munich,' she wrote to Meynell, 'churches and galleries, the funeral procession for the Princess and everything. The evening we spent in a beer-hall among the people.'[16]

Of the Passion Play she wrote in her essay 'The Village of Oberammergau':

What seemed to me strange and interesting, and rather a pity, is to find these earnest villagers, who are a trans-Alpine people and altogether German, making their hamlet subject to the tradition of a classic Italy. The proscenium is painted with a monochrome of Michelangelo's Moses; pediment and pilasters are Italian; the attitude of the groups within is after a Milanese picture or a Tuscan; the grace is that of Raphael . . . The people of the hamlet were as convinced that art and taste dwell beyond their dark highlands as though the second Decline and Fall – that of the art of the South – had never taken place.

But the little village had dedicated its most perfect man to the great part of the Passion Play:

. . . and he, with the utmost simplicity, keeps his brown locks of the length chosen by the painters, and so goes about his daily work, closer to God than is the altar crucifix, and made by German nature and Italian art in the image of Christ.

Not only in the symmetry of the Crucifixion, but in the accidents of every day, shouldering a burden, footing a rough journey in these hard hills, turning his lathe, or gathering a child upon one arm, he carries this perpetual likeness, and turns towards the world this aspect unaltered, until his years shall pass those of the Saviour, when another will take his place. The beating heart, the tide of blood move to the divine purpose, so that the image veiled or scattered among the crowd, distributed, broken, shattered, or grown dull, is gathered up in him, in order and continual consciousness. [17]

Sebastian was now about to set off for Persia, there to work in the Imperial Bank, and his mother heard of his impending departure while she was in Venice. She wrote to him:

Your news affects me very much. All I wish for is your best progress in your calling, because I hope that you may be able, within a reasonable time, to have a wife and home. And I trust that your father and I may be able to help you if our health lasts. An experience of the world is also worth getting, and I trust that you may find much to interest you. But, dearest Bastian, the long separation weighs heavily on my heart. Never let the thought of me fade from your mind. I shall pray for you every single day of my life. [18]

CHAPTER 19

IN 1905 Edmund Gosse published his book on Coventry Patmore. Alice Meynell had been in correspondence with him while it was in preparation, and she had laid stress upon the neglect that she felt had been accorded to the Odes. 'I think no one', she had written to Gosse, 'except yourself, Lionel Johnson, Francis Thompson and two men in America, ever had a glimpse of the greatness of the Odes. Yes, Ruskin did when he wrote one of his letters (I have not that one) saying "The Unknown Eros" was – well – everything. But when the Psyche Odes were published he was very angry, and said C.P. was writing out of his own passions, or words to that effect.'[1]

When the book was published she wrote to Gosse:

All the part about the Angel seems to me more than satisfactory. The brilliant quickness of perception delights me in your appreciation, as well as the gentleness. For you spare many things that are vulnerable . . . All the biographical part I like exceedingly. It is so liberal and large in feeling, and wise, and also buoyant in the writing.

I am disappointed in regard to the Odes, because I think that there are in them lines of the yonder, the diviner poetry, to be heard with an answering rapture:

> Thy breast with dead-winged innocence is filled,
> Even as a nest with birds
> After the old ones by the hawk are killed.

> And burst in wind-kissed splendours on the deafening beach.

> Like sunny eve in some forgotten place.

. . . I think you with-hold that rapture, but I do not guess why. You write in a tepid spirit . . . I am telling you frankly what I think. I know that if you did not feel the perfectly heavenly quality of the Odes you would not have loved the man, nor would you have written the book. But you do not give expression to the homage of your heart.[2]

In the following year Mrs Meynell herself wrote again on Patmore's poems. Her article was published in *The Outlook*,[3] and subsequently reprinted, with alterations, in *Prose and Poetry*, the selection from her work made in 1947. In a passage omitted from the later version she wrote: 'It needs a somewhat vulgar soul to find *The Angel in the House* commonplace, a perfectly vulgar soul to find it contemptible.' No doubt it was to this that she referred when, writing to Wilfrid Meynell shortly before it was published, she said: 'My proof for the

Outlook just come. A good article. I have given some people beans – G.B.S.* By George – beans!'⁴

A tribute paid to her in that year was the dinner given at the Lyceum Club in her honour. She told her mother: 'About seventy or eighty people were there and it was very brilliant. It was given to me in recognition of my work in literature. My health was drunk after the King's, and there were laudatory speeches to which I made a brief reply. Wilfrid was too nervous to go, but I took Viola who enjoyed it.'⁵

Praise, for itself, was not valued by Alice Meynell, nor did it give her particular pleasure; there were only a few whose praise she really cared to have. But she knew that her mother, Mrs Thompson, rejoiced in the admiration accorded to the work of her two daughters; to her, as to no one else, she told the compliments she received. Parties also were described in Alice's letters to 'My dearest little Mama', since these things were of great interest to the old lady, who replied with her usual wild, rapturous phrases cascading over the paper in her thin spidery hand. She moved frequently from one house to another, desiring, wherever she was, to be somewhere else, and spending money with a reckless extravagance from which she could not be dissuaded. Surrey and the outskirts of London were the regions she most favoured, and there were long and complicated journeys for her daughter when she went, as she did frequently, to spent a day with her. A letter of Mrs Meynell's in 1906, when Mrs Thompson was at Farnborough, speaks of travelling home after one of these visits 'in eight conveyances, four trains and four omnibuses.'

All but the two youngest children were now grown up, and they, at sixteen and fifteen, were leaving childhood behind. The exquisite courtesy which Alice Meynell considered was the due of all with whom she came in contact was extended also to her children; their privacy and independence were respected by her, their love not taken for granted but prized as a rare and precious gift. 'My mother', says Francis Meynell, 'maintained a close reticence about her inner feelings . . . A like reticence she allowed to her children; though well aware of their plentiful romances, she did not ask about them.'⁶ It has been said that there were few whose praise she cared to have, and her children were among those few; as the years passed, their judgement on a new poem or an essay was ever more eagerly awaited, and the measure of her happiness in a piece of work was often their approval or their silence. They treated her with a protective tenderness, teased her, adored her, rebelled, often, in their growing up, against her strongly-held opinions. Wisely, but sometimes anxiously, she watched them and said little; sometimes advice proffered in a letter was preceded by a diffi-

* George Bernard Shaw who had made derogatory comments on the work.

dent 'Don't laugh at me' or 'I don't want to preach.' But she knew the strength of the mutual trust that was between them and knew how great a thing in the life of each one of them was the love of her, the desire for her approbation. Their problems brought to her were always met with sympathy; Francis at this time was perplexed by the apparent difficulty of reconciling belief in a merciful God with belief in Hell, and she tried, in a long letter, to explain the view which she now held on this subject after much bewilderment in her own thoughts.

You may guess [*she wrote*] whether or not I have suffered from the thing that is so troubling you. Who has not who has an imagination and a heart? Guard yourself, however, from saying of that doctrine, 'It is a lie.' I am certain that to all eternity I shall never cease to be sorry for some passages in my life, shall never cease to mourn for them. They and their consequences will always be present to me in whatever kind of eternity I may be, even, by the great mercy of God, a happy one. What is this but eternal punishment? All punishment is eternal, and all its consequences are eternal. We are all subject to everlasting punishment because our deeds are irrevocable, because nothing can alter the past, and because we are ourselves for ever. But besides this universal fact, we are to fear the results of an entirely selfish life. It is something to be greatly feared and we ought to fear it. Christ would not have told the story or parable of 'the rich man' if there were nothing to fear. The atonement of Our Saviour is not, however, fruitless, even for 'the rich man'. No doubt the wonderful unselfishness (in spite of a wholly selfish life on earth) that makes him in his place of exile and, no doubt, temporary pain, care for his brethren and wish them to be warned is something divine, won for him by Christ . . . The facts, the truth of moral good and evil, are the important things of our life here. And these the Church holds, for these the Church vouches. Without her we have no law. For what does Nature teach us of moral good? Next to nothing. A sparing of suffering to others because we feel pain to be dreadful – this is the highest, the only, moral thing we learn from Nature – from human Nature – for from animal or inanimate Nature we learn no morality. And how vague in application is this one good law! No, if we are to be in any real sense human, we must begin where Nature leaves off; and there is nothing but the Church to give us this beginning. Grace begins where Nature ends.[7]

Twenty years before, when troubled by her own perplexity upon this point, she had discussed it with Dr St George Mivart, philosopher, biologist, writer, Fellow of the Royal Society, and a close friend of her husband's; and he had written to her reassuringly. Subsequently, after prolonged controversy with the Church, as represented by Cardinal Vaughan, in the correspondence columns of *The Times*, Mivart declared himself an unbeliever, and hastened to preach the new truth that he felt he had found.* This drew from Mrs Meynell a letter in which we see her rare and scathing anger. This, like everything else

---

* Mivart was excommunicated by Cardinal Vaughan because of his articles in the *Nineteenth Century* and the *Fortnightly Review* repudiating ecclesiastical authority.

that she expressed, was light in its touch, but it seared like the flick of a whip-lash.

Dear Dr Mivart,

I should not have offered you my criticism, but in reply to your question I have to say that I do think what you are doing to be wrong.

It seems to me wrong to influence others to give up a faith that is a restraint upon human passions. Your own abandonment of Christianity, however rational you may consider it, is no more than the result of opinion. And there can be no sufficient reason for urging an opinion upon others; whereas the reason for not urging *this* opinion upon others is most momentous. Mankind is absolutely in need of fundamental morality in the first place, and of a code of moralism in the second place. I do not know how much fundamental morality you now acknowledge; probably you still think mere cruelty to be wrong. But the pursuit of pleasure for its own sake leads to cruelty – not merely accidentally, by way of egoism, but directly, as to an end. This is one of the mysteries of human nature, and against this descent into infernal evil mankind needs a safeguard which must be dogmatic from the beginning. I am quite sure it is wrong to take away such a safeguard because *on the whole* you think it is an imaginary one.

Moreover it seems to me wrong and lamentable that a man should be eager to write and talk about his loss when he has lost Jesus Christ. To have to relinquish that figure and that person ought to be a great grief – certainly a grief imposing silence for a time. Only a cold and corrupt heart could fail to suffer. Therefore I think you must suffer more than you know, and I wish I had words to persuade you to respect your own distress.

> Very sincerely yours,
> Alice Meynell[8]

The growing-up of the children and the lessening of her regular journalistic commitments made travelling more possible for her than it had been hitherto, and from 1905 to 1914 there was only one year that did not have its record of a journey abroad.

In the spring of 1906 she went with Everard to Rome, where her friend Mrs Swynnerton had lent them a flat in the Via Montebello. Of the last stages of that long journey she had written on a previous occasion:

The morning and the evening are the day's journey. When you reach the end, each place keeps in your memory its peculiar light on that single day. Genoa *was* the morning, and the Carrara mountains, red, with their veins of white marble, were the golden day; Pisa was the after-glow, as its cathedral, its baptistery, and its leaning tower stood up together in the delicate light against a delicate sky; the Campagna was night, and Rome a violet in the electric light.[9]

A sleeper was a luxury that she never contemplated indulging in for herself. When there was a suggestion of his coming out to join them she wrote to Meynell:

My darling Wilfrid, The thought that you may really come is too happy. I
don't think I can bear to forgo it now I have had the hope. There is nothing
fatiguing in the journey if you sleep (as I think you should) in Paris. I bear
travelling all night sitting up and not sleeping one single half-hour, but you
would not.[10]

She rejoiced in seeing again the many things in Rome that she loved,
and in showing them to Everard for the first time. Lady Butler was
there too, with one of her daughters.

Much is spoilt and vulgarized in Rome, but so much is left! Mimi and I who
feel exactly alike, refuse to see certain things, and keep our eyes for seeing a
hundredfold the loveliness that remains. We *do* see. And so does Everard,
though he sometimes stops himself from giving in to us. Sometimes, however,
he cannot. He is off this morning with damsels to the crypt of St Peter's, the
tomb of the Apostles. Lanciani* thinks the dust of St Peter and St Paul was
scattered in one of the Dark Ages sieges; but here they lay, and at San Pietro in
Montario was St Peter crucified, and you may stand on the stones where he
stood who saw the Crucifixion and spoke with Christ. Constantine built a
chapel to mark the place and there is no reason to doubt it . . .

I hope you got my two articles. If the second is printed, please change the
spelling of 'Bon riposo' to 'B*u*on riposo'. I thoughtlessly spelt it the Genoese
way.[11]

The disappearance of the Religious Orders from the streets** [*she wrote in
her next letter to Wilfrid*] (with the exception of a few Capuchins) makes a
great difference. The people attend the churches in great numbers. The Gesù
was full for a sermon today. The usual grave fathers take their charming little
girls to Mass. In St Peter's it is a lovely sight.

Everard . . . does appreciate Rome and he gathers history so readily, it is a
pleasure to go about with him. Also he finds his way . . .

Remember my question about the jewels – 2 bracelets, a star, a pearl
necklace, a ring – I left them out on your chest-of-drawers and forgot them.

Tell me – as you have done hitherto – everything that happens. We are both
well. As to our crossing, it was decidedly qualmish but I was not ill as most
people were – and very ill. I am no longer the champion. Nor was Everard ill.
We bore all the fatigues and had no difficulties. My dear love to the darling
children. Your Johnson[12]

To her mother she wrote: 'We go about all day. I cannot rest, so do I
long to see things and places, and we come home at night staggering
with fatigue. I am writing articles on Rome as it is *now*. I think I shall
pay my expenses this way.'[13]

And to her daughter Madeline:

* A leading archaeologist of the day. Modern investigations have confirmed, with
moral certainty, the presence of St Peter's tomb under the basilica; but attempts to
identify the bones found there with those of St Peter are unsubstantiated.

** As a result of the abolition of the Papal States and the forcible incorporation of the
city of Rome into the new, secular kingdom of Italy.

My darling Dimpling,

This is the third fine day. Sapphires and diamonds in the pure air. Rome smells of hyacinths. The scent travels all along the streets where hyacinths have merely passed. Yesterday we walked through the most classic Borghese gardens with their pines and fountains. It was a golden evening. Today we are lunching with the Butlers at a *trattoria* at the foot of the Palatine . . . We shall stand on the very pavement where St Paul stood to be tried in the Basilica of the Caesars. This is not legend but history . . .

Viola has written me *delightful* letters, so has Olivia, one . . . Three several times have I asked to be told whether my jewels are all right. I left them loose. Your father does not answer and I shall begin to think something has happened. When one has left loose fifteen hundred pounds' worth of jewels, one wants to know. I do hope I shall hear tonight. I shall begin to think he does not read my letters.[14]

She longed for her husband to join them:

My darling Wilfrid, You say nothing in your last about coming! This rest must be. *Do* come. The sun is streaming over shining Rome. I wonder whether Garvin* would endure four articles. I should like to send one entirely on the Vatican Gardens, and another general one. Tell me whether you received No. 2.

Thank my Viola for her most delightful April Fool letter. Everard had not the heart to make me an April fool so far from home.[15]

And on the following day:

My love to the darlings. Hurry up and come. Your Johnson.[16]

But Meynell was tied in London and his wife finally gave up hope of persuading him to come.

I should like some more explicit news of Monica — how she is. And anything about Francie or Bastian will be welcome.

It is a great disappointment that you are not coming. It is hard that finances or rheumatism should stop you, dearest Wilfrid.[17]

Another letter described a visit to Hadrian's Villa:

Darling Wilfrid, What a heavenly day we have had! It was not precisely sunny, but a lovely light, and much warmer. At 10.30 we started in Mrs Hunter's splendid motor, St Clair Baddeley being of the party. We sped across the Campagna to Hadrian's Villa and I thought of you in that incomparable beauty. The hills were the blue of lapis lazuli, but softer, and when we came near we found the lower cultivated parts all misted with almond blossom. Cyclamen and violets everywhere. St Clair Baddeley gave us a splendid lesson on Hadrian and his time and his works. Here is Roman history for Everard, at

---

*   J. L. Garvin: journalist and playwright; editor of the *Pall Mall Gazette* 1912-1915, and of *The Observer* 1908-1942.

last. We went over all the stupendous remains of that art-city, for a city it was and not a villa, and we pushed through the olive orchards to places whence you see a visionary view of Rome and the three ranges of mountains. We lunched under a giant pine, Mrs Hunter having brought a noble hamper from her hotel, and at leisure we prepared for the homeward journey, putting off the Villa d'Este for another time. So many impressions of vast distance, exquisite colour and mysterious form, were not to be disturbed, and they were enough for one day. Cypress, pine, olive, almond, vine – how lovely are these indigenous things. All the new boulevards are planted with pale plane and palm. It is the darkness of the cypress and pine that gives such fine accents to the pallid scenery, and sends the distance such leagues away.[18]

They were in Rome for Holy Week, and Mrs Meynell wrote to Viola on Good Friday.

My darling Viola, Thank you for your welcome and excellent letter. Yesterday we were three times at St Peter's. It is *the* St Peter's day. At nightfall after Tenebrae the great relics, brought from Jerusalem by St Helena, mother of the first Christian emperor, Constantine, are held up over the thousands of people in one of the loggias under the dome. Outside was a wonderful night of stars.
    This morning we spent in Santa Maria Maggiore. In the afternoon we motor to the villa d'Este. I would not have chosen Good Friday, I need not say, but it was not a thing I *could* refuse – it is too lovely. It is so delightful of Mrs Hunter not to take these long excursions of twenty miles without us.[19]

She was always watchful for anything that would make an article or even a paragraph and thus bring in something to the family purse. 'I think for "Et Cetera". It is exactly four centuries this week since Pope Julius II laid the first stone of the present St Peter's. It was laid under the pier where those great relics now are.'[20]

On Easter Day she wrote to Meynell:

The most beautiful thing I have seen in Rome was ordination at the Lateran yesterday – Holy Saturday. So many young creatures with their snow-white garments and their jet-black heads, in that majestic apse with its eleventh-century mosaics – one of the few mediaeval things in Rome. Spring, or rather summer, has come suddenly, the roses have crowded into flower, the city is overflowing with flowers, the Campagna covered with daisies. Yesterday the priests went about blessing the houses; also the restaurants. Where we had lunch, they had prepared the table of eggs, lamb, salame, and cake, the food which is specially blessed . . . The two young country servants of Miss Baker were weeping on Good Friday because they thought the Romans cared so little. In their village, they said, they thought of nothing all day but the Crucifixion. The Madonna went about their streets all Friday and Saturday looking for her Son. She went through the woods and up the mountains, and at dawn on Easter Day she came into the church where the first Mass was said, and there she found Him.[21]

They called on Cardinal Merry de Val* and evidently hoped that he would procure for them an audience with the Pope (St Pius X), but he made no offer.

He put the whole question of audiences aside, referring to Cardinal Bisletti, the Majordomo, but not giving us his card or any facility. He was quite nice, however, and we talked of Father Rickaby's book which he had that very morning again been admiring. He said he did not know whom to thank. It was a stately occasion. We had to wait nearly an hour, during which now a scarlet presence floated through, now a violet. We stood up, under Pinturrichio's exquisite frescoes to do them honour and their manners are certainly very good.[22]

But the audience was granted after all.

Yesterday, by some mistake, Mimi's invitation to a semi-private audience admitted 'one other lady' so Mimi at once sent to me, and I went with her and Eileen. It was only semi-private, and as His Holiness paused but a few moments with each guest I could not say your nice things. Mimi did not say a single word, being rather afraid of not hearing if he was speaking. But I asked his blessing in choice Italian for you and for all my sons and daughters. He said, with a charming action, 'Tutti, tutti, tutti,.' He is most spiritual and gentle, quite unlike the portraits, but exceedingly sad.[23]

Later Mrs Meynell met the Pope's sisters.

They are not lodged at the Vatican but in a little ordinary house in the street leading from the Piazza. The elder sister whom I saw is Venetian of the gondolier class – much less polished than any Venetian shop-keeper of St Mark's Piazza, but perfectly easy, courteous and simple. Her dialect is of a rough popular kind, with many Genoese words. I could understand and talk to her but Miss Baker and she cannot understand a single word of each other's; they beam at one another. Much the same happened at Cardinal Vannutelli's,** whither she took me. It was an interesting visit. I must say the Italian manner in him made a fine contrast with the English unfortunately exemplified by that extraordinarily disagreeable man Monsignor Stanley,*** to whom she afterwards took me. He did not want to see me in the least, and did not pretend to. I enjoyed my various experiences. Fogazzaro**** is much talked of. I put in

---

* Rafael Merry del Val: 1865-1930. Son of the Secretary to the Spanish Legation in London; educated, in part, at Ushaw College, Durham. Nominated by Leo XIII for the Papal service, he was secretary to the commission which in 1896 condemned – by the narrow margin of one vote – the validity of Anglican ordinations. In 1897 he fulfilled a delicate papal mission in Canada, and in 1903 was created Cardinal and Secretary of State by Pius X.
** Vincent Vannutelli: Papal Legate at the Westminster Eucharistic Congress of 1908, when the public procession of the Blessed Sacrament was prohibited by the Home Secretary, H. H. Asquith.
*** Algernon Charles Stanley, (son of second Baron Stanley of Alderley) a convert to the Catholic Church.
**** Antonio Fogazzaro, author of the famous novel *Il Santo*, at that time in trouble at the Vatican on account of his alleged Modernism.

words for him, very well taken by Cardinal Vanutelli, not at all well by Monsignor Stanley who, I am bound to say, neither asked my opinion nor had the smallest wish to hear it, poor man.[24]

There were many friends to see. They went with Charles Lewis Hind* and Miss Clemson to Frascati and Albano. Hilaire Belloc came to tea: 'He is quite brilliant, though one has to discourage some of his "unexpected" bombs of conversation.'[25]

She wrote articles and despatched them to Meynell, anxious that they should be used to bring in money as quickly as possible. 'Dearest Love,' she said in one letter, 'when I think that it is with labour and headaches that you have gained us this too, too lovely holiday!'[26]

They stayed at Sori on the way back, with Mrs Granet.**

I have prosed about the beauty of Liguria but nothing, nothing, can ever give an idea of it. All the way from Rome the beauty grew and grew – first Campagna and then Tuscany and then this celestial country. Those who have not seen it at the end of April have not seen it at all.

We are very happy with our charming hostess, and I don't know whether our return will be on Tuesday night or on Wednesday night . . .

Many thanks for the cabled money. It is sad how wealth flies in travelling. But as to enjoyment, take my word for it no two people ever appreciated it more. We are just off to Mass at the village I know so well. No factories. How often I have dreamt of it with chimneys – all my life since I was six years old. I have never set foot in it since I was six.[27]

A brief stay at home in Granville Place was followed by another journey – to Jersey, with Viola. Here she saw the house where she had stayed with her parents as a child of ten, and went in search of the shop where she and her sister used to buy peppermints.

In August Alice Meynell went to Scotland and stayed with Mrs Cameron Head at Inverailort, on the west coast. Her letters make it clear that she was not a lover of the Scots, nor even of the Highland scenery. On arrival she wrote to Wilfrid:

Darling Wilfrid, The journey is well over, and it is nice to be in this hospitable house. A hot bath has partly restored the circulation. It is deep autumn here. I need hardly mention that it is raining. From Edinburgh onwards that has been a matter of course . . . My box has remained somewhere, I am sorry to say, but the station master here is seeing to it. Changing in the cold small hours at Edinburgh, I saw it – if my eyes did not deceive me. But anything more barbarous than the porters and officials in Scotland cannot be imagined. They either don't answer you, or don't know. You cannot get information. A worm

---

* Charles Lewis Hind, 1862-1927. Editor of the *Pall Mall Budget* 1893-5 and of *The Academy* 1896-1908.

** Evelyn Pulchérie, daughter of David Ward Chapman, married Colonel E. J. Granet, Military Attaché in Rome.

will turn, and I said on two occasions. 'Is there nobody here to answer questions and to attend to travellers in these places?'

I hope we shall have some motoring after all. The hills are as usual lost in a rag of mist. Oh, the south! . . .

Another visitor arrived with me having travelled in a sleeping car and looking fresh. I look a wreck for the moment.[28]

They went to the Highland Games at Fort William:

It was, of course, a deeply gloomy day but the rain held off. All people over ten stone went by train, but we light ones sped by motor and that I always enjoy. There were all the games one has heard of so often, throwing the weight and putting the hammer, and the caber, and the dancing, with shouts, to me a most offensive performance, though they all think it lovely. Competitions for bagpipes also. Mr Head stalked and got a stag. Mrs Grant Duff is gone and I think Lord and Lady Denman are going today . . . Lord Denman is in waiting. He has very good manners and is a pleasing little man, a strong Liberal.

Let no one ever mention mosquitoes again in a world where there are midges. At least you pay for sunshine with mosquitoe bites (a few). Here, in the perpetual darkness, the midges are quite intolerable . . . There is a good croquet lawn, and the players are excellent but the midges made the game impossible. The others are not bitten like me but they cannot stand it . . .

Mrs Head particularly wants me to stay to meet Lady Lovat a little later. Bridge goes on every evening, and at last I have joined in, as I don't really play so badly, but only with the three who will consent not to play for money . . . The fewness of my evening dresses is becoming almost tragic as no one else wears a dress twice. I don't *really* mind.[29]

Everyone is gone who was here. Today arrive Sir Clement Hill, Sir Alfred Scott Gatty and his wife, and a wonderfully musical cousin of Mrs Head's. So we shall have music instead of bridge and the screaming ping-pong. Everybody is always in fits of laughter, and that to me is a little tiring.[30]

Among other guests in the house was the chief of the Clan Mackintosh, whose title caused Mrs Meynell some bewilderment since, as he was always referred to as 'The Mackintosh', she could not decide what would be the correct way to address him. Finally she asked, and was relieved to learn the proper form of address, which she might at any moment have to use. Another guest she described as 'rather nice' but 'the most imperturbable egoist in conversation I have ever struck. He tells you what he had for dinner during the last few years, and all other intimate but dull details of his life day by day.'[31] Literature was not a subject of conversation in the house-party. 'A young woman, having evidently had me explained to her as an author, asked me whether I read my things after they were printed, and added that she, too, would write but it would bore her so.'[32]

From this uncongenial society Mrs Meynell retired to her bedroom at night to count her midge-bites, which attained, at one point, a total of fifty-three.

To her mother she wrote:

My dearest little Mama, I have been here a week, and shall probably return – staying at Newcastle on my way – on Thursday next.

This is a wonderful coast – in-and-out bays, and mountain beyond mountain, and the islands blue in the lovely weather. But it is not scenery that knocks at my heart, principally because it is 'wild' – that is all the people have been driven away to make room for leagues and leagues of forest for deer. As you know, I love cultivated land or something really great, like the Alps, which this is not . . .

I have greatly enjoyed motoring on the wildest kind of roads – a switch-back with curves of the most abrupt kind. The boating, also, is nice.

I meet Dimpling at Newcastle. She has just had two more offers of marriage and has, I am almost certain, accepted one.[33]

Madeline's engagement was to Percy Lucas, an archivist, and younger brother of the writer and publisher E. V. Lucas. It was a curious coincidence that he, like Wilfrid Meynell, had been brought up as a Quaker, and became a Catholic.

From Newcastle, where she and Madeline were staying with some Meynell relations, Alice wrote to Wilfrid:

Dearest, I find my darling and precious child very happy and well. She is more than resigned to a long engagement. I have no ambitions for fortunes, less than ever after seeing the smart less intelligent than others, though certainly better groomed.[34]

The last journey of that year of travelling was with her oldest daughter, Monica, and her husband, Caleb Saleeby. They set off in December to motor down through France to the Riviera, Saleeby giving lectures at various places on the way. On the eve of departure Mrs Meynell wrote to her mother:

We start early tomorrow morning. Motoring day after day in the depth of winter will be severe – an open motor. My millionaire American, Mrs Thaw, has presented me with a magnificent fur coat, worth sixty or seventy pounds, which wraps me from head to foot. I declined it, and refused to meet her at the fur shop, but she got it all the same. Then I have a fur lining to my motor veil, and a talc window in front. Hot water bottles for our feet, of course. We shall be a fortnight on the journey. We shall see the cathedrals and churches closed. It is the greatest persecution there has ever been . . .*

---

* In 1880 the anti-clerical French government had passed laws withdrawing recognition from Catholic universities, expelling the Jesuits from France, and seizing their property and that of other religious orders. In 1903 the last nuns were expelled, and in the Army a purge was directed against officers known to be Catholics. Later, government committees were set up to take over the ownership and control of churches, church schools, seminaries, and other ecclesiastical property. Pius X refused to recognise the system and forbade French Catholics to have anything to do with it. The churches were then closed by the fanatically hostile government.[35]

I am glad the frost is over. It was terrible for the poor.

Viola and Dimpling are both doing splendid work in this district and in distant slums. What angels those two are! Some days Dimpling never sits down at all except for a brief meal. She has kept many a girl from drink and destruction.[36]

From Folkestone she wrote to Wilfrid expressing her anxious thoughts of the family she was leaving behind. She had made the decision about this journey with difficulty and went only for the sake of Monica, who was in a rather nervous state and dreaded being left alone while Caleb was lecturing. She reports having had lunch 'very pleasantly' at Maidstone, and tea at Folkestone. 'Is it not very stupid [*she asked*] to leave what one loves? . . . I trust you will have slept better, Darling, in the room you like. Don't let dearest Everard forget my Cowley.* You will have Bastian in as much as you can, won't you? It is good for him and he appreciates it more than he seems to do.'[37]

From Beauvais Mrs Meynell wrote to Sebastian:

We have had a long and exciting day from Arras – that beautiful city without one single modern house within its noble gates. No priest in that diocese had submitted to the monstrous law against 'meetings' in church, and they bravely broke the law this morning by saying Mass. They will all be fined, imprisoned and banished for this. And every man and woman going to Mass for three Sundays and after will be fined or imprisoned. The landlady would not speak of it at first – she thought we might inform against her, but at last she shut the door and unburdened herself of her grief. 'It is too frightful' she said. 'Shall we have Mass at Christmas? What will happen? It is appalling.' And how can we expect these people, among whom is an army of small Government employees, to rise in Civil War? The army has been secured because no one brought up in a religious school can hold a commission. And as to elections to the Chamber, the returns are certainly falsified. There never was a persecution more carefully prepared. The Bishop was banished from the town just before we arrived.[38]

Of the mechanics of their journey she reported:

We had a long day's journey through snow and in a piercing wind. Many things happened to the car and Caleb had to get help in strange and remote hamlets. It got dark and foggy and we felt our way by unknown roads . . . We shall have to stay here all tomorrow to clean out our tank. Owning a car is a luxury but travelling by it is not. But we enjoy it very much.[39]

From Macon she wrote to her mother:

We are having a most interesting and delightful journey from one lovely unspoilt city to another, and from one great cathedral to another – Arras, Amiens, Beauvais, Meaux and Sens. Here the Bishop has been expelled, there he has gone into a little lodging house, here again he is leaving. In each case his house has been taken from him . . .

* Her copy of the works of the poet Abraham Cowley: 1618-1687.

The cold is intense. The Saone is frozen over and Burgundy lies under snow. We do about eighty miles a day and are always hoping for something more southern.[40]

Mrs Meynell described the wintry journey in an article in the *Morning Leader*.

We have eight hundred miles of frost and snow behind us – a rather arduous mid-winter journey of nine days under a stooping sky. Ours has not been a jaunt in the closed car that the French seem to use exclusively when they have women with them; we have sped uncovered, with a wild wind in our ears, across the lamentable country of northern France, accompanied by the thin avenue of leafless trees and big ridges of snow and little roadside gullies of frost. The grip of our wheels has been often uncertain upon the furlongs of pavé, and we have climbed the hills of the south, deep in snow, with hard labour for the willing engine. The country has been locked in frost, the golden range of Burgundian hills white beneath their little goblin vines, the Saone frozen, Lyons wrapped in her own industrial breath, the magnificent Rhône and her castled crags in a mist of cold. Frost had even laid a light hand on Avignon on the dark night on which we swept once outside her machicolated walls, and once within them, twice circling the serried city, groping for our hotel . . . That bridge is the oldest thing in the world, not because it was built in the twelfth century, but because as children we were sung to sleep in a song of its name 'Le Pont d'Avignon' . . . The day's motoring from Aix to Cannes is such a journey as Europe cannot elsewhere match; . . . here is the quality which in literature we call style. The colour is wonderfully simple – a slight red for the soil, a slight blue for the beautiful hills describes it; a luminous winter mist lies in the valleys; all the distances are, as it were, kept by cypress and pine; castle walls and villages of stone make crowns for the painted walls; the olive, evergreen, or rather ever-grey, make silver of the sun.

She wrote to Everard on Christmas Eve from Nice, where the great bells of the cathedral were ringing: 'I shall think of you all the whole day tomorrow.'[41]

Two days later they reached San Remo. 'As to the beauty of this region', Mrs Meynell wrote to Viola, 'I say little in my articles, because everybody comes here and nobody cares. It is a heavenly, heavenly coast, made into a playground for the vice of Europe – that upper scum which I think more horrible than the lower dregs. But the splendour of the sun and sea, the moon and stars, the mountain and the after-glow, are not to be described.'[42]

In early January, from Menton, Mrs Meynell sent her husband instructions about the placing of an article that she had sent to him for publication. ' "The Hotel-Keeper" ought to go to the *Pall Mall*, I forgot to say, as it is the only paper that would print my remark about naming French streets after scoundrels. While all the other papers were praising the rascally French Government for "conciliation" – incredible hypocrisy! – the *Pall Mall*, I see by one you sent me, calls them roundly "atheists" which, of course, they proclaim themselves. We have had French ruffianism before, and we have had English hypocrisy before, but have never before had them in monstrous combination and unnatural confederacy.'[43]

After her return she wrote to her mother:

My dearest little Mama,

Here I am at last. I returned alone as Dimpling wanted me. She is to be married at Easter.

Monnie had become so nervous that she could not face the return journey in the motor. I had a final drive up the Corniche road. What a vision! . . .

I am writing so as to pay every shilling of my expenses. I am doing a long article for an American magazine.[44]

Two poems that were written in 1907 recall that winter tour in France. 'The Fugitive', published in the *Saturday Review* in February, was an expression of horror and distress at the religious persecution in France, and was written as an answer to the pronouncement of a French publicist: *'Nous avons chassé ce Jésus-Christ'.*

> Yes, from the ingrate heart, the street
> Of garrulous tongue, the warm retreat
>   Within the village and the town;
>   Not from the lands where ripen brown
> A thousand thousand hills of wheat;
>
> Not from the long Burgundian line,
> The Southward, sunward range of vine.
>   Hunted, He never will escape
>   The flesh, the blood, the sheaf, the grape,
> That feed His man – the bread, the wine.

'In Manchester Square' was written on the death of a crossing-sweeper with whom Alice Meynell had been wont to talk when she passed by the place where he worked.

> *In Memoriam T.H.*
>
> The paralytic man has dropped in death
>   The crossing-sweeper's brush to which he clung,
> One-handed, twisted, dwarfed, scanted of breath,
>   Although his hair was young.
>
> I saw this year the winter vines of France,
>   Dwarfed, twisted goblins in the frosty drouth –
> Gnarled, crippled, blackened little stems askance
>   On long hills to the South.

Great green and golden hands of leaves ere long
    Shall proffer clusters in that vineyard wide.
And oh, his might, his sweet, his wine, his song,
    His stature, since he died!

It is probably true to say that Alice Meynell never really understood the English populace, and that they remained, in some sort, foreigners to her all her life. It was the Italian *gente del popolo* that she knew best in her childhood, and it was their humour, their way of life, their emotions, and their mode of expression that ever afterwards seemed to her the most right and natural. Those impressionable years of absence fixed a gulf between her and the people of the London streets that she never bridged, and it was further widened by her remoteness from the practical business of living. She knew what it was to need money, she worked hard for most of her life, she made sacrifices, lived austerely – yet she rarely thought about cooking or sewing or cleaning, and never understood the importance of these things in other women's lives. She maintained – though involuntarily – a certain aloofness. Her family teased her for saying politely 'I beg your pardon?' to a bus conductor who remarked jovially, 'Now we shan't be long!', and the story is expressive of her beautiful manners and her bewilderment.[45] In her essay 'Popular Burlesque' she wrote: 'Bank Holiday courtship (if the inappropriate word can be pardoned) seems to be done, in real life, entirely by banter . . . We have to believe that unmocked love has existence in the streets, because of the proof that is published when a man shoots a woman who has rejected him; and thus also do we learn to believe that a woman of the burlesque classes is able to reject. But for that sign we should find little or nothing intelligible in what we see or overhear of the drama of love in popular life.'[46]

Yet with this curious incomprehension existed such thoughtfulness and such courtesy towards people of every degree that she could trouble to write this letter to the crossing-sweeper: 'I shall not be passing your corner for some few more Sundays, and I don't like to think you will forget me, nor do I like you to think I have forgotten you.'[47] And now, when he died, it was the dwarfed and twisted vines of the French winter that she remembered in thinking of his poor crooked body, and the magnificent green and gold of the vineyard's spring that she compared to his new glory.

CHAPTER 20

MADELINE was married to Percy Lucas that spring. The new son-in-law was welcomed into the family most joyously. Afterwards Alice Meynell wrote to Madeline:

My own Darling,
   Don't think that your happy marriage leaves us too sad. I don't lose you, sweetest and best of daughters. The tie between us is too old and too sacred.[1]

And for Madeline's birthday, a few weeks later, her mother wrote to send her loving good wishes and to comment on the visit that had evidently been paid by a number of Meynells to the young couple in their new home.

My darling Dimpling,
   Many most happy returns to the sweetest and best of daughters, of this first of married birthdays.
   I wonder whether you will have begun to rest, when you get this, from the washing-up! What an invading army we were! We devoured and consumed, and left havoc, (cracked) wedding presents and knives to clean behind us, banana skins, egg shells, and work for a week.[2]

Sir William and Lady Butler were now settled at Bansha Castle, Tipperary, and in July 1907 Mrs Meynell travelled to Ireland to visit them.
   Writing to Wilfrid and to Sebastian she told them:

The air is full of meadow-sweet, honeysuckle, lime blossoms and hay. The showers in this heavenly country wing their way from the distant sea and are gone again. What a lovely country! Tell Viola that it is very like England, inevitably, because the trees, that make so large a part of landscape, are the same – elm, lime, ash, beech, and the rarer pine – but it is *more country*. The quality that makes country different from town or marsh is more intense.
   About that telegram, it is surely rather characteristic that the guard of the train at the harbour deliberately edited it. I may have my faults, as Viola says, but I don't send 'kindest love' to my family. The guard insisted on writing my message down for me. When I showed him that he had mis-spelt a word, he said he would copy it right. And he wrote down exactly what I told him. 'Very good passage. Love.' He looked at it critically and asked whether they would know whom it came from. I reassured him. It does amuse me that he not only interpolated 'kindest' but changed 'very good' to 'splendid'.[3]

Loving the country, she cared little for the people and always asserted that the Irish had no sense of humour. 'Last night', she wrote to Meynell, 'there was a dinner party of the parish priest – all platitudes – and the very nice young Anglican clergyman, and Major Serocold, posted here because he is "on the staff" whatever that may be – I think perhaps constabulary. The talk was fairly lively on account of the intelligence of Mr Johnstone, the clergyman. He has a congregation of three in the awful little Strawberry Hill gothic church. The Catholic church is even worse – of the most modern gothic of 1830 or so. The priest apologises for it because it is old.'[4]

Soon after Mrs Meynell's return from Ireland Francis Thompson's always precarious health became so bad as to cause great anxiety. He had left London at the end of 1905 and had lodged for a while near the Franciscan friary at Crawley, in Sussex; but he had soon returned to London, to lodgings near the Harrow Road, and had divided his days, as before, between Granville Place and the British Museum Reading Room. Meynell suspected that the drug habit had once again got firm hold of him, and his sharply deteriorating condition seemed to confirm his suspicion. In August Everard Meynell took him down to Newbuildings Place, where Wilfrid Blunt installed him in a cottage on his estate with a servant to care for him; but two months later he was brought back to London, iller, weaker and thinner than before. He was in an advanced stage of tuberculosis. He entered the Hospital of SS. John and Elizabeth, in St John's Wood, and there, on 13th November, he died, at the age of forty-eight.

His loss was deeply felt by all the Meynell family, but especially by Wilfrid, who had borne for so long the often demanding charge of the poet, and had given unsparingly of friendship, encouragement, time, money, and practical aid. Now, more than ever, it became his first task to ensure that Thompson's poetry should be acknowledged in what he believed its rightful place—the front rank of English literature.

In his *Life of Francis Thompson*, which was published in 1913, Everard Meynell wrote:

But, for all that friends were at hand, the nurse tender, and the priest punctual, his passing was solitary . . . The fires quenched were his own. It seemed to his friends as if it were a matter personal to himself; while their sorrow for their own loss was mixed almost with satisfaction at something ended in his favour, as if at last he had had his way in a transaction with a Second Party, who might have long and painfully delayed the issue . . .

His features, when I went to make a drawing of him in the small mortuary that stood among the wintry garden-trees, were entirely peaceful, so that I, who had sometimes known them otherwise, fell into the mood of the cheerful lay-sister with the keys, who said: 'I hear he had a very good death.' To the priest, who had seen him in communion with the church and her saints at the moment which may be accounted the most solitary possible to the heart of man, no thought of especial loneliness was associated with his death.

In the *Dublin Review* Alice Meynell wrote:

Francis Thompson's friends were few, and such as survive him should take the occasion while it is given them to record him as a living poet; as a poet of the past he will have a nation, a literature, a language, to record him, as a man he has not a score of women and men. When he died, many who for the first time heard his name, gave him, imitating one another, the name and fame of a kind of outcast or minor criminal. Perhaps the tragic tone of much of his poetry, forbidding the conjecture of jovial sin, yet suggested that of long remorse. But he was a man of singular innocence; he had what some schools of Christians place in the forefront of the Christian life – a 'conviction of sin'; nothing that concerns the world or its judgments. But he was not singularly, or often, unhappy. He had told all readers, with a perfect freedom of communication all his own, what was the deprivation and the chief distress of his life. It is the deprivation that is the equally noble privilege of many thousands of women in our present civilization; without avowal even to themselves they endure the lack of the love that is between man and woman. The avowal made in his whole poetry by this solitary man implied no lapse of dignity.[5]

A time of rare pause had come now to the pen of Alice Meynell. She was writing little, either of prose or poetry: a few reviews, descriptive articles on her travels, the usual *Daily Chronicle* paragraphs, a translation of René Bazin's *L'Isolée* which Eveleigh Nash published under the title of *The Nun*. That was all, and she was not happy in this uncreative period. 'I don't think I shall be quite well', she wrote to Meynell, 'so long as my poor literary career is so at a standstill. It makes me unhappy.'[6]

In the spring of 1908 she went with Wilfrid, Olivia, and Everard to Paris. Everard was doing research for the life of Corot which he was writing. They stayed at an hotel in the Rue Corneille, where, she wrote, 'we have French, Germans, Americans and several of those cosmopolitan Englishwomen who travel alone and have seen all countries under the sun and talk until one wishes one were dead.'[7]

'We tramp from morning to night', she told Viola. 'We have only once, when hopelessly lost and unable, owing to the biting wind, to consult maps in the street, taken a cab. I am delighted to find that your father can bear all the walking without any fatigue to speak of. The sky is as gloomy as that of London, and the cold intense.'[8]

She went on alone to Italy and stayed with her American friends the Thaws at the Villa Aurora in Rome. A dinner party of twenty was given for her on her arrival.

A splendid party. A dash is no word for what the Thaws are cutting here. And cutting it so joyously with thanksgiving. They stand and look at their new motor and say it is too much joy. And the same with their palatial house – the real very actual Villa Ludovisi once the centre of the most adorable garden in Rome – another Borghese – now the centre of the smart quarter. I lie in 'palace chambers far apart' (how finely Tennyson says things!). My vaulted ceiling is frescoed by seventeenth century masters and portraits of popes. A great cedar and ilex (last of that garden) stand guard at my window. The sun is incredibly, indescribably golden. All Rome is gold. This old palace, thank goodness, is yellow.

Wilfrid, I have lost my ticket. Fool is not the word for me. It was in the moment of meeting Mr Thaw and paying my porter with loaded hands, thinking I grasped my ticket just received from the collector, I really grasped only my silly purse. I have been twice to Cooks to see what could be done to safeguard it, and, of course, to the station, interviewed everybody and had notes made. Did I sign it at Cook in Oxford Street? I can't remember. I won't let this disaster poison my joy here but it requires an effort. Nor do I let the Thaws see how much I feel it, for fear lest they should want to frank me home. Ah, forgive me. Johnny.[9]

Happily, the ticket was found and returned in answer to an advertisement.

The Thaws had a great many friends and acquaintances in Rome, and there were numerous parties. To one of these came Sir Edward and Lady Elgar, and afterwards they took Mrs Meynell back to their flat, and Elgar played for her some recent compositions. She met Carolus Duran (the French painter) and Bjornsen, the Norwegian writer and Nobel prize-winner, went to a musical party at Sgambati's,* lunched and dined in some of the great Roman palaces. 'There is a kind of excess in the luxury of society here', she wrote to Sebastian: ' – the canopies of flowers, the regiments of tall servants, the gold and silver plate – which I don't and never shall really enjoy in such a world of want.'[10]

Describing a large afternoon party which was 'full of Roman princesses', she commented that 'The Roman ladies have a most overwhelming style of dress; their hair is brought down in a black roll well on to the bridge of the nose.'[11] And to Wilfrid she wrote:

There are society things – afternoon dances at private houses, or Beneficent teas (*thes di beneficienza*) at the great hotels every day; and the dressing is preposterous. I think the great Roman princesses are the worst in their loading of diamonds, furs, feathers and flowers. It is only their being in the last fashion that saves them from being grotesque and it hardly does . . . Tomorrow evening I promised to go to the Keats-Shelley house with the secretary. The Shelley cult makes me laugh internally. With Mrs Thaw it is a craze, and I say nothing. But I did tell the astonished secretary something of what I thought of Shelley. They have my Red Letter booklet there. I have been of enormous help to Mr T. in correcting his awful mistakes in metre in an ode to the two poets; and to Mrs T. in correcting the equally awful French in which she writes her invitations. They are everything that is sweet and kind. But oh, the swans that all friendly geese are made to appear! I do so love your letters. I want details

* Composer and pianist, b. Rome 1844, d. 1914.

about everything . . . If I could but import to you some of these lunches and dinners, alas! alas! You *must* come to fetch me. Your Johnnie.[12]

Many years before, when lamenting the frustration imposed upon women by denying them 'work for the mind', she had written: 'O my Shelley, if you were alive you would help me to fulfil my golden dream.'[13] But a closer knowledge of his life, while it had not affected her love for his poetry, had made her dislike and despise him as a man. Writing to Wilfrid Meynell about an article on which he was at work, she said:

> I cannot find the passage in Browning's life or letters in which he renounced Shelley 'as a man' after forty years' devotion. I am perfectly certain that I read it not long ago. But where? . . . If there were any signs of regret for Harriet's fate! But I never found any.
> Shelley's respectability is bad enough but not so bad as Godwin's who writes to announce the walking out to her marriage in church of his 'tall daughter' to the son and heir of the baronet, as though the damsel was a maiden come to a young bridal: she had been living with Shelley until Harriet's death. I think it was Matthew Arnold who said of them all 'what an unclean company! . . .'
> As to Shelley's whimperings in the Bay of Naples, I cannot think of anything more unmanly and false.[14]

With Mr and Mrs Thaw, Alice Meynell dined with Count and Countess Pasolini, and she described the Count's somewhat eccentric English. 'The Conte is a great friend of mine. He tries to talk English and says his wife is "respectable but violent". Also that he has not "annoyed God" by praying too urgently for children though he would have liked some.'

Three Americans whom she met at a luncheon party 'did not catch my name, but we got on exceedingly well at table. Then they severally learnt it and ran to me, crying out: 'Is it really you?" They knew my works – this one the verse, that one the prose – so genuinely that they quoted it with sweet enthusiasm. One had been saying to herself my essay on bells, listening under a village belfry. Another had lately heard Kipling reading my poems aloud. He said they "rent his heart in two".'[15]

In the Thaws' car she went to Ostia, to Subiaco, to Lake Nemi, and to the Sabine hills to look for the site of Horace's villa. 'It is all very doubtful, but some Roman house was there. A bit of pavement has been uncovered and we picked up little fragments from the olive grounds. I will have one set as a pin for Bastian as he loves Horace.' She confessed that to her Horace stood, as far as she knew him, 'for good mediocrity – but I may be wrong. At any rate, I compare our interest and toil in climbing mountains for his villa with the small interest taken by those I know here in the divine author of that chapter

"Though I speak with the tongues of men and of angels – ". The "hired house" in which he lived a year is here, well attested, under a church in the Corso, and he trod the Appian Road on his way to death.'[16]

After her visit to the Keats-Shelley memorial she wrote: 'I am just home from the Keats house where I stood in the tiny scene of his suffering. He prayed, says Severn, at the last.' The light of Roman skies and the beauty of Roman skylines struck at her heart always. 'It is almost a relief', she exclaimed, 'to look at the gasworks and the palms, when one almost aches with love of the pines and belfries.'[17]

In August Mrs Meynell was at Wilmington, in Sussex, with some of the family: 'The children have arranged a dinner to the Newtons tonight. As a woman says frequently in *Alice for Short*,* "I was not consulted" or I should have suggested luncheon. The gripping chills of dinner in the dew are severe treatment for guests. And then people who dress every night (even though they will not on this occasion) look for a dinner different from ours. But I was not consulted! Viola is gone to get a bottle of claret (Heavens, what will it be like?) at Eastbourne, and some bananas.'[18]

Spring of the following year took her again to Italy, this time accompanied by Olivia, with whom she visited Rome, Florence, and Venice. She wrote to Wilfrid:

All goes well with us. Olivia is the sweetest companion, always considerate and complaining of nothing. How wise is she who chooses not only her husband but her children's father, and thus has such daughters and sons as ours.

The weather is so perfect that we expect nothing else. We have strolled through the morning. What enchantment is a stroll in Venice, what dim rosy corners in a sparkle of water-light, what little bridges somewhat too small for the people, as in the back places of a stage, and yet in such a reality of sun!

We are very quiet in our little rooms, and sleep well. They are only 3 lire each a night, and we live very frugally. It is too hot for real dinners or lunches.[19]

They were guided in their explorations of Venice by Carroll Brent Chilton. To Madeline Mrs Meynell wrote:

My darling Dimpling,
. . . We have Mr Chilton all day long and his conversation on the True Meaning of Life and the influence of someone upon someone, which had never been suspected until his discovery. He is very nice, but his mind is so entirely that of the commentator that I cannot think he will do much. He interests Beelie, and when I am threatened with nervous prostration she is still fresh. We contrived to bore *him*, for once, by reading Ruskin to him in front of pictures of which he really knows nothing whatever.[20]

* *Alice for Short* by William Frend de Morgan, 1839-1917, associated with William Morris; noted for his decorative tiles, also stained glass and pottery.

In a letter to Wilfrid Meynell she said: 'It was curious to meet the grand-daughters of Mrs Jackson, Coventry Patmore's first friend, at the house of Mrs Ross, the daughter of Meredith's first friend, I being the latest one dear to both (not that I compare those two affections).'[21]

After her departure to Italy, Meredith, writing to thank Meynell for a gift of Thompson's poems inscribed from the whole family, said: 'The love of all the Meynells, let all the Meynells know, is very precious. And the book of poems was very welcome, though a thought of the poet's broken life gives pain . . . Our Portia, I may suppose to be now in Italy, and Italy seems to me her natural home. For me, I drag on, counting more years and not knowing why . . . Though I see little of my friends, I live with them.'[22]

Meredith's ill health had made his meetings with Mrs Meynell very few in recent years, and his letters, too, had become rare. He had written to her: 'You are with me daily, at the finish of most of my readings, when I compare our views';[23] and, 'I do not see you but I look about for your work, to see where the mind of Portia is active.'[24] Now, during this absence of hers in Italy, Meredith became suddenly worse and died.

She wrote to her mother: 'My loss in George Meredith is very great. I am annoyed at the many silly things written about him. No one knew him as I did. He told me that I only could have made him what he should have been and could not be without the real mate. He calculated whether there had been a time when he was a widower and I unmarried when we might have met. A retrospective offer! I had a happier fate, for he was, I am told, a rather perverse husband.'[25]

To Meynell she wrote: '*The Morning Post* on dear Meredith is good – I skipped the literary estimate, however. I think no one living knows him as I did – for only a woman could know parts of him, and the other women have not the brains. Nor can he have loved many as he loved me.'[26]

That summer the critical study of Swinburne already referred to was published in the *Athenaeum*. 'It will make me many enemies' Mrs Meynell predicted, with a touch of defiance; and it did, in fact, provoke much controversy and some censure; but the other viewpoint is shown in a letter from Lady Butler to her sister in July 1909. 'We have just returned from a visit at Castle Bellingham in County Louth. There I met a Miss Charlotte Dease who told me when she last saw Wilfrid Ward* he burst out in enthusiastic praise of your Swinburne, almost before he shook hands with her.'[27]

---

* Wilfrid Ward: son of William George Ward, Tractarian divine and Roman convert. Wilfrid Ward, who had philosophical interests, wrote the first biography, still in some ways the best, of John Henry Newman, and also lives of Nicholas Wiseman and others.

In the autumn of 1909 Constable and Company published *Ceres Runaway*, a new volume of essays by Mrs Meynell. The essay from which the book took its title was on 'the Roman growth of green in the high places of the city', the grass and flowers with which Nature everywhere defeats the tidying hand of a Municipality. 'The Little Language' and 'Anima Pellegrina' were concerned with words and their uses, 'Harlequin Mercutio' and 'The Audience' treated of the drama. 'The Tethered Constellations' described the starry sky to be seen in the waters:

The stars in the stream fluctuate with an alien motion. Reversed, estranged, isolated, every shape of large stars escapes and returns, escapes and returns. Fitful in the steady night, those constellations, so few, so whole, and so remote, have a sudden-ness of gleaming life. You imagine that some unexampled gale might make them seem to shine with such a movement in the veritable sky; yet nothing but deep water, seeming still in its incessant flight and rebound, could really show such altered stars.

The book was highly praised by the press, though here and there were discordant voices. The *Morning Post's* critic wrote: 'Mrs Meynell is a delicate thinker and delicate writer and perhaps the most sincere and uncompromising of those authors who appear to believe that Walter Pater wrote good English . . . She is able to do what few but the best thinkers can do, to start upon a common subject at a new point and to maintain an untrammelled line right to the end.'[28]

Sending this to her mother, Alice Meynell said: 'I am glad you take so rosy a view of my notices. It seemed to me that I had a very cool reception. The triumph I had in 1893 and 1896 was a very different thing! I send you the *Morning Post* notice which is clever and cold and quite amusing. When the reviewer calls me a writer in Pater's manner, he makes a curious blunder; I am the only literary person now alive who has never read Pater at all.'[29]

Ceres Runaway was the last of her daughter's books that Mrs Thompson was to see. Early in 1910 she became gravely ill; Mrs Meynell, who was on the point of starting for Italy, cancelled her journey and hurried instead to the little house at Camberley where her mother was then living, there to sit by her through long and painful nights. She died in March.

Lady Butler wrote from Portofino: 'Oh! Alice, what wringing of the heart must yours have been by that bedside. It is inexpressibly touching to me to think of her here where I remember her in her prime. Her face of those days is as vividly before me as the poor distressed one I last saw, overshadowed by the fast approaching end.'[30]

Mrs Meynell, writing to her husband in the interval between her mother's death and her return home, said: 'I never wished her to live when I saw how grave her illness was. It seemed too dreadful that all would have to be gone through again so soon. But no one knows what those nights were – or rather seemed, for they were not as terrible as they seemed, I firmly believe. It would have broken my heart if she, so affectionate in health, had responded to any signs of my love then, but she never did. We ought all to be prepared for a curious change of character in those last days.'[31]

In this same year Sir William Butler also died, and Mrs Meynell made the journey to Bansha again to be with her sister. She helped her in another way besides that of companionship in her time of grief, for she took on the work of correcting the proofs of the autobiography that Sir William had finished shortly before his death.

A happier journey in this sad year was taken with Wilfrid and Olivia to the beloved Ligurian coast, and in the following spring there was a visit to friends at Mentone, whence Alice wrote to her husband:

Darling, We had a most comfortable journey, thanks to your great cares and kindnesses.

This is a dream of beauty and vulgarity mingled in proportions quite peculiar to the French Riviera. Oh, the mountains and the sun! and the little white, old, lovely houses on the steep! Cypresses and pines above, and the celestial blue. Flags and the battle of flowers and motors below. *Do* come.[32]

In June she was staying with Mrs Charles Hunter at Hill Hall in Surrey, and the house party included Sargent, Cassals and his wife, Viola Tree and her husband, Robert Ross,* Henry James, and Wilson Steer: an interesting collection upon which, unfortunately, we have no comment from her.

Viola was now established as a writer, and Everard, who had originally intended to be a painter, had now turned to writing about art, with volumes on Corot and Bellini. He also started and ran successfully the Serendipity Shop, near the British Museum, for the sale of rare books, prints, and manuscripts. In 1908 he had married Grazia Carbone, a singer of Italian parentage who had been born and brought up in America.

Two literary employments that occupied Mrs Meynell during 1911 were the writing of the text for an illustrated book called *Mary, the Mother of Jesus* and the making of a selection from the works of Dr Johnson. The contract for the former was concluded in February and provided that she would be paid £78.15s. for an essay of 25,000 words, the manuscript to be delivered by 1st November. Lee Warner was to publish the book for the Medici Society. The Johnson selection was for Herbert and Daniel's 'Regent Library', and G. K.

---

* Robert Ross 1869-1918. Journalist and art critic, friend of Oscar Wilde and editor of his collected works.

Chesterton was to write the introduction. The meeting of the work of these two writers within the covers of this volume was one of the few personal contacts between them. They had many friends in common in literary London and it might easily have happened that their paths crossed often, but with equal ease it happened that they did not, and both lamented that their slight acquaintance never developed into friendship.* They met a few times, but only two of these occasions have been recorded. In 1900, when Chesterton had just published his first book of poems, he wrote to the lady who was to become his wife: 'I have been taken to see Mrs Meynell, poet and essayist, who is enthusiastic about *The Wild Knight* and is lending it to all her friends';[33] and in 1912, when they were both guests at a dinner of the Ladies' Pioneer Club, Chesterton offered high praise to Mrs Meynell in his speech, causing her to write across the invitation: 'One of the happiest evenings of my life followed, for Chesterton spoke of me.'[34] He was one of the few whose praise she really valued; and later, at a time when a new volume was being lauded by the critics, she wrote to Meynell: 'Better than my excellent reviews I have loved a word from Chesterton in the *Illustrated***.'[35] His admiration for her work was expressed, to her joy, several times in her life, but it was after her death that he wrote of her in the highest terms. In an article in the *Dublin Review* in 1923 he said:

All the talk about her fastidiousness and fine shades and delicate verbal embroideries is quite beside the mark. The point of her poetry was not that she chose this or that sort of adjective, or even cast it in this or that sort of style. The point about her poetry, as compared with most modern poetry, was this; that she never wrote a line, or even a word, without putting brains into it; or, in the most exact sense, meaning what she said. She never wrote a line, or even a word, that does not stand like the rib of a strong intellectual structure; a thing with the bones of thought in it . . . Therefore in any anthology or magazine of minor poets, her work always stood out as something inevitably and imperatively interesting. It was like being startled amid the chatter of birds by the spoken words of a man.

After her death Wilfrid Meynell wrote to Sebastian: 'Among the wonderful tributes is Chesterton's. I wish she had known in her life that he thought her "the first mind of her time" and also that if ever there is a Catholic England "she will have made it".'[36]

In his *Autobiography* Chesterton said of her:

She was strong with deep roots where all Stoics were only stiff with despair;

* The main reason for this was that in 1909 Frances and Gilbert Chesterton left London to live in Buckinghamshire.

** *The Illustrated London News*: Chesterton contributed a weekly column, 'Our Notebook', to this paper for over thirty years.

she was alive to an immortal beauty where all the Pagans could only mix beauty with mortality. And though she passed through my own life fitfully, and far more rarely than I could wish, and though her presence has indeed something of the fugitive accident of a bird, I know now that she was not fugitive and she was not shadowy. She was a message from the Sun. [37]

Viola Meynell has written:

The chief enthusiasm in the contemporary reading of all her later years was this for Chesterton. She found him to be at once the wittiest and the most serious of living writers. The habit he was charged with of turning things upside down was to her mind the setting right of things that had been standing on their heads . . . 'If I had been a man, and large, I should have been Chesterton' she asserted with a smile, really feeling that there was something more than mere agreement between his mind and hers. [38]

That remark of Mrs Meynell's, at first sight so astonishing, sets one to the fascinating game of comparing and contrasting those two. There were such differences that, for a moment, there seems no possible likeness between the huge figure of Chesterton, swinging along Fleet Street in his great black cape, and the slender, delicate woman of Sargent's drawing, with her large, thoughtful eyes; no likeness between the author of *The Rhythm of Life* and the author of *Orthodoxy*. And, indeed, one looks in vain for any similarity in their literary styles, as in their physical appearances; both had an extraordinary ability in their writings of hitting the nail on the head, but Alice Meynell never stayed for more than one light tap while Chesterton went on hammering at it with zest and enjoyment until London rang with the blows. But Chesterton's wild and, at the same time, reverent enjoyment of the ordinary things of life looks out sometimes between the lines of Alice Meynell's letters; and when she went careering along in open motor cars, with her heart yearning for even greater speed, when she rode up the mountain face above the Yosemite Valley, or expressed her pleasure at being thrown out of a carriage, there, surely, is a touch of Chesterton. Their ways of making people laugh were directly opposite, but the things they laughed at were the same. And both had a rare gift of seeing things and ideas freshly, as if for the first time, so that they often saw them in a different shape, and made other people do so too. The most obvious of the things that they had in common – their Catholicism – only became established fact a few months before Alice Meynell died, for Chesterton did not become a Catholic until 1922. There is no word of Mrs Meynell's on that occasion; but in 1914 she had written to her husband: 'What is the news about Chesterton? I can think of nothing better than his reviewing me – except his reception into the Church. I love him so.' [39]

In this year – 1911 – the *Saturday Review* published 'To Sylvia two years old', a poem which she addressed to her little grand-daughter, child of Percy and Madeline Lucas. In it she spoke of the sentiment often expressed by poets about children who will not live to grow up, that 'No autumn will destroy this lovely spring', and declared that she too could say that:

.   .   .   .

> For there's another way to stop thy clock
>   Within my cherishing heart,
> To carry thee unalterable, and lock
>   Thy youth apart:
>
> Thy flower, for me, shall evermore be hid
>   In this close bud of thine,
> Not, Sylvia, by thy death – O God forbid!
>   Merely by mine.

At Christmas time she turned again to the thought of the countries from which Christ was driven out, and looked forward with sorrow to the reign of persecution:

IN PORTUGAL, 1912

> And will they cast the altars down,
>   Scatter the chalice, crush the bread?
> In field, in village, and in town
>   He hides an unregarded head;
>
> Waits in the corn-lands far and near,
>   Bright in His sun, dark in His frost,
> Sweet in the vine, ripe in the ear –
>   Lonely unconsecrated Host.
>
> In ambush at the merry board
>   The Victim lurks unsacrificed;
> The mill conceals the harvest's Lord,
>   The wine-press holds the unbidden Christ.[40]

CHAPTER 21

THE YOUNG MEYNELLS, their London childhood left behind, made frequent visits to the country on walking-tours, and there now grew among the family a desire to have a home in the country, preferably in Sussex, the county which they knew best. Percy and Madeline Lucas had a cottage near Storrington; in the summer of 1911, after months of fruitless searching, Wilfrid Meynell heard from Percy of a property at Greatham, three miles from Storrington, which was shortly to be sold by auction. This property he was able to secure. It consisted of a small seventeenth-century farmhouse called Humphrey's Homestead, and eighty acres of land, on the further extremity of which was an old cottage. Round the farmhouse were the garden and orchard, then a field, an oak-wood, a little pine-wood, and some rough grazing land which had earlier been common land. After the purchase Meynell went down to look at it, with Everard and Percy. The latter wrote to Madeline: 'My darling, Your father, Evvie and I have all been to Greatham and I am writing this in the train home. It was all delightful and improved on acquaintance. Your father is most enthusiastic about it and even Evvie, too, though applying a damper now and then.'[1]

Wilfrid Meynell, perhaps even more than the rest of the family, was delighted with the purchase. Shortly afterwards he was staying at Newbuildings with Wilfrid Blunt and they drove over to look at it. Wilfrid wrote to his wife: 'W.B.'s opinion may be gathered by his saying about the other bit of outlying common, "If you don't buy it I will." He thinks the place perfect, and that we must have used some magic to get it at the price or indeed to get it at all . . . I made some observation and the more I see the Property the more I like it.'[2]

Alice Meynell, who was staying at Leith Hill, near Dorking, motored over to see it. 'The beauty of England between here and the Downs', she wrote to Meynell, 'is quite overpowering. The lovely uplands over Arundel, the entirely unspoiled villages and village greens, the old tiled houses, and the immense and glorious trees! What a country! Too little tilled, and too long spaces between the villages – that is the only fault. Oh, signs of man, the traces of his brown hand, how I love them!'[3] After a momentary misgiving as to whether it was not, perhaps, too isolated and remote from humanity, the Property, as it was called in the family, was taken to her heart.

In July some of the children went down with her to Alfriston, from where, in turn, they could visit Greatham. To Meynell she wrote:

204

'This is so lovely a place that I hope they will think the Property lovelier, but I am not quite sure. But what a journey! Nearly an hour to wait at Lewes. And then you make yourself a figure of fun by asking for the Ber-wick train, whereas, being civilized, the porters say "Ber-rick" . . . All are well. A trifle of stiff back and muscular rheumatism contracted by me . . . in sitting out in the garden, wrapped up, hardly counts . . . When I look back upon the severe diseases I have sustained, all my life, in English gardens after sunset, I sometimes wonder what is to happen to me on the property.'[4]

Some alterations were made to the house, and a library was built on, with capacious bookshelves, long windows opening on to the garden, and a huge open fire-place like the seventeenth-century ones in the other rooms. Meynell planned to give pieces of land on the property to some of his children, on which they could build houses for themselves. His first idea was that these should be at some distance from the main house, but Alice wrote asking him, in the most gentle and tactful way, if he would reconsider it, and group the houses together in a triangular area nearer to Humphreys.

My darling Squire,

I had wheels and consequently a bad night, so gave up the journey today, much as I wished to see Crickmer.* You know by heart what I like – length rather than right angles; and the Western outlook contents me because of the road, the elms, the field beyond, which our darling house commands. I was sorry to be tired, but tussocks beat me. Wilfrid Blunt's coachman told me that the horses 'don't take no notice of 30 or 40 miles.' I don't take no notice of 3 or 4 on your turnpike road but your tussock gets the better of me . . .

I want you to be so very kind as to give mature reflection to these here following remarks. In the first place, you as master and giver (besides you as father) would be pleased with the acknowledgement of your gifts made to me by all. So much for the point of feeling. On the point of fact it is not necessary to say that all must submit to your veto. *But.* After you who earned the place and me who loved it, – yes, and after Dimpling and Viola have lived in it perhaps a lifetime, and when their children inherit it, all these people except me will have inhabited sites disliked by all but you. (I think I can answer for Sylvia!) The ground is your kind gift; but the sons and the sons-in-law are to invest difficult moneys in the building of their houses. All the pleasure is gone from the colony for them. They have not asked me to say so. But I perceive their feelings to be feelings of pain. So are Viola's. Dimpling I have not seen since she has been told that the Isosceles Triangle was withdrawn. Remember, that whole triangle was explicitly given to Percy, here, on the sofa.

Your objections to the little group of houses gathered modestly in the triangle or its immediate vicinity quite back from the road . . . are three:
1.   'That they would be ugly as cottages.' Not so, believe me. They will all be beautiful cottages. I have heard the materials and styles discussed, and I know.

---

*   Courtney Crickmer, the architect who designed the addition to the main house.

2. 'That ugly or pretty, buildings at all in sight would impair the beauty of the estate.' Now this is a matter of taste. For your taste at this moment (taste prompted, I cannot but perceive, by the crotchets of a most interesting and excellent but crotchety friend) any buildings would impair that beauty. But is that your perdurable taste? You have 'come round' to me in other artistic matters. Now for me, for Dimpling, for Viola, for Everard, for Percy, for Bill,* for all the rest as far as I know their minds, the beauty of that lovely place would not be marred but enhanced by good building – nay, by indifferent cottage building so strong is the feeling of all these human beings that what the colony wants is the blessed cottage touch. And to be somewhat near a road is as dear to them as it is to me. I can't say more. I should not love my Humphreys (except in as much as you loved it) if it had not that road. Realise this little fact – that none of us much love bracken. It is a little fact of great significance.

3. 'Houses in sight would deprive you of your right of complaint if others built houses on neighbouring land.' Of what use would be complaint, if people came who wanted to build? Whether our property were a desert or colony, they will build if they will build. Your only defence would be in something more practical than complaint.

Will you let Monica and Beelie read this? You know I wrote to you before Percy had chosen, and received, the Isosceles Triangle, that Monica should have the first pick. She can still have this, and be near us in home as well as in heart, and yet the others can be happy too. There is plenty of good room.

O my Squire, think again. I do want you to be satisfied in your dear Property, but I want the others not to be so sadly dissatisfied. They don't love bracken as you do. Think, then, what it would be to have to gaze on bracken at close quarters and in the middle distance always. Frankly, I should not like it.

But if on pondering every word of this letter (written motu proprio, ablative case) you don't change your mind, I, at any rate, will not tease you. But keep this letter. Don't tear it up. Put it away for a week and then read it again. If you could understand our aesthetic unanimity, you would be quite surprised.

Your Johnson[5]

The 'Isosceles Triangle' was a piece of land of about two and a half acres at the far end of the property. A cottage stood there which was occupied at the time of the purchase by a shepherd; but while plans for building were being considered[6] the shepherd vacated Rackham Cottage, as it was called, and so it was decided that the Lucases would restore it, and would add some more rooms to the existing house in preference to building a new one. For the other houses Alice Meynell's ideas prevailed. During the next three years the cow-shed was converted into a house, ever afterwards to be known affectionately as Shed Hall; another house was built close by for Monica, and a bungalow to be a home for someone who would help in house and garden. A croquet lawn and tennis court were laid out, and after the war a swim-

* 'Bill' was Charles Stabb, a young artist who was unofficially engaged to Viola for some two or three years.

ming pool was added, making it a perfect place for the grandchildren's holidays.[7]

Monica's marriage to Dr Saleeby had, sadly, broken down, and her parents were worried about how she would manage her life. It was therefore an arrangement welcome to both sides that she and her two daughters could be near the country home and in close touch with her family.

While the work of building and alteration went on there was much visiting and inspecting and discussing of the Property, and letters flew to and fro between London and Greatham. Meynell was already in occasional and uncomfortable occupation there by the winter of 1911, while he kept an eye on the progress of his various plans. 'Dearest,' he wrote to his wife, 'I cannot be away from you for a day without feeling lonely, and I hope you will think this is a true testimonial of an admiration and appreciation that is not denied even an occasional and quite uncontradictory smile.'[8]

'Forgive my telegram', Mrs Meynell wrote to him. 'I am more than ever anxious that the colony's water should be directly heaven's. I am uneasy about the danger of well-holes in the garden or near it; and, besides, there are all the metallic or mineral things that are in all well-water . . . I know I prose, but it is with good reason.'[9]

An amusing account of an unexpected visitor at Granville Place was sent to Wilfrid Meynell in his absence. The man, Mrs Meynell said, was 'so stout and elderly that I should not have known him but Nora has the virtue of pronouncing names correctly and clearly. What puzzled me was that he used to have one arm and now he had two. Mechanism must have gone far, to produce such a hand and arm; for he had tea, and never faltered with either hand, not to speak of his hat and stick. He staid a long time and told me some curious things about Portugal. But he is wooden in manner. I am glad you are not. (If one of his arms had been wooden in manner I should not have wondered.)'[10]

Under Meynell's careful and loving eye the work went forward, and soon it was possible for the family to gather at Greatham. Of them all, it was perhaps he who loved the Property best and whose brain was most prolific with ideas for its improvement, so that Alice Meynell, writing to him from there when he was in London, would say, 'Your Greatham is looking heavenly.' But for her, too, this country home was a great delight. She had lived so little in the country in England that she was by habit and custom a townswoman; but she loved country things, and she observed them with a keen eye, unclouded by the prejudice and sentimentality that so often hampers the townsman's view. Her eyes and ears were eager and alert; she watched the landscape changing as the seasons passed, marked the unfolding pattern of the flowers, listened to the varied birdsong, and wrote these things down with the naturalist's accuracy and the poet's discernment.

Of blackthorn she wrote: 'The blossom is shaped like that of may, but it is much more fragile; its white is almost grey with transparence, and it seems to open more flat and wide. It does not come in large clusters but in single rows, or knots of two or three, close against the winter black of its thorny branch. There is nothing else quite like this tender and shuddering flower, leafless and fine . . .'[11]

And of the blackbird: 'The blackbird is generally in the major, but he knows the minor scale, and now and then sings a more than usually lovely phrase in it . . . By listening you may hear the same phrase for several successive days, especially from such a tree at such an hour; but it is not certainly, though it is probably, the same bird every time. He comes while the dawn is still dark and cool, and sings his few and intelligible notes aloud, in their definite shape and form. Other kinds of birds are still whispering, without rhythm or rest. He is the only singer of perfect and valued pauses . . .'[12]

Seeing a weasel, she could describe how it 'went undulating, with life in every wave',[13] and watching some hens she noted that they were 'wearing their unrivalled feminine air of practical life'.[14]

She thought the view of Sussex from the top of the Arundel hills to be among the finest views in the world, and in that first summer of belonging to Sussex she wrote, exulting in its beauty:

What is the most beautiful thing to be seen on the face of the flowering earth? In this present week of June most unquestionably a buttercup field in the lovely low-lying land near Pulborough, over against the South Downs. All through England are buttercups, thank heaven; Somersetshire is spread with sheets; let us say, for the love of round numbers, of about a hundred thousand million of them, more or less. Everywhere, as Tennyson says, 'you scarce can see the grass for flowers'. But in this Sussex field you cannot see grass because there is no room for a blade. The buttercups stand shoulder to shoulder, close; and about the middle there is a kind of nucleus, many yards large, where, thick as they are, they thicken . . . In the buttercup is the utmost beauty of the most glorious colour given to earth.[15]

Mary the Mother of Jesus, published early in 1912, was well received by the press. Some disagreement had arisen before publication between Mrs Meynell and the publisher as to whether she had taken a sufficiently undenominational line in writing of the Virgin Mary. 'As to Lee Warner,' she wrote to her husband in December 1911, '. . . I think a man who could say that I undertook to write a book which "could not possibly provoke any feelings" is out of all reasonable dealings, which is a good rhyme.'[16]

Press notices of the Johnson selections had also been good. 'I hope I shall see the *Pall Mall* on Johnson', she wrote to Meynell. 'There is nothing to say on my part of the work, except the inevitable complaint of omissions, which no doubt I too should make in reviewing. I shall get the *Sphere*. I hope the papers are both nice to "my Chesterton".* He is mine much more, really, than Belloc's.'[17]

In 1912 the *Fortnightly Review* published Alice Meynell's poem

CHRIST IN THE UNIVERSE

With this ambiguous earth
His dealings have been told us. These abide:
The signal to a maid, the human birth,
The lesson, and the young Man crucified.

But not a star of all
The innumerable host of stars has heard
How He administered this terrestrial ball.
Our race have kept their Lord's entrusted Word.

Of His earth-visiting feet
None knows the secret, cherished, perilous,
The terrible, shamefast, frightened, whispered, sweet,
Heart-shattering secret of His way with us.

No planet knows that this
Our wayside planet, carrying land and wave,
Love and life multiplied, and pain and bliss,
Bears, as chief treasure, one forsaken grave.

Nor, in our little day,
May His devices with the heavens be guessed,
His pilgrimage to thread the Milky Way,
Or His bestowals there be manifest.

But, in the eternities,
Doubtless we shall compare together, hear
A million alien Gospels, in what guise
He trod the Pleiades, the Lyre, the Bear.

Oh, be prepared, my soul!
To read the inconceivable, to scan
The million forms of God those stars unroll
When, in our turn, we show to them a Man.

---

* A reference to Hilaire Belloc's well-known lines: 'Remote and ineffectual Don That dared attack my Chesterton'. (*Lines to a Don.*)

Many of her letters at this time tell of the work that she was doing for the women's suffrage movement. All her life she had felt keenly the injustice that was done to women by denying them the opportunity to work alongside men in the professions for which intellect rather than physical strength was required. She believed that a woman's brain should be judged by the same standard as a man's; and it infuriated her when a critic called her 'the best of women poets', or by some such condescending phrase made it plain that allowance must be made for her sex. In some ways the mind of this most feminine of women had a quality more usually found in men, and in general she talked more easily with men than with women; but wherever she saw, or thought she saw, her own sex being slighted or insulted or patronised she was there to do battle, and her anger was very real. Militant suffragism was something that she could not approve, and the window-smashers did not have her support; but she worked for this cause that was so near her heart, writing and speaking and marching with the suffragettes, and her family, too, were enlisted to help. 'You would not think', she wrote to Meynell after one meeting, 'from the wretched reports what a magnificent meeting it was at the Opera House yesterday. Nearly all the speakers good – Miss Abadan and Granville Barker splendid – and the house crammed, unanimous, and (I am sorry to say) militant. They made me sit in the front of the platform, but you know that I am *not* militant.'[18]

She was on the platform again at the Hyde Park demonstration in July 1912; before this event her sister, Lady Butler, wrote to her: 'I am curious to learn how the great suffragist meeting next Sunday in Hyde Park will go off. Massed bands, playing the "Woman's March", led by the composer, Ethel Smyth, in a "Cap of Liberty". The papers say all the marchers will wear "Caps of Liberty". I hope there will be some exceptions if you are one of the marchers.'[19]

In an important letter to *The Times* Alice Meynell replied to a letter to that paper from the distinguished physician Sir Almroth Wright. In his letter Wright had deplored the idea of male doctors having to collaborate with female doctors, and had said that 'the mind of woman is always threatened with danger from the reverberations of her physiological emergencies'.

Sir Almroth Wright [*she wrote*] avers that modesty is injured by consultation of a man doctor and a woman doctor. But what of the colloquy of a man doctor with a nurse? It is the nurse who has the most intimate and painful knowledge of her male patients' diseases, and must discuss them with the male physician. And that of the woman patient who is, or was until this more decent time, obliged to give every privacy of her nature into the medical hands of a man? It is her modesty that has brought the woman doctor into office, but that is a modesty which Sir Almroth Wright ignores. The different modesty

Humphreys Homestead, Greatham, showing the newly-built wing
containing the library on the right, before it was whitewashed

Alice Meynell, 1921, drawing by Olivia Sowerby

assigned to the woman doctor who is to be condemned and to the nurse who is to be used must be explained by the difference of a social caste. Fastidiousness as to the modesty of a lady is not respect for purity, but respect for caste.

As to Sir Almroth's estimate of the normal insanity of women, it is surely the disproportionate estimate of one who has to deal with the abnormal. Sick women gather – out of the innumerable multitude who are not sick – in the consulting room. But we had hitherto believed that the physician had eyes and judgment for the outer world.

It is a fact of human life that 'sex' troubles man at least as much as it troubles woman, but it does not disfranchise man. The foolish habit of our speech almost confines the word to womanhood. But George Meredith was delighted when a woman who was his friend interrupted a remark about 'the sex' by the question 'Which?'[20]

Alice Meynell had, all her life, an extreme modesty that was partly attributable to her generation and partly inherent in her personality. That she could accept, without demur, Coventry Patmore's ruling that it was indecent to mention legs in an essay showed, as well as her absolute trust in his judgement, her respect for the conventions of her own time. But the strength of her dislike, made plain in the letter just quoted, of being attended by a male doctor was part of her general dislike for any violation of physical privacy. She managed, in the house crowded with children, never to be seen by those children except when she was prepared to receive all comers. She accorded to her children and to her grandchildren the privacy which she desired for herself. Her grand-daughter tells how once, as a small child, staying at Greatham, she was in the bathroom when Mrs Meynell, opening the unlocked door, found her in a state of undress. She said, 'Oh, I *beg* your pardon', and instantly withdrew. It made a keen impression on the child thus to be treated and addressed as if she were grown up.[21]

It is made plain in her essay 'A Point of Biography' that she hated to hear the details of an illness revealed; for by this, as by every denial of the right of privacy, she felt that human dignity – the general as well as the particular – suffered some diminution.

But with the kind of nineteenth-century convention that found it immodest for a lady to concern herself with any but the respectable Mrs Meynell had no sympathy. Having woken one night to hear screams in the street outside her house, she asked the policeman whose beat it was what had caused the disturbance; she repeated, with anger, the reply he had given her: 'Oh, you don't want to trouble about that – it was only women. Ladies didn't ought to have nothing to do with women.' To her, womankind was as much injured by the rough treatment of a prostitute as that of a duchess. She had that truest kind of charity that made her unable to feel herself a member of a race apart from the outcast, the transgressor, the failure; and one of the rare occasions when she found any fault with Patmore was when she deplored 'the scorn which he flings, not reluctantly or with any fear, upon evil and base men as well as evil and base things.'[22]

In April 1912 the terrible *Titanic* disaster brought a personal loss to the Meynells besides the shock that was felt by the whole nation. Among those drowned was W. T. Stead, who was well known to them since he had been on the staff of the *Pall Mall Gazette*, first as assistant editor and then as editor, from 1880 to 1888. 'I wish I had gone to St Paul's', Mrs Meynell wrote after the Memorial Service for the victims. 'Surely there will be a Requiem at Westminster. I think of Stead constantly. He told me I needed courage and hope. How much he had! What a splendid death! Far, far better than the deathbed distresses and farewells. A quick end and a short prayer, who would not wish for this, even in terror and calamity? It is the survivors I weep for.'[23]

Her birthday, in October of this year, 1912, was greeted by Wilfrid Meynell with a note that preceded him from Greatham.

Dearest and Dearest,
 Though I am coming up to keep your young birthday, I must just send this line of greeting for your – shall I say, breakfast table? I do not dare to begin to think of the things I could say to you of congratulation, of thankfulness for your past, hope for your future. So I say no more than this – that I am
Your W.[24]

In January 1913 Mrs Meynell went to Rome with her sister. She had been rather unwell, and troubled with arthritis in her knee, and it was partly to escape this worst part of the English winter that the journey was taken. It was her last visit to Italy. She wrote to Meynell: 'My delight in the sun is perhaps extravagant – the mere reflection from one side of the street to the other – the look of the profound ilexes and cypresses in the sunshine – all is a perpetual surprise to my heart, although this is my sixth stay in Rome. Never, never have I seen it more radiant.'[25]

The light of Roman skies, always beloved, was on this visit such a joy, such an astonishment to her, that it was as though she saw it for the first time, and she spoke of it in letter after letter. 'The sky is clear aquamarine blue, the sun gold, the air diamonds . . . I have been walking all the morning, after Mass, in this shining city.' And: 'In the many Januaries of my life I have never seen the like of it in any country. The purity of the sky is such as to move one almost to weeping.'[26]

They went by car to Ostia, and she wrote to Wilfrid: 'Ostia, where St Monica had her last colloquy with St Augustine and where she died, is now a great uncovered city with its league-long streets towards Rome laid bare and some fine statues discovered now and then.'[27]

It was at this time that she visited Frascati, and the novelist Phyllis Bottome*, who happened to be there too, has related her first impression.

[One day,] as we were having tea on the hotel terrace, two unknown ladies decided to follow our example . . . We could not see the faces of the two women . . . but we could hear their voices. One of them made a cheap and easy sneer against the English suffragettes and their – as she thought – foolish and unnecessary sufferings. The other began to answer her . . . Never had I heard so beautiful a voice, so rich in quality, so varied in cadence; merely listening to the sound of it would have been pleasure enough, but it was the words that caught us – unpredictable and jewelled words, sentences in which verbs had an active quality that stung the mind like a whiplash.

The speaker was, of course, Alice Meynell.
The writer continued:

Each time I saw Alice Meynell I felt that I was watching a magnificent creature – a tethered angel – suited for enormous distances and stately freedoms, closed into a narrow space behind the iron bars of a cage. The sense of this disciplined self-control was so severe, and yet so impassioned, that it hurt me. I wanted to break down the bars and I knew that I never could. A.M. meant never to have the bars broken down.[28]

There were, as on the last visit to Rome, many people to see, friends and acquaintances who were anxious to entertain her. 'People are really too nice', she wrote; 'they keep one from the real Rome.'[29] She enjoyed meeting interesting people, and so could not bring herself to forgo the social round; but there was much of it that she hated. The grandeur oppressed her, the false values of some of the people she met irritated her, and the luxurious, hot-house atmosphere of the great Roman hotels was unpleasant both to her mind and to her lungs. 'The smart hotels . . . have those infernal round doors that keep out the air. If Dante had known of them he would have made them the gates over which the famous inscription was placed.'[30] And after a tea-party at the Excelsior, which she called 'that Vanity Fair', she wrote: 'Talk rather lively but gossipy – nullities,** separations, the Rodds' fancy-dress ball, which is the topic. The sky, the evening star, the wonderful, wonderful evening sufficiently rebuke an Excelsior tea.'[31]

Some months previously Olivia had become engaged to Murray Sowerby, and Alice wrote to her from Rome for her birthday:

*   Phyllis Bottome: 1884-1963; b. Rochester, Kent, daughter of a New York clergyman and his English wife. Her most famous novel, *The Mortal Storm* (1937), deals with the rise of National Socialism in Germany.
**   Nullities: i.e. annulments of marriages by the ecclesiastical court, the Sacred Roman Rota.

My darling Olivia,

Many happy and ever happier returns of the beloved day that gave you to us
and Murray . . . This is the last of your few birthdays under our roof.[32]

Viola's novel, *Lot Barrow*, was published now, and Wilfrid sent his wife
the review from the *Manchester Guardian*. She replied: 'You are too
delightfully kind to write constantly. The enclosure today made my
morning joyous indeed. I think the *Manchester G's* review is without
exception the most intelligent review I have ever read. It fills me with
happiness to think that Viola's meanings have found such a reader. I
have had equal praise, but never, no never, in any paper, praise so
worth having as this blessed man's. If she got no other for Lot she
might well be satisfied.'[33]

Of Viola's next book, finished but not yet published, she wrote to
her: 'I *like* [it]. It is very well thought out . . . On the first page there is
a little (inherited) complexity. How well I see myself writing just that,
with effort. But I should have gone back after finishing the last page
and re-written the first more simply.'[34]

Mrs Meynell longed for her husband to join her and to share the
beauty that she was so much enjoying. 'Willie, just you pack a few
things' she wrote, '. . . and come jolly well straight out. You have
never really seen Rome as you never saw it in this weather.'[35] She
could not bear to feel that she alone was spending the money which he
had earned. 'I have ever so much of the original £15 left – fully
half – and I have paid up my first week here. Oh, might your generous
cheque help to pay *your* score here too. Chuck some things into a bag,
why not? I do feel selfish, and we should be so happy together.'[36] But
Meynell was not to be coaxed away from his work, and she was obliged
to desist from her efforts to persuade him to come. 'I have loved Rome
much', she wrote before leaving. 'I thank you for the joy of it, which
perhaps you can hardly understand. Nothing but Italy could have
drawn me away from all I love – not any number of aches. But really
that arthritis is wonderfully quiet now.'[37] She discovered that she was
not alone in her infirmity, and told Meynell: 'The Pope has a K-nee
also. He told Mrs Rawlinson, who has long talks with him, . . . that he
can admit no more strangers to his Mass because he cannot genuflect
and it would cause wonder.'[38]

On the way back she stayed in Genoa to see her half-sister, Fanny.
'Ah, what dear friends I leave in Rome!' she wrote. 'How generously
loving to me!'[39] But she was happy to see the beloved coast once more.
'The sea lying absolutely still and silent, as though it were a little lake
and did not clasp African shores and Cretan and Greek – a tender
white-blue seen through pine and cypress – made me think yesterday as
I travelled along the coast that there is no beauty in Rome or anywhere
equal to this beauty.'[40]

In the spring of 1913 Alice Meynell's *Collected Poems* were published by Burns and Oates, and she arrived back in England in time to read a host of interesting and laudatory press notices as they appeared. One article that had been printed in her absence was that by Professor Albert Cock* in the *British Review*, which he had sent her some time before and of which she had written to her husband: 'Did I tell you that Albert sent me his essay on me and my work? I have very nicely asked him if he will omit the personal description and tone down the ecstasies.'[41] Professor Cock spoke of 'the austere character of Mrs Meynell's love lyrics', and said that the characteristic of her work was silence. He likened her and Francis Thompson to St Teresa and St John of the Cross. 'A remarkable parallel here. Two English poets, man and woman united in closest bonds of sympathy and friendship, supplement and co-ordinate in a native and unconscious way the life work of the two Spanish saints, who were also poets.'

From Rome, when the essay was published, Mrs Meynell wrote: 'I think Albert says very over-strained and exaggerated things about St John of the Cross and St Teresa, and about my austerity. I am not so very austere and I do not write with renouncement. I renounce nothing that would make the poem a good one. It is only that my opinion of what is a good poem is rather strict and simple. There is no sacrifice in that.'[42]

The conviction that the very greatest things in poetry could only be reached by way of simplicity had grown stronger in her mind, and the thought is implicit, and sometimes expressed, in her critical judgements at this time. Sending to Wilfrid two poems that she had written, she said: 'Thinking them over, I am as much pleased with "The First Snow" as with "Maternity". The pleasure of having done something good has nothing to do with the desire for praise. And what pleasure is like it? The more undecorated, henceforth, my poems, the better. It is the undecorated that will live.'[43] In 'The Courts' she used a beautiful metaphor to illustrate her point, giving the poem the sub-title, 'A Figure of the Epiphany'.

> The poet's imageries are noble ways,
> Approaches to a plot, an open shrine,
> Their splendours, colours, avenues, arrays,
>   Their courts that run with wine;
>
> Beautiful similes, 'fair and flagrant things',
> Enriched, enamouring, – raptures, metaphors
> Enhancing life, are paths for pilgrim kings
>   Made free of golden doors.

* Professor of English Language and Literature at University College, Southampton.

And yet the open heavenward plot, with dew,
Ultimate poetry, enclosed, enskied,
(Albeit such ceremonies lead thereto)
    Stands on the yonder side.

Plain, behind oracles, it is; and past
All symbols, simple; perfect, heavenly-wild,
The song some loaded poets reach at last –
    The Kings that found a Child.

The new volume contained almost all the poems of *Preludes* and all those of *Later Poems*, together with the more recent ones that had not yet appeared in any book. There had been some discussion over the arrangement of the collection; for Mrs Meynell, who held a very low opinion of her own early poems, had expressed a wish that these should be relegated to the back of the book, thus defying chronology; while Meynell, who valued her early work much more than she did, favoured the chronological order. In literary as in other matters his judgement was final, and she yielded. 'Yes, place them as you like best', she wrote to him. 'I cannot say I like that order but I can sincerely say that I trust your judgement. Or perhaps, even more truly, that making you unhappy about the book is intolerable to me. Oh, let the word *Early* be conspicuous!'[44] After she had gone to Italy Wilfrid wrote to tell her that part of the edition would be printed in the way she wished and part with the poems in their chronological sequence. She commented: 'So some of my volumes have the cart before the horse and others the spirited, thoroughbred horse before the rather conventional old cart. Think of that now!'[45]

In one of the later poems, 'The Unknown God', she approached the mystery of God's union with each of his children.

One of the crowd went up,
And knelt before the Paten and the Cup,
Received the Lord, returned in peace, and prayed
Close to my side. Then in my heart I said:

'O Christ, in this man's life –
This stranger who is Thine – in all his strife,
All his felicity, his good and ill,
In the assaulted stronghold of his will,

'I do confess Thee here,
Alive within this life; I know Thee near
Within this lonely conscience, closed away
Within this brother's solitary day.

'Christ in his unknown heart,
His intellect unknown – this love, this art,
This battle and this peace, this destiny
That I shall never know – look upon me!

'Christ in his numbered breath,
Christ in his beating heart and in his death,
Christ in his mystery! From that secret place
And from that separate dwelling, give me grace!'

J. L. Garvin, reviewing *Collected Poems* in the *Pall Mall Gazette*, in May 1913, wrote: '. . . We are even tempted to wish that the poems of Mrs Meynell were written by another in order that she might have been their due critic in her own prose. Only that could assure the memorable and delicate thing about them which still waits to be said . . . With an exquisite singleness of genius, she stands apart and escapes the categories. She has few affinities, and none of this day.'

In the *Times Literary Supplement* Walter de la Mare said:

Out of the hurly-burly of ephemeral books and hardly less ephemeral literary reputations live quietly on a few names and a few achievements that are of significance and value not only in themselves but for the high isolated standard they represent. There have always been a few writers who, like far-beaming candles in a noisy and naughty world, are an encouragement and an assurance to their fellows. Mary Coleridge, Francis Thompson, Father Tabb – one could not but be reminded of such names by this collected edition of the poems of Alice Meynell . . .

Even in the earliest sonnets, with all their delicate sensitiveness, their restrained ardour, we are always conscious of a kind of native wisdom of thought that is not so much the chance and sudden flower of a happy and unforeseen moment, but that has been pondered over and proven. 'But not a flower or song I ponder is My own, but memory's.' It is this serene poise of mind, this consistent refusal to fall captive to caprice of mood and wandering impulse, that gives Mrs Meynell's verse its rarest quality. It is a restraint not only of art, but of life; a selection not only from among the richer things of a personal life, but from among the rarest . . . But though Mrs Meynell is one of the comparatively small number of poets who actually think in verse, and though now and then her poems are weighed down with their burden, her work is always lyrical. There is nothing far-fetched, only the close-treasured; nothing obscure or learned or exotic, only that which is abstruse because it needs diligent search to find it and to be sure of it . . . There is sadness in her verse, but no melancholy; resignation but not despair. Above all, her poems are, we feel (in spite of the exquisite craftsmanship of a true artist that ensures for the moment lastingness), only notes, as it were, by the way. They tell much, not all. And as each poem's essential beauty dwells behind rather than in its expression, so her work in its completeness is only the partial witness to a life's whole trend, a rare spirit's daily experience.[46]

Writing to Meynell after this notice appeared, she said: 'The Times was [good] wasn't it? I think I have never had anything so good, so *interested*. Three cheers. I wonder who wrote it. I hope you will find out.'[47] He had been unwell, and apparently appendicitis was suspected; her letter ends: 'Oh, Willie, take care of yourself. What is *The Times* or poetry or anything compared to one small appendix? Your Johnson.'[48]

In this year there appeared also another book of Mrs Meynell's essays on children, *Childhood*, which was published by Batsford. While she was preparing it she had written to Meynell from London, where she was alone in the Granville Place flat. 'I am getting on well with my "Childhood" (the cheerful book for Batsford), so that the solitude has not been really unwelcome . . . In my old Autolycuses are several capital columns on children (1897 and 1898) written after my book "Children". I am sure you would agree with me that they could go in bodily or with very little recasting? They are quite forgotten and really ought not to be lost. By their aid I have done more than half the booklet.'[49]

Her accounts for 1913 show that in that year she earned £465, of which more than £400 came from the sale of *Collected Poems*. At the foot of the page on which her earnings were entered she wrote: 'I think this must have been one of my best years.'[50]

In June she was the guest of the Poetry Society at a dinner given at the Café Monico. Her health was proposed by Father Vaughan*, but she could not face making a speech in reply, so her son Francis did it for her.

In July Wilfrid Meynell was ill with an ear infection, which prevented him from travelling in the car which they had now acquired and which was, of course, an open one. Alice wrote to Olivia, who was in Italy:

Beelie, you don't know how delightful the motor is. I took her down to Greatham, a trial trip. It was glorious weather and the hay was being carried everywhere . . . How much I hope your father will soon be able to use his car. At present, of course, it is impossible. I long to see him on the road to Greatham. She is a great bargain and a genuine one . . .

Dick Tobin turned up today. He says ex-President Roosevelt and Mrs R. want to come when they arrive in England, Mrs R. being a reader of mine. She invited me to the White House when I was in America but I had an eye. I hope you will meet Theodore.[51]

Within a week or so Wilfrid Meynell was recovered and they were motoring in the Greatham area. 'A West Sussex motor map from

* William Vaughan, S.J., one of the Vaughans of Courtfield (Herefordshire), and a brother of the Cardinal. Famous for his sermons at Farm Street church; especially those on 'The Sins of Society'.

Selfridges is indispensable to us', Alice wrote to Viola in London. 'No one knows the road to anywhere and we do nothing but lose ourselves for miles and miles. The local chauffeur knows rather less than your father and I could not say anything more than that.'[52]

Following the death of Alfred Austin, there was much discussion at this time about who was to be the next Poet Laureate, and Mrs Meynell's name was frequently mentioned in the press in this connection. The *London Budget* published her photograph under the heading 'Suggested Successor to Mr Alfred Austin'; the *Daily Citizen*, the *Pall Mall Gazette*, and the *Daily Mail* all advocated the bestowal of this honour on her. *T.P.'s Weekly** ran a ballot among its readers for the most popular choice; Kipling came first, Alice Meynell second. Sir William Robertson Nicholl wrote in the *British Weekly*: 'Would it not be a graceful and righteous thing to put the wreath on the brows of a woman poet? I will not go so far as Mr Garvin and say that Mrs Meynell is the greatest of living poets, but I will say that she ranks with the very best, and I will believe there will be no disposition to dispute her claim.'

The Times, after listing other possible candidates in a third leader, remarked acidly: 'Feminists would add, and not without some reason, that there is Mrs Meynell; perhaps to make her Laureate would help to satisfy those eminent persons who wish to admit more women to the Civil Service.'[53]

On the whole, it must have been something of a relief to Mrs Meynell when the matter was settled by the appointment of Robert Bridges.

---

* A popular magazine edited by the Irish Nationalist M.P., T. P. O'Connor.

CHAPTER 22

IN 1913 an accident befell Sylvia, the five-year-old child of Madeline and Percy Lucas, to whom Alice Meynell had addressed the poem 'To Sylvia, Two Years Old'. She fell on a sickle that was lying in the long grass, and injured her leg so severely that for a considerable time there was danger of losing not only the limb but life itself. Percy Lucas was in Italy with his brother, E. V. Lucas, at the time. He hurried home, but arrived only after an operation had been performed at a London hospital. Alice Meynell suffered both for the suffering of the little girl and for the anguish of Madeline and Percy. She made frequent visits to her in hospital, and wrote her letters in which she called her 'dear dear priceless lovely Mrs Badleg'.[1] When the initial danger to her life had passed, and after two operations, there remained the painful anxiety as to the future of the injured leg. A number of doctors were consulted. 'It is a great relief', Mrs Meynell wrote to her husband, 'that Elmslie ratifies Trotter's judgement. But he does not think the knee will ever be quite normal The new splint is being made. Dimpling is heroic. I have made her a present of my new five-guinea costume for indeed I did not need it.'[2] And to Madeline, when a new doctor had been called in:

Darling Dimpling,
　　It was a great pleasure to see Percy today and to hear from him that, to his eyes, Sylvia could bend her knee and move her toes *more*. I am sure that you are right to give this man a good trial. I have had the idea of asking you to let me take you and Sylvia to Paris if there is not a marked progress.
　　You, darling, who have withstood so much, will bear these three weeks too, I know. We who have to take the severe part of our religion must take the kind part as well; and you and Sylvia have much treasure laid up by what you have suffered. May all now go well with you and that beloved child.[3]

There was another grave anxiety at this time. Sebastian suffered a nervous breakdown. His life, up to that time, had not gone smoothly; work in banking had proved quite unsuitable, and after a period at Newcastle, working at journalism under Garvin, he returned home to work with his father at Burns and Oates, but living chiefly in the main house at Greatham. Alice wrote to him:

My dearest Bastian,
　　It was a great pleasure to have your letter and to know first hand how you have felt. Your letter reads to me most excellently and speaks of a real cure. Remember your illness was one of the *nerves* only . . . Be of good cheer. I look forward to seeing you very soon. I long to do something to make you happy. I hope we may soon be together.[4]

To Meynell she wrote:

My darling Wilfrid,

Thank you for your most welcome letter giving news of Bastian's further progress. I am full of hope now. If he can accept Bognor as an intermediate step, it will be an excellent thing. Of course there may be some difficulty in finding good rooms. I should suggest an hotel. This place is, of course, so much quieter that in a week or so I think Bastian might venture on it, with a different room, and you and me and Viola only as inmates . . . Quiet for Bastian is the first consideration – but of course not dullness. We must watch his inclinations.[5]

But there was no quick solution. An undated letter from Wilfrid Meynell to Olivia from Greatham tells of a relapse.

I am here because Bastian has been less well . . . Your mother and Prue are in town. Don't say anything to your mother about Bastian. I came away suddenly from town without telling her that there were very bad reports which, however, have greatly improved. I have his work to do, of course – he cannot even open a paper. But his sleep is better.[6]

The slow recovery was to be complete, but for a long time Sebastian's health was an anxiety, and great vigilance and tact had to be used in dealing with him. A letter from Alice Meynell to her husband suggests that even in that most happy, loving, and united of families his nervous condition caused some tension: 'Dear Darling Wilfrid, In deeds you could not be kinder and more tender to Bastian. Am I wrong in asking you to be a little more affectionate in words? I know he would appreciate it more than you think.'[7]

Olivia was now married to Murray Sowerby and living at Clifton. Alice Meynell was with her in April 1914, while Olivia was having her first baby, when she wrote to tell Meynell of a letter that she had received from Agnes Tobin's sister, Celia, now Mrs Charles Clarke.

My darling Wilfrid,

Celia writes that I am to be invited to visit the Panama Exposition next year – one of four women: Mme Curie, Mrs Sidney Webb and Helen Key* being the others. These are the first names. In case of refusals others would be substituted . . . Celia is on the Women's Committee and sends me this preliminary notice. I can't go, can I?

The whole expenses are paid, of course, and a week at San Francisco, but Celia asks me stay with her, extra. I have to answer at once. If I were a little younger, so as to be more presentable, I should fly. What do you think? Send me a line by return.[8]

To Viola she wrote: 'Shall I go to San Francisco? I say Yes and No all day. Murray says "Yes". Lobbie says "No". I must write tomorrow.'[9]

---

* Presumably Ellen (not Helen) Key, Swedish writer 1849-1926.

She longed to go: 'I have written my formal refusal very regretfully, but I was afraid if I did not clinch it I should say yes'[10] – and the decision was unmade again. 'Well, there! I am cabling acceptance to San Francisco. I am writing to Celia also to say that of course illness (but nothing less) would stop me. You see it is nearly a year off! I shall be a year older!'[11] But the terrible events still hidden in the future, though not far off, were to prevent her from going.

Her heart still yearned for travel and adventure, still felt young, but her physical heart was no longer strong. She was beginning to be frail, finding herself obliged to treat her body with a consideration she had not previously accorded it. But nothing had grown stale to her, and her world was a world full of matchless beauty. 'I did three calls without a taxi', she wrote to Meynell at this time, 'and I find the shining streets intoxicating and love walking in them.'[12]

Early in 1914 Burns and Oates published her *Collected Essays*. The book bore, as frontispiece, a reproduction of Sargent's drawing of her, and the last lines of each essay were arranged in diminishing length down to a point in the centre of the page. To both these embellishments she objected, although she was otherwise pleased with the book's appearance. 'My "Collected" are out', she wrote to one of her daughters. 'If I could suppress the portrait I should be wholly pleased for the book is exquisitely produced.' And to Wilfrid Meynell: 'Delighted with the look of my book (except the hideous tailing off of lines) and with the sales. Oh, if I can make another nimble ninepence to help with Sylvia!'[13]

The essays were collected and selected from *The Rhythm of Life, The Colour of Life, The Spirit of Place, The Children*, and *Ceres Runaway*, with four more added which had not previously been published in any book: 'The Seventeenth Century', 'Prue', 'Mrs Johnson', and 'Madame Roland'.

In her essay on the wife of Dr Johnson Mrs Meynell did honour to poor Tetty who had been jeered at and abused by other writers. '. . . Not to any writer has it occurred that if England loves her great Englishman's memory, she owes not only courtesy, but gratitude, to the only woman who loved him while there was yet time. Not a thought of that debt has stayed the alacrity with which a caricature has been acclaimed as the only possible portrait of Mrs Johnson . . .'

This volume, in which were collected the finest things in twenty years of fine essay writing, was naturally reviewed at great length in all the important papers and periodicals, and was the occasion for the critics to attempt an assessment of Alice Meynell's place in English literature. *The Times Literary Supplement* said that the wisdom of these essays was independent of fashion and ways of thought. 'Their delicacy – of scrupulousness, balance, fineness, skill – is as rare in life and in art as ever it was.' This critic, speaking of her censure, said: 'If Mrs Meynell's shafts have any target, that (comparatively spacious) target is certainly Man. She may add a chillish word of comfort to her suggestion that he should make a strenuous effort even at this late day to attain to "a certain human dignity in the clothing of his natural body" – "the best leg is the man's" . . . But whether she is considering him as "a sensitive Municipality in tears" over the grass that defies forbiddance to spring up in its tramways, as the poet who says nothing in terms of the eternal or wastes his craft on a common hoard of erotic remembrances, or as a critic who for dapper sentimentality's sake would dismiss Swift's beloved Dingley from all share in his idolized "M.D.", or who lavishes cheap satire at the expense of the all-consoling wife of Johnson, Mrs Meynell shows no mercy. Poor Gulliver writhes under whispering volleys of wit, irony, raillery which he is powerless not only to repel but to locate.'[14]

Of this, Alice Meynell wrote to Viola: 'In case you didn't see *The Times* I enclose it. A very fine article and uncommonly well written, but the suggestion that when I censure a municipality or a painter I am censuring him as a *man* (and not a woman) is most wrongheaded. Of course the conspicuous things have been done by men, and one has to criticise them for that reason.'[15]

She was delighted with a review in the *Liverpool Courier*. 'A lovely, lovely review in the *Liverpool* something – ', she wrote to Meynell; 'not all praise, but such as an author loves. Viola is ordering some copies and I will send you one tomorrow.'[16]

Dixon Scott, in this article, wrote: '. . . I am soberly convinced that the prose of Alice Meynell is absolutely the most perfect produced in our language for at least the last twenty years. There have been louder instruments than hers; there has been orchestration more complex; and there have been artists, no less honourable, who have parted with some purity of tone for the sake of a wider range of keys or strings. But unless it be some of the early work of Mr W. B. Yeats (the essays he wrote in *Ideas of Good and Evil*) I can think of no prose-tissue – no, not even that of Mr James – which presents a surface so free from the faintest falsity or blur, and that clings with so exquisite a closeness and transparency to the rippling body of the swiftly moving thought.'[17]

Mrs Meynell's letters to the family when they were at Greatham and she in London tell of some of her activities in the early part of 1914. She had been to a performance of *Parsifal*, and wrote to Meynell:

Even though one whole act was, as music, entirely unintelligible to me, and as spectacle distressingly ugly, I found the rest one of the greatest works of man. It is overpowering . . . It is significant of Wagner's curiously austere mind that the act which presents the delights of the senses and of unspiritual love – the temptations through which Parsifal comes – is ugliness itself, in music, decoration, action, and the female figure and face – extraordinarily fat and German. Not one note or movement of charm. But the religious motive – the wounded soul and its sorrow and final redemption – to this Wagner has given all his gigantic power and tenderness.[18]

After a dinner at Mrs Hunter's London house, she wrote to Olivia: 'I had an interesting dinner last night with Mrs Hunter and Sargent and their "Magic" and G. B. Shaw's imbecile buffoonery at which Sargent's temper and endurance gave way.'[19]

Her poem 'Free Will' was written at this time and sent to Meynell for his judgement. He suggested some alterations, and she wrote again, returning it to him.

Please read the altered poem. I have taken out the comparison with other men, which I think was beside the simple issue. And I have restored some good to the speaker's memories, as you suggested. But remember it is a poem of self-accusation, and expresses the simple thought that it is in the free will of our own old transgressions that we find humility. There is a slight paradox in the idea of those evils as a treasure, which is a paradox of poetry, it seems to me, and makes the poem a poem.'[20]

Meynell suggested that the sentence from her letter, 'It is in the free will of our own old transgressions that we find humility' should be put at the head of the verses. 'If I need this key,' he wrote, 'whom you have brought up by hand, how much more the heathen.'[21]

The poem contained an allusion to Meredith under the name by which she sometimes spoke of him, 'the Master'.

FREE WILL

Dear are some hidden things
  My soul has sealed in silence; past delights;
Hope unconfessed; desires with hampered wings,
  Remembered in the nights.

But my best treasures are
  Ignoble, undelightful, abject, cold;
Yet oh, profounder hoards oracular
  No reliquaries hold.

There lie my trespasses,
  Abjured but not disowned. I'll not accuse
Determinism, nor, as the Master says,
  Charge even 'the poor Deuce'.

Under my hand they lie
  My very own, my proved iniquities;

And though the glory of my life go by
I hold and garner these.

How else, how otherwhere,
 How otherwise, shall I discern and grope
For lowliness? How hate, how love, how dare,
 How weep, how hope?

Visitors were reported and sometimes described in swift, amusing little sketches. A caller at Granville Place was 'quite an interesting woman, talks very well, wears a single eye-glass and has the walk of a groom'; and from Greatham to an absent daughter went a description of a visit from a local celebrity who 'had that terrible coiffure of bell-pulls on either side pulled out horizontally and a toupet on top. This did not exactly match.'[22]

From Greatham, too, Mrs Meynell reported on the work of conversion that was being done to make the old cattle-shed into Shed Hall. 'I think we must be a little under-manned; and a large piece of soap let into the drains from the wash-house has caused a digging-up of the garden.'[23] The stationery supply in the Sussex house was always running out, and when Alice Meynell was there her urgent appeal would be written on the backs of envelopes or across the tops of letters to Granville Place: 'Envelopes please', or 'More Greatham paper'. An even more urgent appeal went to Wilfrid Meynell in the early days of settlement at Greatham: 'All is very well here except fleas. Will you tell my Viola that in addition to the Selfridge things I asked for I should love a tin of Keating's insect powder. I am told that though it does not slay the flea it discourages her coming.'[24]

It was from London that she wrote on 30th July: 'All the papers alarm us this morning'; but she was at Greatham when, a few days later, it became certain that war was coming. 'All are well here', she wrote to Meynell, 'and keeping up each other's hearts. It is heavenliest weather. How we hope you will come tomorrow, bringing the last news. But we no longer hope for peace.'[25] The day after war was declared, she wrote: 'My darling Wilfrid, It *will* be a pleasure to see you tomorrow. I do want to keep together as much as possible, so that I long for the Everards and Francis to be stowed here somehow.'[26]

At this time, harrowed by the terrible happenings in the world, her more personal anxiety was for her scattered family. Not because of dangers, but for some reason that she could not define, she longed for them all to be together under one roof, and dreaded separations. 'I bear absences less and less well', she wrote to Meynell; and added: 'It is all over with that engagement. Don't speak of it yet to anyone. I will tell you all when we meet. Viola feels it deeply.'[27]

She was convinced of the rightness of going to war now, of the justice of the Allied cause, and deeply stirred by the response of the nation. 'Everything adds to the security of our conscience in this war,' she wrote, 'and defeat itself will not degrade us now.'[28] 'I do think that Christianity is so rooted in our nation and our hearts that it grows, strangely, side by side with the ethics of war.'[29] 'What shall we not do for the splendid Belgians if the Allies are finally victorious!'[30] 'I hope you all saw *The Times* full report of the Notes between Grey and Berlin. Nothing could be more honourable to us. I do think there is such a thing as distinctively English honour.'[31]

She remained at Greatham through the last days of that summer and the early autumn, and the serenity and beauty of the Sussex country-side made a strange background to the violence and horror going on across the Channel and filling all minds at that time. In her letters talk of the war alternated with talk of the round of work in farm and garden. 'Aeroplanes often go over us, night and day', she wrote to Viola. 'Their sound a mile off is much like that of a humming bird in the Californian flowers. How one blesses the brave hearts that are in them, and all brave hearts . . . We are overwhelmed with plums. What a year!'[32] 'We have wind and rain, which makes things sadder; bad for the harvest, but good, on the other hand, for the "winter keep". In the intervals of rain, I weed as usual.'[33] 'We are flooded with sunshine, and the skies are enormous, heroic skies.'[34] 'The great field across the road is reaped, and we see the welcome sight of stubble in many lands – nearly a month earlier than usual.'[35]

It was in that summer of curious contrast that Alice Meynell wrote 'Summer in England, 1914', which was published in *The Times* on 10th October:

> On London fell a clearer light;
>   Caressing pencils of the sun
> Defined the distances, the white
>   Houses transfigured one by one,
>   The 'long, unlovely street' impearled.
> Oh, what a sky has walked the world!
>
> Most happy year! And out of town
>   The hay was prosperous, and the wheat;
> The silken harvest climbed the down:
>   Moon after moon was heavenly-sweet,
> Stroking the bread within the sheaves,
> Looking 'twixt apples and their leaves.
>
> And while this rose made round her cup,
>   The armies died convulsed. And when

This chaste young silver sun went up
   Softly, a thousand shattered men,
One wet corruption, heaped the plain,
After a league-long throb of pain.

Flower following tender flower; and birds,
   And berries; and benignant skies
Made thrive the serried flocks and herds. –
   Yonder are men shot through the eyes.
        Love, hide thy face
From man's unpardonable race.

      *   *   *

Who said 'No man hath greater love than this,
   To die to serve his friend'?
So these have loved us all unto the end.
      Chide thou no more, O thou unsacrificed!
The soldier dying dies upon a kiss,
   The very kiss of Christ.

In a letter to Viola in September Mrs Meynell wrote: 'Wilfrid Blunt has been here to lunch . . . He brought the *New Witness** with G.K.C.'s article on Louvain and me! It is delightful about me but *too* wrongheaded and unjust about the Germans. He must have no music in him when he says they have created nothing – music being the *one* creative art and German music the greatest that is or, surely, can be.'[36]

The Royal Society of Literature honoured her in November by electing her to their Academic Committee. In his Address of Reception Sir Henry Newbolt said: '. . . It would be impossible to over-estimate the value of Mrs Meynell's Essays to the general public. For these small studies of things apparently small, with their Athenian ingenuity, their Spartan terseness, their mediaeval clearness and profundity, were, at their first appearance, read and marked, not by a narrow circle of the initiated, but by a crowd which looked eagerly for them week by week.'[37] Of her poetry he said that here was to be found 'a union of wit and religious emotion as rare now as it was characteristic of the seventeenth century in England'.[38]

'That Literary Society affair was lovely', she wrote afterward to Olivia. 'I could not have wished for a better welcome than Gilbert Murray's and Newbolt's.'[39]

---

*   The weekly paper edited by Cecil Chesterton, Gilbert Chesterton's younger brother.

CHAPTER 23

AT THE END OF 1914 Wilfrid Meynell published a little book called *Aunt Sarah and the War*, which became immediately popular and went through many editions. He now became a regular contributor to the weekly review *Land and Water*, and Alice Meynell wrote to him:

I am overawed by your triumph – for triumph it is; beyond the dreams of avarice, at any rate of your journalistic avarice twenty, thirty years ago. What a sum! Bastian is only afraid that it will overwork you, B[urns] and O[ates] work being now thrust back upon you. But surely you will let me help you with L and W. Did I not do smart topical paragraphs for *The World* for years? So smart and topical that you virtually left *The World* to me at one time . . . On the strength of our great gains I want a present from you of a sports coat. It costs about £1.15. This, worn with my short skirt, will make my garden outfit for the summer, this grey alpaca being somewhat too shabby for visitors.[1]

The war now directly touched the closely knit family. Percy Lucas volunteered for military service, in September, and Mrs Meynell wrote from London to Madeline: 'I have heard all the history of your great courage and dear Percy's. I confess I was sorry at first, but conscience must be the last law in all of us, and I cannot tell you how I admire him for doing what is to him the right thing, and therefore the only thing. I give him a mother-in-law's blessing from my heart! Some people would think that comic; I pity them.'[2]

Everard wrote of Percy's departure to France in May 1916: 'He left us humbly and cheerfully. Having no thought for any of the lesser awkward chances, he refused, at the last moment, to take a reserve of money. That the main ill chance was in his mind and faced with supreme courage, we all knew, even while he bade us goodbye without a flicker of regret save such as was sufficient for the day and a temporary absence.'[3]

Shortly after his going, Alice Meynell wrote to Wilfrid:

Dimpling has no letter today. Yesterday she heard from Percy that he was joining his regiment, so his fears of delay were in vain. She feels it, but is very courageous, and busy all day sewing and teaching her children and bringing them up well.[4]

An illness in the winter of 1914-1915, though not itself dangerous, had been an indication of Alice Meynell's failing health. She was frail now, slept badly, felt the cold acutely; but she wrote cheerfully: 'I am going on well. I believe I am as well as I was in the summer, when I remember telling people about my rag-time heart.'[5]

The business of the Greatham garden claimed her as soon as she was up and about again in the late spring. She weeded, Viola Meynell tells us, 'with an amateurishness of attitude beyond that of most amateurs even, but certain to get her root',[6] and she was immensely proud of her success in this task. Her eldest grandchild, Mary Saleeby, who loved gardening, worked hard in the garden when she was at Greatham. Alice Meynell wrote to her:

Greatham is very eager to see you back. Agriculture is the order of the day, for we found chaos. The potato patch was a kind of small forest, in which potato plants were hardly perceptible. You should see it now – orderly rows of flourishing banked-up potato-plants, promising Irish stew for months, and not a weed to be seen. Prudie has been particularly masterly, but I must say I bore my part. I do *eradicate*.[7]

And to Olivia she wrote: 'All is well, and beautiful here. The few rains have made the weeds grow so fast that I can't keep ahead of them. Nobody can stop weeding who once begins because they are so nimble and lively. The wet earth is hot to the touch.'[8]

More of her time was spent at Greatham than in London now, and her joy was great when she could gather some of her family round her. 'O my Lobbie,' she wrote, 'what a pleasure it is, even in this unhappy year, to see my beloved children, and to have the assurance of their love – so much more than I have ever deserved.' And again: 'How I look forward to your coming, Beelie! I think no woman ever had such daughters.'[9]

There were other family anxieties besides the concern for the son-in-law at war. Monica's matrimonial troubles were unresolved and she was ill. Alice Meynell wrote to Wilfrid when she was briefly in London:

The darling, darling Monica. How we shall look for news. I am sure you are doing right to stay and give her a rest cure. We must certainly try to arrange her life so as to guard against these over-strains. Mary ought to go to school. Perhaps Monica will see this soon. Even if they have to be here and Mary to go to a day school. It might make such a difference that they might afterwards resume life together.

I am grieved to think of your fatigue and anxiety too. I am going on *well* . . . My ever darling, keep up your invaluable heart.[10]

Francis had married in August 1914 a young pianist called Hilda Peppercorn (her professional name was Hilda Saxe). He felt very strongly against the war, and was writing and speaking publicly against it. Since 1913 he had been working for the *Daily Herald*, as well as running a small private printing press at his house in Romney Street; and he was becoming known for his very left-wing opinions. He now felt that for him to remain with Burns and Oates would be an embarrassment for his father, so he left the firm and started the Pelican Press, financed by Lady De La Warr and Miss Dodge, who were also dedicated socialists.[11]

Alice Meynell, despite anxieties and distractions, was writing poetry again. She, whom the Muse visited fitfully and infrequently, had entered upon the last and greatest creative period of her life. Ten of the poems written between 1913 and 1915 were privately published by Francis at the Romney Street Press in 1915. Among them was 'A Thrush before Dawn', in which she wrote of the splendour of the voice that she heard as she lay awake in the dark early mornings when other birds were silent.

> A voice peals in this end of night
>> A phrase of notes resembling stars,
> Single and spiritual notes of light.
>>> What call they at my window-bars?
>>>> The South, the past, the day to be,
>>>> An ancient infelicity.
>
> Darkling, deliberate, what sings
>> This wonderful one, alone, at peace?
> What wilder things than song, what things
>>> Sweeter than youth, clearer than Greece,
>>>> Dearer than Italy, untold
>>>> Delight, and freshness centuries old?
>
> And first first-loves, a multitude,
>> The exaltation of their pain;
> Ancestral childhood long renewed;
>>> And midnights of invisible rain;
>>>> And gardens, gardens, night and day,
>>>> Gardens and childhood all the way.
>
> What Middle Ages passionate,
>> O passionless voice! What distant bells
> Lodged in the hills, what palace state
>>> Illyrian! For it speaks, it tells,
>>>> Without desire, without dismay,
>>>> Some morrow and some yesterday.
>
> All-natural things! But more – Whence came
>> This yet remoter mystery?
> How do these starry notes proclaim
>>> A graver still divinity?
>>>> This hope, this sanctity of fear?
>
> *O innocent throat! O human ear!*

In this year Alice Meynell began a correspondence with Mother St Ignatius, an American nun, who was writing a life of Emily Patmore, the daughter of Coventry Patmore who had been a nun and had died in 1880. Mother St Ignatius was a woman of brilliant intellect as well as very fine character, perceptive, devout, and with a great sense of humour. She had long admired Mrs Meynell's work, and the correspondence that started when she sought permission to quote, in her book, from the introduction to *The Mount of Vision*[12] led to a close friendship that lasted until Mrs Meynell's death. They did not meet until 1918, and then their meetings were few; but they loved and understood each other, and in her last years Alice Meynell opened her heart to this friend as, perhaps, to no other.

Writing to her in 1916, Mother St Ignatius said:

I wonder if you would be glad to know this. Some one, a soul in great storm and stress, a religious soul in the Dark Night, in a moment of dire temptation, suddenly remembered one little separate line of yours: 'Access, approach Art Thou, Time, Way and Wayfarer' (Is it correct?) and the realisation of it was borne in upon her at a real crisis in her spiritual life. It just made the difference. Things of that sort go on and on and live and reach out and do God's work long, perhaps, after the writer has ceased to live here in the Vale of Tears, and things go on happening because of it.[13]

Of their first meeting Mother St Ignatius wrote long afterwards to Wilfrid Meynell:

She was so exactly like what I expected from my own imaginings and the impression of her writings that that first seeing her at Cavendish Square in 1918 was hardly a first meeting . . . Our short but intimate acquaintance greatly enriched my life. She told me many things about herself in a quick swift-worded way – but was there ever anyone who could get more meaning in a few words? The great drawback to all biography is that the most vital and interesting things simply can't be told – it might do in mediaeval times but one would not bear the beautiful intimacies and depths and heights in our artificial day.[14]

And in an earlier letter to him she said: 'I was reading Catherine Brégy's *Poets' Chantry* the other day – I like it very much. She says some true and lovely things about Mrs Meynell. People are generally at their best when they speak of her – she uplifts by the most passing mental contact.'[15]

A more prosaic and less rewarding result of being an author was the subject of a humourous complaint in one of Alice Meynell's letters to Olivia at this time: ' "The Pleasures of Illness" did appear, I remember, in *The Queen*, but the editor thought the title horrible and changed it to "The Compensations of Illness" or something like that, losing the point. *The Bookman* has a laudatory page or two on me with a quotation vilely misprinted in a way to destroy a good sentence. It is not all porter and skittles being a fairly successful author.'[16]

The tercentenary of Shakespeare's death fell in 1916, and Mrs Meynell wrote to her husband: 'That swankish body the British Academy are getting up a general committee for the Shakespeare tercentenary. It is no distinction to be on it ("no duties") or they would not ask me. Am I to say Yes or No?'[17]

The poem that she wrote on that occasion she called 'my one, *one* masterpiece'.[18] It was printed in the *Observer* on 1st October, 1916. In it she reflected that her own age was now greater than that of Shakespeare when he died. Time, and the tricks that it played, and the pattern of relative age changed by death, were subjects that always fascinated her.

The Two Shakespeare Tercentenaries
OF BIRTH, 1864; OF DEATH, 1916

TO SHAKESPEARE

Longer than thine, than thine,
Is now my time of life; and thus thy years
Seem to be clasped and harboured within mine.
Oh, how ignoble this my clasp appears!

Thy unprophetic birth,
Thy darkling death: living I might have seen
That cradle, marked those labours, closed that earth.
O first, O last, O infinite between!

Now that my life has shared
Thy dedicated date, O mortal, twice,
To what all-vain embrace shall be compared
My lean enclosure of thy paradise:

To ignorant arms that fold
A poet to a foolish breast? The Line,
That is not, with the world within its hold?
So, days with days, my days encompass thine.

Child, Stripling, Man – the sod.
Might I talk little language to thee, pore
On thy last silence? O thou city of God,
My waste lies after thee, and lies before.

In July 1916, aged thirty-six, Percy Lucas died in France of the fatal wound which he had received when, as a subaltern, he was leading his men to the attack on the first day of the Battle of the Somme. The Meynells lost a beloved son-in-law, and suffered doubly in watching the anguish of a beloved daughter. All that they could do to help her, distract her, comfort her, they did in full measure. Alice Meynell wrote to her husband:

My darling Wilfrid,
I think that by the slowest degrees our poor girl is becoming more normal. I suppose it is a good thing that she cries at intervals all day. She speaks more. A letter from the Nurse has taken away her great hope that Percy died under the anaesthetic. She felt so sure of it. But evidently he did not. I think they must have decided against the operation. The Nurse says he was 'very quiet and peaceful' and the Priest sat by him till the end. Are these not blessings? But Dimpling had so hoped he did not know he was to die.
Dimpling said she would go out today but she has not left her room yet, and it is raining hard. All the comfort she seems to have is in letters. She sees the children very little.[19]

Some time later Alice Meynell wrote to a friend: 'My poor Dimpling has borne her affliction throughout with splendid fortitude, but it has quite changed her.'
The shuttling to and fro of parts of the family between London and Greatham now became to some extent influenced by the occurrence of air raids. To Madeline, who was in London with the children, Alice wrote from Greatham:

My darling Dimpling,
How near did they come? And how much were you and the little ones frightened? It was dreadful to get no news here – telegrams are held up – until dear Viola's welcome letter this morning telling us that the families were safe. We had heard from the postman the most frightful accounts, on Saturday evening.[20]

And when she was herself in London she wrote to Olivia:

Now as to that old Raid, nearly forgotten. It is impossible to forget that at every bump *someone* is being hurt; otherwise I must confess there is a pleasure I cannot account for in the danger. We had listened for some time to the bumps getting nearer until the big one came (Edgeware Road) and then we went down to the cellar for an hour or two. That is all. I am glad Viola was at Greatham as she does not enjoy raids so much as I do.[21]

And to Viola she wrote: 'Your father wanted me to think the great thuds were guns, but I do know a bomb and I always shall.'[22]
In winter Mrs Meynell exchanged Greatham for London, in search not of danger but of warmth. 'I have decided to go up on Monday', she wrote to Meynell. 'The damp is so deep, the hurricanes so cold! I should not complain of such a little thing as lack of exercise, seeing

what others are suffering, but for your sake and the children's I think I ought not to encourage and cultivate gout, rheumatism and arthritis. Ours have indeed been happy years, my most Dear, and I like to continue them by moderate care.'[23]

A strange interlude was a luncheon in London. 'Your father and I lunched with Mary Barwell at an altered Claridges. No men in livery and powder and fairly bad luncheon. I wonder if those will have been the very last powdered footmen in London for ever.'[24]

In 1917 were published *Hearts of Controversy*, a book of essays, *A Father of Women and other Poems*, the ten poems from the Romney Street Press, and *Poems of the War*, privately printed by Clement Shorter. Shorter, writing in *The Sphere* on *Hearts of Controversy*, called Mrs Meynell 'one of the finest of living essayists, matchless in the grace of an incommunicable style, restrained, keenly analytical'. In one of the essays she attacked Swinburne, and Shorter commented on this: 'She writes amazingly well, and she has brought the whole of her powerful artillery against Swinburne in words singularly eloquent and forcible. Never was there so telling an indictment of any popular writer, and let it be admitted how much of truth there is in this indictment.' But he went on to qualify his remarks: 'A great critic should never be affected by the personal equation, yet one finds it possible that Swinburne's irrational and ignorant hatred of the Roman Catholic Church has influenced Mrs Meynell. In any case she has avenged her Church upon him with an essay that will be read long after these lines of mine have passed into the oblivion which comes to all journalism.'[25]

J. C. Squire, writing in *Land and Water* on *A Father of Women*, spoke of detached meditation as Bacon wrote of it in *The Advancement of Learning*, and said: 'Mrs Meynell too, after her manner, retires into the immensities of Time and Space and contemplates pain and pleasure, birth and death, as small and transient things: not for perverse amusement or the consciousness of superiority, but for a refuge and a consolation. She has at once an extraordinarily sensitive heart and a perfectly balanced brain: a capacity for an intolerable excess of feeling but a permanent check in the steadiness and sagacity of her thought.'[26] 'I like Squire in *Land and Water* on *A Father of Women*', Mrs Meynell wrote, 'better than *The Times*, better than *The Manchester Guardian*. I think no author has had an appreciation so to the *full* as I have now.'[27]

In a letter to Monica's daughter Mary she wrote: 'Tell your darling mother that my tiny book has had a quite disproportionate reception of *columns* in *The Times*, the *Manchester Guardian* and *Land and Water*. I forgot to tell her. Long ago, when she had passed an excellent examination in the University Extension, she once wrote to me (she was very young) that she felt *exillerated* . . . I feel exillerated at having reviews that will sell my book.'[28]

But to Sebastian she wrote: 'Better than my excellent reviews I have loved a word from Chesterton in the *Illustrated*.'[29]

Meanwhile there were family worries. In August 1916 Francis had received his calling-up papers, and duly appeared before a local tribunal to declare himself a conscientious objector. He was offered non-combatant service in the R.A.M.C., but insisted that he would not accept any service remotely connected with the war. He appealed against the local tribunal, and was heard a month later by a national one. Again he was told that he could be exempted on conscientious grounds from *combatant* service only, and in January 1917 he was arrested.[30] Writing to Sebastian to thank him for some kindness to Wilfrid, Alice Meynell said: 'Your considerateness especially touches your father because he is hurt by Francis involving his family in his conscientiousness. Your father had asked him not to do so. A paragraph is in all the papers today naming his case as that of my son, and I think I shall have to write to *The Times* a line, disclaiming. I honour Francis for his conscience, but he ought to consider his father's feelings in regard to publicity . . . He is at Whitehall, and to be taken to Hounslow – what prison I don't know. He says he is very happy.'[31]

'There are two months of absolute *solitary* confinement without any letters to or fro', she wrote in another letter. 'A book is allowed besides a Testament but you cannot choose it. It is dumped on you – generally a novel of Miss Braddon's. That is only part of the time. And altogether it is a hard experience. And a man undergoes it because he is intensely convinced that we ought to have allowed Belgium to be sacked, murdered, tortured and ruined. There is nothing more idiotic than a conscience *can* be.'[32]

Francis at once started a hunger strike, not even taking water, but concealing his fast from the prison authorities until he was too weak to be forcibly fed, and collapsed. After three weeks in prison he was discharged as 'unlikely to become an efficient soldier'.[33]

Francis was uncertain of the reception he would get from his parents. His mother wrote to Olivia:

I confess I have been unhappy about Francis. But when he decided to come, and sent Everard to me to see how he would be received, I did not hesitate, and he is on the old terms, unchanged. But I don't at all allow that we are at 'liberty' to think what we happen to choose as to right and wrong.

The Prior here* sent a message to Francis (quite on his own impulse) congratulating him on his courage in following what he believed to be right. I cannot understand this. He might believe swindling or murder to be right.

I may say that I hold the administration of morals to be of such vital importance that for its sake I accepted, and now accept, dogma in matters of faith – to the last letter.[34]

* The Prior of the Premonstratensian canons at Storrington.

In another letter on the same subject she said:

To make my preachment clearer; Right and Wrong (Morals) are the most important, or the only important, things we ever know or can know. Everything depends on them. Christian morality is infinitely the greatest of moralities. This we know by our own sense and intellect, without other guidance. The Church *administers* that morality, as no sect does or can, by means of moral theology. And there you are. The world is far from living up to that ideal, but it is the only ideal worth living up to.[35]

So the relationship with Francis was restored; but public opinion was strong and had to be considered, particularly for the sake of Sebastian, who was unable, because of his nervous illness, to serve in the armed forces. 'How much I wish', Mrs Meynell wrote, 'that Francis and Hilda could come this summer. But I see that it is inadvisable. There is so much excitement of feeling here about exemptions and the Tribunes, which are accused of partiality. On that account poor Bastian is looked at with suspicion in public. I greatly fear that Fulton may have to give his reasons for exempting him publicly. But the coming, in motors, of a younger brother would really cause talk at the least and it would be bad for Bastian who is feeling the situation, as it is, so much that he does not, for the moment, go to Church.'[36]

There was anxiety, now, for Everard. He had closed down his shop and joined the Artists' Rifles. 'Everard', his mother told Sebastian, 'looking most unlike anything in the world, bearded and in khaki, has to go before his tribunal on Thursday. Meantime he is attending operations and giving baths to the slightly wounded. I walked after him a little way to see him salute in Oxford Street.'[37] And to Wilfrid Meynell she wrote: 'I shall be very anxious for news of Everard, whether he passed that examination. And yet whatever would detain him is what would make me happy! I know he is anxious to pass, but I don't know the sequel of it.'[38] She was at Greatham in that summer of 1917:

It's hot here because of the magnificent sun. Do you remember our Wigonholt summer, when the commons were catching fire? It is not so hot as *that* for that is the greatest heat I have known out of Italy.

If you had seen dearest Dimpling laden with gooseberries, flowers, butter, children, cream, cabbages, eggs, a toad, a newt, caterpillars and responsibility, you would have hoped, as I did, that some of the most enormous flowers would be left behind somewhere. The toad, the newt and some of the caterpillars did, to my relief, escape as they were setting out. Those dear infants were indeed happy. Christian told me that though school was nice it was not so nice as this.

I have been digging like anything. I think we may have to transfer our strawberry bed where it can have real care, like the vegetables. The alder-roots go right under the strawberry roots, like our tunnels under the German tunnels at Messines, so that I cannot hope to extirpate them.[39]

The letters travelled to and fro between London and Greatham, for there were usually some members of the family at each place for at least part of the week. Alice, in London, related how she had been perplexed by an unexpected visitor:

> Yesterday there were a good many random visitors, among them Mr Lessore. I received him beautifully, talking to him cordially, extra cordially in case he should be a long-lost friend. Oh, I did cudgel my brains. As he went out and spoke of his sculpture it flashed across me. No one guessed I didn't know who the deuce he was.[40]

The aftermath of some other callers took a good deal of sorting out.

> The drawing-room is in a state of chaos quite indescribable since the *Dublin Review** is edited on the writing table, the piano and the chairs and the floor and in the fender. I have no ink . . .
> But it is a dreadful scene of umbrellas. Mrs Spicer's — a very special one — has been taken, probably by Mrs Craies, and Ida Taylor's by Viola or Dimpling. I went to Euterpe's [Mrs Craies'] and hunted up all hers and found one with a name and address engraved on the silver band. Tiny engraving, and we had up the porter and the housekeeper but they could not read it, and at last, with glasses, I managed it, and the name was Craies.
> The lack of ink or a corner of a writing table to answer the letters about the umbrellas is maddening . . .
> Dick Tobin had written to me for an autograph for a friend, and in answering I told him his President was wrong to treat the war as though it were a quarrel on equal terms, whereas it was justice and a kept word on one side and perjury, treachery, murder and theft on the other.[41]

At Greatham Mrs Meynell had to contend with three unexpected visitors.

> Today I had asked the village school marm to luncheon, and the party was increased by the arrival of Wilfrid Blunt, Miss Carleton and Lady Margaret Sackville.** Happily there was enough to eat and all went well. Lady Margaret has written great things about some work of mine, but I know little of hers. Happily your father has all her books, and she autographed them. She is very pretty. The schoolmistress had the time of her life.[42]

Remembering poor Francis Thompson's description, years ago, of the Palace Court food as 'shocking', one wonders if the guests were as convinced as their hostess that 'there was enough to eat'.

Mrs Meynell's birthday — her seventieth — found her at Greatham, and she answered her husband's letter of loving good wishes:

---

* An influential theological and literary quarterly, founded by Cardinal Wiseman, but published in London by the firm of Burns and Oates. It continued in publication down to the 1950s.

** The Lady Margaret Sackville: 1881-1963. Youngest daughter of the 7th Earl de la Warr. A famous beauty, and a prolific poet of considerable merit, her last published work being *Quatrains and Other Poems* (Llandeilo, 1960).

My darling Wilfrid,

My warmest loving thanks for your precious letter. Yes, I *am* a thanksgiver, and our union and your goodness are the subject of my gratitude.

Bastian's powder evidently worked well. At present he *is* better. He says so and has all the signs of it. We are still advising bed.

What do you think of Von Knelmann's admission that there is no obstacle to peace except Alsace Lorraine? That implies the restoration of Belgium. Are our hearts to be broken for the sake of the covetousness of France? How much I feared when that wretched Edward made his Entente, little knowing even then what I *had* to fear.[43]

Now, with two homes, things were even more likely than of old to get mislaid or forgotten about. 'If you will look in my Where is it? book', Mrs Meynell wrote to her husband, '(shabby, red, in my room) without dropping out a single paper, you will find, I think, either Tollast's address or his married son's at Putney.'[44] And to Olivia, who was at Granville Place, she wrote from Greatham: 'I have just remembered my gold thimble. If you did not return it to me, all right. Otherwise – that is, if you did give it back – please look in the left-hand small drawer of my looking glass to see that it is safe. I prize it because Coventry Patmore gave it to me before he thought much of my authorship.'[45]

The entry of America into the war was for her, even more than for most people, a matter for rejoicing, since she loved the New World and had so many friends there. She sent a cable to the Tobins which arrived as 'Hurry delicate cluster victories' and puzzled all except Agnes, who understood it as a quotation from Walt Whitman: 'Hurrah! for the delicate cluster victorious!'[46]

From her many American readers there came in the post, from time to time, expressions of their admiration. She reported to Wilfrid Meynell:

An ecstatic letter from a young American admirer of 'Superfluous Kings' who ends by wishing me a happy and successful career!

I am giving my days, not to careers but to making beautiful patches on your under-garments. You will find several restored to use and vigour.[47]

In February 1918, when staying at Clifton with Olivia and Murray Sowerby, Mrs Meynell had an illness which caused some alarm to her family. She was in danger for several days, but then began to recover. Olivia telegraphed daily to her father. It brought to them all an awareness of how little reserve of strength she had, and some anxiety about her was to remain with them always from now on.

From London, after her return there, she wrote to her half-sister, Fanny, in Italy:

Monica is gone to Clifton, out of the reach of raids, because her eldest girl has grown nervous. Dimpling remains in town for the present, but I think she, too, will take her little ones into a safer place. The responsibility for children makes all the difference. Otherwise I confess there is an excitement in the raids that is not without pleasure. I have been through a couple of them. This is not exactly courage on my part, for under this house is a fine cellar of masonry and cement . . .

Everard is still in camp; he is a 'gunnery instructor' to the flying corps. Bastian is exempt for health and Francis still 'conscientiously objecting' but not yet a second time in prison.[48]

In July 1918, writing again to Fanny, she said:

On this heavenly Sunday afternoon here in Sussex, we can hear the guns in France. Most people here think the War is within sight of the end, but I cannot see the process of peacemaking.

Lobbie and her two lovely children are here, and Madeline and her three, and Monica and her two arrive next week for the holidays. Everard's family remains in town, so as to be in touch with him in his camp. He poor fellow, is less unhappy under the perpetual hard work and the insults. But the separation from his adored wife and children is as hard as ever.[49]

But the war was indeed nearing its end. It was, Viola Meynell tells us, in the train between Greatham and London that the news of the armistice reached Mrs Meynell, 'conveyed by the wild hooting of the engines'.[50]

CHAPTER 24

MRS MEYNELL accepted now that she was physically frail, and as much as that she minded the fact that she was growing older in appearance. She wrote to Wilfrid: 'I have had a better head yesterday and to-day. But I am not strong and such a scarecrow of thin-ness that I have bought a large hat-shape (12/9) to shade my face. As you like brims, you will not be sorry to see me in it.'[1]

But she was working steadily. Her accounts for 1919 show payments for two poems in the *Dublin Review* and one in *The Sphere*, prose articles in the *Observer* (a review of Binyon's poems), the *Atlantic Monthly* and the *London Mercury*, editorial work on the *Dublin Review*, and royalties on her books, the whole amounting to £110.11s.7d.[2]

Financial matters were easier now for the Meynells with all the children grown up; but it was their joy to help those children whenever help was needed. Mrs Meynell wrote to her husband after hearing from him of some less favourable prospects at Burns and Oates.

My darling Wilfrid,
   I am grieved, though not depressed, by your bad B. and O. news. That you should be worried, and the children with children less helped by you in future, must be a sorrow to me, but even of such precious things as our ability to suc-cour these children we must say 'Fate may take them but she shall not snatch them by violence from us.'
   I think Bassie's article the best I have seen of the present *Dublin*. It is in places over my head, of course, but even in these interesting. He can write.[3]

Francis's enthusiastic espousal of the cause of the Russian revolu-tionaries puzzled and distressed her. She wrote to Wilfrid:

Francis writes to ask me to write a George Eliot centenary article for the *Herald*.* I cannot and I am replying 'I would not write for any white paper that seemed to excuse, and was at any rate so prejudicial as to disbelieve, *attested* acts of cruelty on the White side.' This means, of course, that I cannot write for a 'red' paper that does the same, *mutatis mutandis*.[4]

Later she wrote:

Francis has been here two evenings . . . He has fully and frankly explained himself to us, especially as regards Bolshevism proper, as opposed to the detestable Red Bolshevism. I understand, after a hard scolding from Viola and Lobbie, and a quieter explanation from him, his position better. I would even

* The *Daily Herald*, a Socialist newspaper.

write his George Eliot article, only I suppose you would not wish it. Anonymous? Let me know.[5]

Francis now became editor of *The Communist*, and undertook to smuggle diamonds from Europe which were sent by the Communists to subsidise the *Daily Herald*. He brought the diamonds on several trips and handed them over to the Russian Trade Delegation in London, but their existence was discovered and the manner of their arrival revealed. There was a burst of publicity, and Francis resigned from the *Daily Herald* since he had acted without the knowledge of George Lansbury, who was its editor.[6] His mother wrote to Olivia:

I have a very dear and loving letter from Francie. I trust his conscience in all the larger questions. It was the jaunty brag and the ignoble action of that jewel incident that seemed to me degrading. I think it is worse than degrading to have dealings with the Soviet Government. But that is a matter for him and his convictions.[7]

She went on in this letter to speak of a discussion between herself and Olivia regarding the Old Testament. 'Darling, as to the "divine" teachings of the Genesis allegory, I cannot withdraw the word. I have to remember that all the morality worth having – the morality that led on to Christianity – had its origin in that parable.'[8]

Francis now again struck the headlines because J. H. Thomas* sued him for libel in his capacity as editor of *The Communist*; he lost the case and was ordered to pay damages of £2000, which meant that he was bankrupt. Lady De La Warr and Miss Dodge, who were anxious not to attract publicity themselves as past subsidisers of the *Daily Herald*, paid the damages for him.

These events must have been specially painful for Alice Meynell, for she, who loved so deeply all her children, had perhaps a special tenderness for this youngest son. Years before, when he was at school, she had written to him:

When you last wrote you had not been well, and I very much want to know about this – what it was, and whether you are strong again. Do tell me everything. Darling, I count upon your full confidence, not only now but later. I hope to know every trouble you may have, spiritual, mental or bodily.

There has always been a great sympathy – I will call it a friendship between us, and I expect even more than the confidence between ordinary sons and mothers.[9]

And in another early letter:

My beloved last Child, many will love you but none more than does your

---

* 'Jimmy' Thomas, the 'Railwaymen's M.P.'; later a Cabinet Minister, and Chancellor of the Exchequer. His political career was ended through his inadvertent disclosure of 'Budget secrets'.

mother to whom you have never, since your tumultuous childhood, brought any grief.[10]

She valued his criticisms of her work, and in an undated letter she wrote:

My darling Francis,

Your letter gave me great joy and happiness, more than you know and more than I can tell. I seem to have come into nearer relation with my child and critic and reader through these late songs of mine.[11]

In these last years of her life Alice Meynell did not go about much, and the great social and literary gatherings of London seldom saw her. Her family, her work, her letters, absorbed her. At Greatham she still worked in the garden, but with less vigour. 'The whole company of dandelions is seeding by many thousands', she wrote in the summer of 1919, 'and I give up the fight. I think a whole lawn of them would be the most beautiful thing in the world – though not exactly a lawn. It is a word my Tennyson loved, and I don't.'[12]

Visits to the Sowerbys at Clifton accounted for most of her infrequent absences from the two homes, since the rest of the family were all to be seen constantly either in London or at Greatham. In the course of these visits she made friends with Mr Aubone Hare, who was a great admirer of her writing, and with whom she had long talks on literature and philosophy. The one was more pleasure to her than the other, for she had a curious conviction that her mind was incapable of grasping the profundities of philosophy. 'Mr Hare got me out of my depth with philosophy. I really have no intellect for it. If I seem to have in my work, it is only philosophers who think so. *I* don't.'[13] 'Last night we dined with the Hares. Mr Hare tried to make me understand Relativity. But as you want, for that, metaphysics *and* mathematics, and I am incapable of both, it was rather a monologue.'[14] 'I find Einstein exciting though unintelligible. Mr Hare says it is the crushing blow to materialism, and makes man centric as he was before Galileo. How, how, I ask with my incapable mind.'[15] 'Albert Cock writes in great mystic or philosophic ecstasies with my Times verses and other things. I am no philosopher and no mystic.'[16] 'Two things I have not touched and I am sorry for it. All my life I have neglected philosophy and mathematics.'[17]

To Albert Cock she wrote:

You have never realised how incapable I am of philosophy. I really cannot answer your questions. I can only say that when I find a thought worthy of poetry I immediately give thanks for it, and also for such expression as I may have achieved. But this is not at all subtle and not very conscious. I'm afraid that I don't refer (as you do) all beauty to the 'First and only Fair'. I merely refer what I may either write or read to the relative beauty of literature. A

Jesuit long ago told me that I alighted and settled on mere 'Participations'. No doubt I disappoint you.[18]

Her work was a frequent topic in her letters of this time; she was preparing a book of her essays for the Oxford University Press, doing some sub-editorial work for the *Dublin Review*, and writing poetry. 'To Antiquity' and 'Reflexions' were printed in the *London Mercury* in 1920, and 'To "A Certain Rich Man" ' in the *Dublin Review*. To Olivia she wrote: 'I am disappointed to find that no one here *begins* to understand my Mercury poem* – the antithesis between the human, *local*, new single human poet and the birds who are *general*, all over the world and in all times. I should have thought nothing was plainer or more direct.' And to Viola she wrote: 'If no one ever cares for "Reflexions" it is written. And it has succeeded in *singing* the highest thought of intellectual passion and imagination of which I am capable.'[19]

Entries in a notebook of that time consist of possible ideas for poems or essays, theories that interested her, incidents that amused her. Of the latter variety was a paragraph that tells how she recounted to Padraic Colum an alleged remark of Max Beerbohm: 'When I awake in the middle of the night it is such a comfort to think that Mrs Humphrey Ward is not working.' Colum thought for a time and then said: 'I suppose they were staying at the same country house.' 'I had long thought', Mrs Meynell commented, 'that the Irish had no sense of humour. Nor have they.'[20]

Other notebook entries were concerned with that discipline which she held to be indispensable both in life and literature. 'All true poets love the bonds of prosody and, in lyrics, of rhythm; because all true poets have something of the wild at heart that looks for bonds. But those who have nothing to control, nothing to hold, are they who call for liberty. No quantity, no stress, no rhyme, no numbers.'[21] Then, quoting Matthew Arnold who said: 'The strongest part of our religion today is the unconscious poetry . . . Poetry is able to interpret life for us, to console us, to sustain us,' Mrs Meynell wrote: 'Interpretation because we are puzzled, sustentation because we are feeble, consolation because we are dismal? Not guidance, not discipline, not a rule of conduct, not consequences, not retribution, not pardon? No commands in the face of moral good, no prohibition in the face of moral evil? Does man need none of these?'[22]

Discussing politics in a letter to Olivia, she reiterated this theory. 'As far as I know Bolshevism, it is heretical in the practice of right and wrong. I don't at all allow that we have "liberty" to think what we happen to choose as right and wrong.'[23]

* 'The Poet to the Birds'.

In youth she had been fervently interested in politics; later she had become less so; but she had always been, though without great enthusiasm, a socialist. Many years before, she had written:

Solitude in art is like the solitude of the conscience – inviolable. While this is so, and while so much isolation implies a liberty equally inviolable – an inner and a secret liberty – I do not understand why there is so much fear of outward control. Individualistic as is my Faith in regard to thought and Art, I am politically rather inclined towards Socialism than towards Individualism. I do not love political liberty much. The State is welcome to order my affairs far more closely than it has ever done yet, for the good of the majority, and especially for the good of the unfortunate. Men are separated from one another by an unalterable boundary of personality; let them none the less live in order, and in relation to one another; that relation is civilization and political vitality.[24]

Now, in another letter to Olivia, she wrote:

Unfortunately I don't *like* the international politics of Labour. It seems to have solidarity with the execrable bolshevism of Russia. As to its home programme, I hear much of wages but nothing of drink and the social evil. I think Coalition is more promising on home questions. It is not that I care for Lloyd George. I do think him rather a dodger. So I am uncertain . . . I am sorry to differ from you, my Lobbie, but Labour, with its peculiar group tyrannies, is the one thing I cannot vote for.[25]

A separation that brought great anxiety as well as its own inherent sadness was caused by the discovery in 1921 that Everard, who had been unwell for some time, was suffering from tuberculosis. He was ordered by his doctors to go to America, and he left England with his wife and children in July. In September, after a visit from some American friends, Alice Meynell wrote to him:

Now these two would really do a great deal to serve me, and they promise me all kinds of things if I should go to America. I need hardly say that the desire to see you, and to belie the fear I had, when you left Greatham that my weak health and other disabilities might make our reunion very uncertain, has had a great part in my desire to accept an invitation to give a lecturing tour. Your father thinks the idea is mad. But I may be heard exercising my voice in the garden. It is as strong as ever. I will let you know what is finally decided. When the agents first asked me, I thought I was too old and ill, and now they are asking me again I don't think so – which I suppose proves that I *am*.[26]

A few weeks later she wrote sadly: 'I have today at last decided against my dear lecture tour and visit to you. I am really not well enough for unusual exertion. (Nothing to be alarmed at.)'[27]

The new book of essays was published by the Oxford University Press under the title *The Second Person Singular*. Shortly before its appearance she told Everard: 'My little book is in the printers' hands at last. I have made many changes. When Viola tells me that an essay is confused or obscure, I know it *is*. Ten of the twenty essays, as they stand, are up to my little high-water mark, and the other ten are not contemptible second-class.'[28]

Besides the essay of the title there were studies of Patmore, Meredith, Joanna Baillie, Gibbon, and Robert Greene; 'Waterfalls' and 'Superfluous Kings' were also in this volume. It was well received; but Alice Meynell was not much concerned with what the critics had to say. Perhaps the greatest happiness the book brought her was that of being able, in the following summer, to send a cheque to the beloved sick son in America. 'I enclose a cheque for £300 with my great love. This includes the whole earnings of *Second Person Singular* so far – and £75 that I am to receive for my Child's Anthology by Christmas. Dearest, I wish my love could have a richer expression.'[29]

In that year Mrs Meynell made a last visit to Ireland to stay with her sister, Lady Butler. The day after her arrival she wrote to Wilfrid: 'It is charming to be here and the day is breathless. If only yesterday had been! Shall I draw a veil? It was worse than the Atlantic or anything within my experience. I was borne half lifeless to the train, a figure of fun.'[30]

The scattering of the family meant that the young population in the two houses was reduced not only by their own absence but by that of their friends. Nevertheless there were still visitors of every generation who found in Mrs Meynell the graciousness, kindness, and understanding that she had always extended to people of every age. Sylvia Lynd remembers her at that time as a 'faded, remote, slowly-speaking woman, with her sweetness, keenness and unexpected humour';[31] and J. C. Squire wrote of her in the *London Mercury*:

There, in her London flat or in the ample library-living-room of her country cottage, she would sit in her corner; a woman with unwhitened hair, very upright and calm. Her skin was withered with age, but her eyes were large and lustrous; at seventy she still gave an impression of youth and beauty. She was usually in black, her only little coquetry a velvet ribbon around her neck. She sat quiet, Roman dignity in her mien, vivacity, feeling, mockery, sympathy in her eyes; a saint and a sibyl smoking a cigarette: with a young girl's sensitiveness, an old woman's insight, a man's strength . . . She detested vulgarity and cruelty; she excused ignorance. At the back of all her judgements, invariably convincing, was a mind not merely exquisitely discriminating but uninterruptedly aware of the unseen behind the seen. She, a religious ascetic, practised 'art for art's sake' as ruthlessly as any despairing hedonist of them all; and, naturally fastidious, she had no tinge of niceness or superiority. She was proud to the world but humble before goodness; she enjoyed small things but eternity was behind them all. I have never known anyone so ageless. Youth, maturity and fullness of years were here strangely at one. At her death nothing of young freshness or wonder had gone from her. In her home, humourously intent upon the succession of family cares and gossip, she was yet the seer always. To be with her was to be at ease in the presence of a great lady. Let the talk be what it might, she was never withdrawn or indifferent; but behind the gayest of her occasions there was a quietness of mood that gave precision and authority to everything she said . . .[32]

That she possessed in full measure that indefinable thing called charm, and that it was felt by people of all ages, is shown again and again in letters that she received. Her capacity to inspire devotion in those who knew her was intensely strong all her life. Viola Meynell quotes a letter which was written by a young friend, Ann Sedgwick, after a visit to Greatham.

My dearest Mrs Meynell,
    In this letter I can only send you my love. I am unable to express or think of anything else, except perhaps the individual parts of which it is composed. It was so perfect to be with you; I can never quite recover from the wonder of coming into a room and finding you there. Do you remember how Donald Goring wrote to Monica telling her how perfectly he had enjoyed his time there, and describing as an instance of it one day when he and some others were gathered on the grass outside the library door, and suddenly you came out and said 'Come along in, all of you'? We laughed a little when it was read out, but to Donald that was his climax; and it is that sense of climax which I feel, though neither he nor I are able to express it. But it is always connected with you.
    I can envy no one. Only myself at Greatham is inexpressibly envied by myself elsewhere.[33]

Early in 1922, while staying with the Sowerbys at Flax Bourton, where they now lived, she again had some heart trouble. 'I whistled before I was out of the wood when I said my cold was better', she wrote to Viola. 'It is all back with three recurrences of that trouble which sent your father out in London in the small hours of the morning looking for a doctor's doorplate. But these three together hardly equalled that one.'[34]

On this visit she met Dr Edridge who was going to lecture on her work to Bristol University students. 'I would prefer', she wrote, 'in the case of enthusiasts, to remain unseen, for fear they should say (mentally) "Oh" – or words to that effect.'[35]

In March Viola was married to John Dallyn, a neighbour at Greatham. She, the last of the daughters to marry, was so often with her mother that there were not a great many letters between them in the last years. But those that there are speak again and again of the mother's tenderness to this child, as to all her children.

My darling, [*she wrote for a birthday*]
    What happy returns I wish you, my Treasure! What gifts I should like to pile on you, but they would be terrestrial and commonplace, because you have

received what is important from God and Nature. Grace, and Literature, and I think probably Art. (And beauty and charm in the lower world.) Don't think I am writing inordinately. I believe that to know and acknowledge one's gifts makes for humility and not for vanity, still less for pride.[36]

She was ill at the time and wrote the letter when lying in bed. The handwriting was as exquisite as always, but she felt that it was not up to her high standard, and put at the end: 'I am writing vilely, on my back. Burn this as I care so much about handwriting.'[37]

In a letter to Mother St Ignatius Mrs Meynell wrote; 'Yes, Viola looks young but she is curiously wise, wiser than her books seem to represent her, written as they are in that now prevalent impartial mood that commits the writer to nothing. But she has committed herself to great principles in life and she is steadfast. A more loving and self-forgetting daughter no woman ever had.'[38]

That spring, the last of her life, Alice Meynell was busy in compiling an anthology for children which had been commissioned by Collins. She was also planning, when that was finished, to work on another, to be called *Escape*, which would contain the rarest jewels of poetry, all those that expressed the 'wildness' that was for her an integral part of all great poetry. And the flow of her own verse increased. 'It is a joy', she wrote to Viola, 'that you and Francis and Green-Armytage and Dr Edridge care for my last three poems . . . Francis wired "Marvellous poems the best of your best" . . . I tell you this because I want you to share my pleasure, or rather my consolations which I need. And "The Wind" will be in the June *Mercury* I suppose. Francis thinks these late things are high water mark (*my* h.w.m.), so does Everard, which is a comfort.'[39]

In the *London Mercury* for July, August, and September, appeared 'Thetis', 'To the Mother of Christ', 'Prometheus', 'Surmise', 'The Laws of Verse', 'Everlasting Farewells', 'The Voice of a Bird', 'To Winter Trees', 'The Winged Victory', 'The Marriage of True Minds' and 'By the Threshing Machine'. 'Christmas Night', and 'The October Redbreast' were printed in the *Observer* in December 1921 and October 1922.

This creative fervour at the end of her life, this singing of the swan, brought her, seemingly, more happiness than she had ever had from her work before; it was one of her 'consolations which I need'. There were sorrows, regrets, anxieties to which she was rendered especially vulnerable by her frailness, and which she endured, for the most part, in silence, as she had done all her life. To Mother St Ignatius she confided the things that troubled her spirit. A few years before, she had spoken of her grief at having lived what she thought of as a selfish life, and the nun had answered her: 'You could not make me believe you are selfish – or that your life has been selfish as you say. I don't quite

see how you could help feeling vain – you couldn't be so feminine and
so gifted without knowing your own power. What I know is that you
have been kindness itself to many – of whom I am one – and that is
what matters more than all gifts.'[40]

In answer to a letter in which Mrs Meynell had asked for guidance,
Mother St Ignatius said: 'It is the really right and true thing to believe
all that the Church teaches (which includes the fact that God is love)
and leave it alone – We are neither more loving nor more merciful than
God – that is certain. But do formally make your inclusive act of faith
and don't be analytic . . . You are wise and know deep things because
you have lived . . . It took me so long to learn to live.'[41]

Now Alice Meynell told her: 'All my troubles are little, old, foolish,
trivial, as they always were – the troubles of my spiritual life, I mean.
But as to sorrow, my failure of love to those that loved me can never be
cancelled or undone. So I never fail in a provision of grief for any night
of my life.'[42]

Her nights in these last years were rendered painful by being often
almost unblessed by sleep. 'The human mind', she had once written,
'has in the hours proper to sleep (whether it wakes or sleeps in them) a
different temper; and the undefended, unshielded, and helpless heart of
terror, sorrow, anger, or tenderness of the sleeper's dreams has little
help when the dreamer wakes, if it is night.'[43]

Now she addressed her plea 'To Sleep':

> Dear fool, be true to me!
> I know the poets speak thee fair, and I
>   Hail thee uncivilly.
> Oh, but I call with a more urgent cry!
>
>   I do not prize thee less,
> I need thee more, that thou dost love to teach –
>   Father of foolishness –
> The imbecile dreams clear out of wisdom's reach.
>
> Come and release me; bring
> My irresponsible mind; come in thy hours;
>   Draw from my soul the sting
> Of wit that trembles, consciousness that cowers.
>
> For if night comes without thee
> She is more cruel than day. But thou, fulfil
>   Thy work, thy gifts about thee –
> Liberty, liberty, from this weight of will.

· My day-mind can endure
Upright, in hope, all it must undergo.
   But oh, afraid, unsure,
My night-mind waking lies too low, too low.

   Dear fool, be true to me!
The night is thine, man yields it, it beseems
   Thy ironic dignity.
Make me all night the innocent fool that dreams.

In September Wilfrid Meynell went on a short visit to Venice and Ragusa. He wrote from Venice to his wife: 'Your poems are my atmosphere here. I find myself quoting them to myself at every corner. The line "Bending these knees, and feeble knees, I pray" reconciles me to the feebleness of mine. What an achievement!'

Alice Meynell replied: 'I was very glad of your letter this morning, albeit written in pale pencil. Is there no inchiostro, no calamazio, anywhere? If you knew the trouble when I have a packet of letters to go through, I have in decyphering your handwriting, you wouldn't do it.'

The pale pencil was not used again. 'My darling Wilfrid,' she wrote in her next letter, 'Your lovely letter has just come. I could read it – it was written in ink!'[44]

Looking forward joyously to the return of the traveller, she wrote:

My darling Wilfrid,
Two dreary days and then your coming! My darling Dimpling and her three left early this morning. She had hoped to see you all here. I can never tell you what she has been to me. And as to finances, my 'keep' with the quarts of milk and the eggs every day (a little more than a quart of the former and two of the latter) and the Bovril and the Ovaltine is something inordinate! She is always working like a horse, and she looks worn. She is trying to save up so as to treat herself to a charwoman.[45]

Alice Meynell recognised her failing strength and wrote down her wishes concerning her still unpublished poetry. Fearing to distress him, she forbore to speak of this to Meynell, but gave her instructions to Albert Cock.

In London, early in October, she became so ill as to make hope of her recovery impossible. Many years before, she had written, in 'A Point of Biography', of Nature's reticence concerning the death of wild things, and had pleaded that biographers should 'take the hint of Nature'.

Even more wanton [*she wrote*] than the disclosure of a death is that of a mortal illness. If the man had recovered, his illness would have been rightly his own secret. But because he did not recover it is assumed to be news for the first comer. Which of us would suffer the details of any physical suffering, over and done in our own lives, to be displayed and described? This is not a confidence we have a mind to make; and no one is authorized to ask for attention or pity on our behalf. The story of pain ought not to be told of us, seeing that by us it would assuredly not be told.

Let it, then, suffice to say that after seven weeks of illness she died at dawn on 27th November, 1922.

In the year following her death Mother St Ignatius wrote to Wilfrid Meynell: '. . . She grows more and more vivid to me as time goes on. As I see her now, she was the most beautiful and interesting and gifted personality ever found in or out of a book. As if God had given her all he could because of her strange humility. I understand why she went through the dark night of the soul in which I found her. It was "the last rub that polishes the mirror" '.[46]

Last Poems was published in 1923. In one of them she spoke her farewell, she, the poet whose song was soon to cease, addressing the birds whose song continues while the world endures:

THE POET TO THE BIRDS

You bid me hold my peace,
    Or so I think, you birds; you'll not forgive
My kill-joy song that makes the wild song cease,
    Silent or fugitive.

Yon thrush stopt in mid-phrase
    At my mere footfall; and a longer note
Took wing and fled afield, and went its ways
    Within the blackbird's throat.

Hereditary song,
    Illyrian lark and Paduan nightingale,
Is yours, unchangeable the ages long;
    Assyria heard your tale;

Therefore you do not die.
    But single, local, lonely, mortal, new,
Unlike, and thus like all my race, am I
    Preluding my adieu.

My human song must be
    My human thought. Be patient till 'tis done.
I shall not hold my little peace; for me
    There is no peace but one.

SELECT BIBLIOGRAPHY
NOTES
INDEX

SELECT BIBLIOGRAPHY

This does not give the many editions, some of them privately printed, of Alice Meynell's work, but only the main collections of her prose and poetry, together with the books that I have read while doing my research on her life.

A. C. Thompson. *Preludes* (Henry S. King, 1875)

Alice Meynell. *Essays* (Burns & Oates, 1914)

Alice Meynell. *Poems* (Burns, Oates & Washbourne, 1923)

Alice Meynell. *Prose & Poetry* (Jonathan Cape, 1947). Introduction by V. Sackville-West

Viola Meynell. *Alice Meynell – A Memoir* (Jonathan Cape, 1929) (referred to in notes as V.M. *Memoir*)

Viola Meynell. *Francis Thompson & Wilfrid Meynell* (Hollis & Carter, 1952)

Alice Meynell Centenary Exhibition Catalogue. National Book League 1947

Alice Meynell Centenary Tribute edited by Terence L. Connolly, S.J. (Bruce Humphries Inc. Boston 1947)

Anne Kimball Tuell. *Mrs Meynell & her Literary Generation* (E. P. Dutton and Co. New York. 1925)

*   *   *

Mrs. Belloc Lowndes. *The Merry Wives of Westminster* (Macmillan 1946)

Wilfrid Scawen Blunt. *My Diaries* (Martin Secker 1932)

Phyllis Bottome. *The Challenge* (Faber & Faber 1952)

Osbert Burdett. *The Idea of Coventry Patmore* (Humphrey Milford 1921)

Lady Butler. *Autobiography* (Constable 1922)

G. K. Chesterton. *Autobiography* (Hutchinson 1936)

Richard Le Gallienne. *The Romantic 90s* (Putnam 1926)

Major Fitzroy Gardner. *More Reminiscences of an Old Bohemian* (Hutchinson 1926)

Edmund Gosse. *Coventry Patmore* (Hodder & Stoughton, 1905)

Philip Hughes. *History of the Catholic Church* (Burns & Oates 1939)

E. V. Lucas. *Reading, Writing & Remembering* (Methuen 1932)

Everard Meynell. *The Life of Francis Thompson* (Burns & Oates 1913)

Francis Meynell *My Lives* (Bodley Head 1971)

David Paroissien. *Dickens Studies Annual*, vol. 2. (South Illinois University Press 1972)

Derek Patmore. *The Life & Times of Coventry Patmore* (Constable 1949)

Siegfried Sassoon. *George Meredith* (Kennikat Press 1969)

John Evangelist Walsh. *Strange Harp, Strange Symphony* (W. H. Allen 1969)

John Evangelist Walsh. *The Letters of Francis Thompson* (Hawthorn Books Inc. New York 1969)

Maisie Ward. *Gilbert Keith Chesterton* (Sheed & Ward 1944)

NOTES

As the research for this book was started a long time ago when the many papers relating to Alice Meynell's life were in the care of her daughters who have since died, it is possible that some of the letters etc. that I saw at Greatham were subsequently dispersed. The sources given were accurate at that time, and I have brought them up to date to the best of my knowledge.

The following abbreviations are used throughout:

Alice Meynell: *A Memoir* by Viola Meynell (Jonathan Cape, 1929): V.M. *Memoir*
Pall Mall Gazette: P.M.G.

Introduction
1 *Sunday Times*, 18 January, 1953
2 *Dublin Review*, 1923
3 *Daily News* 26 February, 1923
4 *The Child of Subsiding Tumult* in *P.M.G.* 6 July, 1898
5 Ms letter from Mother Ignatius to Wilfrid Meynell, Greatham
6 Ms letter, Greatham
7 V.M. *Memoir*

Chapter 1
1 V.M. *Memoir*
2 *Dickens Studies Annual* vol. 2 by David Paroissien
3 Ibid
4 V.M. *Memoir*
5 Ibid
6 Ibid
7 *Dickens Studies ut supra*
8 V.M. *Memoir*
9 Ibid
10 Ms letter, Greatham
11 Mrs Thompson's Diary, Greatham

Chapter 2
1 *P.M.G.* article, Dember, 1904
2 Ibid
3 Mrs Thompson's Diary, Greatham
4 Ms letter, Greatham
5 *Scots Observer*, August, 1890
6 *The Child of Tumult*; Ms Greatham, omitted from this essay in *Ceres Runaway* (Constable, 1909)
7 *Daily Chronicle*, 18 September, 1911
8 V.M. *Memoir*

9   Lady Butler's Autobiography
10 Mrs Thompson's Diary, Greatham
11 Ms letter, Greatham
12 'Wares of Autolycus' column, *P.M.G.* date unknown
13 Ibid
14 'Wares of Autolycus' *P.M.G.* 26 January, 1898
15 Ibid
16 'Wares of Autolycus' column, *P.M.G.* 'Near the Ground' 7 Nov. 1898
17 Mrs Thompson's Diary, Greatham
18 Lady Butler's Autobiography
19 Ms letter, Greatham
20 'W. of A' column, *P.M.G.* 'In Process', 27 April, 1898
21 Lady Butler's Autobiography
22 Mrs Thompson's Diary
23 Ms letter, Greatham

Chapter 3
1   *P.M.G.* 'A Palace in a Garden', date unknown
2, 3, 4, 5 Mrs Thompson's Diary, Greatham
6   'W. of A' column, *P.M.G.* 20 April, 1894
7   Ms letter to Miss Anne Kimball Tuell, 14 December, 1921, in Boston
    College Library
8, 9, 10 Mss Greatham
11 Draft essay, 'Little Girls', Greatham
12 Lady Butler's Autobiography
13 Ibid
14 and 15 Mrs Thompson's Diary, Greatham
16 Article in *Youth*, 1918
17 and 18 Mrs Thompson's Diary
19 *P.M.G.* 'The Englishwoman Abroad', date unknown
20 'Wares of Autolycus', *P.M.G.* 20 April, 1894. (Reprinted in *The Children*)
21 Lady Butler's Autobiography
22 Mrs Thompson's Diary, Greatham
23 Meynell papers, Greatham
24 Notebook, Greatham
25 Ibid
26 Lady Butler's Autobiography
27 Ibid
28 'Wares of Autolycus' column, *P.M.G.* 20 April, 1894
29 Lady Butler's Autobiography

Chapter 4
1   Mrs Thompson's Diary, Greatham
2 and 3 Ms letter, Greatham
4 – 11 inclusive Ms diary, Greatham
12 Ms letter, Greatham
13 – 20 inclusive Ms diary, Greatham

Chapter 5

1 Ms notebook formerly the property of Sir Francis Meynell
2 Ibid
3 Ms at Greatham
4 – 8 inclusive Ms letters, Greatham, dated 1866
9 V.M. *Memoir*
10 Ms letter, Greatham
11 Autobiographical letter, property of Ann Kimball Tuell
12 Ms letter, Greatham
13 Ibid
14 V.M. *Memoir*
15 Ms letter to Olivia Sowerby, undated but c. 1917, at Greatham
16 and 17 Ms notebook, Greatham
18 Ms letter to Mrs Chandler Moulton, in the Library of Congress, Washington, D.C.

Chapter 6

1 – 5 inclusive Ms letters, Greatham
6 Information from Father Arthur Kavanagh, S.J.
7 Ms Greatham
8 Article in *P.M.G.* 'A Palace in a Garden' (date unknown)
9, 10, 11, 12 Lady Butler's Autobiography
13 Ms diary, Greatham
14 and 15 Lady Butler's Autobiography
16 'On Keats' Grave'
17 Lady Butler's Autobiography

Chapter 7

1 Ms letter to 'Elma' 15 September, 1873, at Greatham
2 Ibid
3 Ibid
4 Draft letter to Aubrey de Vere, Greatham
5 Draft letter, Greatham
6 Ms notebook, 1873, at Greatham
7 'The Mystical Lyric'; introduction to *The Mount of Vision* by Adeline Cashmore (Chapman & Hall 1910)
8 Ms letter, Greatham
9 Lady Butler's Autobiography
10 and 11 Ms letters, Greatham
12 Ms letter to Miss Anne Kimball Tuell dated 14 December, 1921, in Boston College Library
13 V. M. *Memoir*
14 Ms letter, Greatham
15 Lady Butler's Autobiography
16 Ms letter to Wilfrid Meynell, undated, Greatham
17 Ms letter, Greatham
18 *Francis Thompson and Wilfrid Meynell* by Viola Meynell (Hollis & Carter, 1952)

19 Ms note by Wilfrid Meynell, Greatham
20 Ibid
21 – 26 inclusive Ms letters, Greatham
27 Lady Butler's Autobiography

Chapter 8
 1 – 5 Ms letters, Greatham
 6 Information from Mrs Hardie
 7 *Francis Thompson & Wilfrid Meynell* by Viola Meynell
 8 Ms letter, Greatham
 9 Ms letter to Mrs Alfred Pollard, Greatham
10 *My Lives* by Francis Meynell (Bodley Head, 1971)
11 – 20 inclusive Ms letters, Greatham

Chapter 9
 1 26 January, 1878
 2 Ms diary, Greatham
 3 V.M. *Memoir*
 4 Ms diary, Greatham
 5 and 6 Ms letters, Greatham
 7 V.M. *Memoir*
 8 and 9 Ms letters, Greatham
10 Account book, Greatham
11 – 14 inclusive Ms letters, Greatham
15 'Mrs Meynell, Poet & Essayist', *Fortnightly Review*, Dec. 1892
16 *Francis Thompson & Wilfrid Meynell* by Viola Meynell
17 Ibid
18 'Wares of Autolycus' in *P.M.G.* 3 November, 1893
19 'Solitude' in *The Spirit of Place*
20 Ms note, Greatham

Chapter 10
 1 *My Lives* by Francis Meynell
 2 *The Life of Francis Thompson* by Everard Meynell (Burns & Oates Ltd.
      1913)
 3 Francis Thompson & Wilfrid Meynell by Viola Meynell
 4 Letter to Canon Carroll begun in May, 1890, and finished in August
    1890. *The Letters of Francis Thompson* edited by John Evangelist Walsh
      (Hawthorn Books Inc. 1969)
 5 Ibid
 6 Ibid
 7 Ibid
 8 Ibid
 9 Ibid
10 Ibid
11 Ms letter, Greatham, dated 15 March, 1890
12 Ms letter, Greatham, dated 21 May, 1891
13 *Letters of F.T.*, Walsh

14   V.M. *Memoir*
15   Ms letter, Greatham
16   *The Album*, 14 October, 1895
17   Ibid
18   Ms letter (undated) to Patmore, Greatham
19 and 20   Ms letters, Greatham
21   Article, 'Children and their Ways', *The Delineator*, 1897
22   'Wares of Autolycus' in *P.M.G.* 'A Young Child.'
23   *My Lives* by Francis Meynell
24   V.M. *Memoir*
25   Ibid
26   Ms letter, Greatham
27   'Wares of Autolycus' in *P.M.G.* 23 June, 1893
28 – 31 inclusive   Ms letters, Greatham
32   Letters of F.T.

Chapter 11
 1   *Coventry Patmore* by Edmund Gosse
 2   *The Idea of Coventry Patmore* by Osbert Burdett
 3 – 6 inclusive   Ms letters, Greatham
 7   *The Life & Times of Coventry Patmore* by Derek Patmore
 8 – 20 inclusive   Ms letters, Greatham
21   Ms letter in Boston College Library
22 – 34 inclusive   Ms letters, Greatham
35   V.M. *Memoir*
36   Ibid
37 – 43 inclusive   Ms letters, Greatham
44   *The Life & Times of C.P.* by Derek Patmore
45   Ibid
46   Ms letter, Greatham
47   *Life & Times of C.P.*
48   Ibid
49   Ms letter dated 16 June, 1892, in Boston College Library
50 and 51   Ms letters, Greatham
52   V.M. *Memoir*
53   *Life & Times of C.P.*

Chapter 12
 1 – 4 inclusive   *Letters of Francis Thompson* edited Walsh
 5   Ms letter, Greatham
 6   *Letters of F.T.* edited Walsh
 7 and 8   Ms letter, Greatham
 9   Notebook, Greatham
10 – 13 inclusive   Ms letters, Greatham
14   *Letters of F.T.* edited Walsh
15 – 18 inclusive   Ms letters, Greatham
19   Ms letter to Mrs Chandler Moulton dated 6 January, 1897, in the
     Library of Congress

20 – 25 inclusive   Ms letters, Greatham
26   Ms letter in Cambridge University Library
27   Ms letter, Greatham, dated 22 August, 1893

Chapter 13
 1   Ms letter, Greatham
 2   V.M. *Memoir*
 3 – 5 inclusive   Ms letters, Greatham
 6   Ms letter, Cambridge University Library
 7 – 10 inclusive   Ms letters, Greatham
11   *The Merry Wives of Westminster* by Mrs Belloc-Lowndes
12   Ibid
13 – 21 inclusive   Ms letters, Greatham
22 and 23   *Letters of F.T.*
24   Telegram in Greatham papers
25   V.M. *Memoir*
26   Ms letter dated 3 December, 1896, at Greatham
27 and 28   Ms letters, Greatham

Chapter 14
 1   'Unlinked'; published in *Merry England*, January 1884, as 'A Poet's
     Sonnet'
 2   Ms letter to Edmund Gosse, 30 December, 1896, University of Leeds
 3   Ms letter, Cambridge University Library
 4   Ms letter, Greatham
 5   V.M. *Memoir*
 6   Meredith letters, University of Texas
 7   *Reading, Writing & Remembering* by E. V. Lucas
 8   *My Diaries* by Wilfrid Blunt
 9 – 24 inclusive   Ms letters at Humanities Research Center, University of
     Texas at Austin
25 – 27 inclusive   Ms letters, Greatham
28   Ms letter at University of Texas
29   Ms Greatham

Chapter 15
 1   *Daily Mail* 16 December, 1903 (Series 'The Best Woman's Book of the
     Year', reviewing *Other Poems* by Mrs Le Bailly)
 2 – 4 inclusive   Ms letters, Greatham
 5   *Tomorrow*, 'Ex Cathedra Mrs Meynell's Cowslip Wine' by Max Beer-
     bohm
 6 – 9   Ms letters, Greatham
10   Meredith letters in University of Texas
11 – 17 inclusive   Ms letters, Greatham
18   Ms letter in University of Texas
19   Katherine Tynan's Ms notes, Greatham
20   Ibid
21   *Daily Chronicle* paragraph, November, 1904

22 Katherine Tynan's Ms notes, Greatham.
23 Related by the late Olivia Sowerby
24 *My Lives* by Francis Meynell
25 *Daily News*, 11 May, 1905
26 Ms letter, Greatham
27 V.M. *Memoir*
28 Ms letter, Katherine Tynan to A.M., Greatham
29 *The Romantic 90s* by Richard Le Gallienne
30 *Reading, Writing & Remembering* by E. V. Lucas
31 *More Reminiscences* by Major Fitzroy Gardner
32 – 34 inclusive   Ms letters, Greatham

Chapter 16
1 *My Diaries* by Wilfrid Blunt
2 Katherine Tynan's Ms notes at Greatham
3 V.M. *Memoir*
4 *Academy*, 2 June, 1900
5 Ms letter at University of Texas.
6 Ms note Greatham
7 *Athenaeum*, October, 1900
8 Ms letter, Greatham
9 Ms letter at University of Texas
10 Ms letter dated 9 August, 1899, Greatham
11 and 12   Ms letters at University of Texas
13 'The Lesson of Landscape' in *The Rhythm of Life* (Elkin Matthews &
     John Lane 1893)
14 Ms letter, Greatham
15 *P.M.G.* 17 August, 1900
16 Ms letter at University of Texas
17 Ms letter, Greatham

Chapter 17
1 Ms letter, Greatham
2 Ms letter at the University of Texas
3 – 11 inclusive   Ms letters, Greatham
12 *Daily Chronicle* 20 September, 1911
13 – 35 inclusive   Ms letters, Greatham
36 Ms letter dated 22 January, 1902, in possession of Mrs Wall
37 Ms letter, undated, property of Mrs Wall
38 – 52 inclusive   Ms letters, Greatham
53 Ms letter, University of Texas

Chapter 18
1 'Chimes'
2 V.M. *Memoir*
3 and 4   Ms letters, Greatham
5 'Swinburne' in *The Athenaeum*, 1909, subsequently in *Hearts of Con-
     troversy* (Burns & Oates 1917)
6 Ibid

7 – 9 inclusive   Ms letters, Greatham
10   V.M. *Memoir*
11 and 12   Ms letters, Greatham
13   *Daily Chronicle* (date unknown)
14 – 16 inclusive   Ms letters, Greatham
17   'In the Village of Oberammagau' in *Wayfaring* (Jonathan Cape 1928)
18   Ms letter, Greatham

Chapter 19
1   Ms letter to Edmund Gosse, University of Leeds
2   Ms letter, 11 March, 1905, University of Leeds
3   *The Outlook*, 10 November, 1906
4 and 5   Ms letters, Greatham
6   *My Lives* by Francis Meynell
7 and 8   Ms letters, Greatham
9   *P.M.G.* 5 May, 1897
10 – 13 inclusive   Ms letters, Greatham
14   Ms letter, property of Mrs Wall
15 – 36 inclusive   Ms letters, Greatham
37   *History of the Catholic Church* by Philip Hughes
38 – 44 inclusive   Ms letters, Greatham
45   V.M. *Memoir*
46   'Wares of Autolycus' in *P.M.G.*
47   V.M. *Memoir*

Chapter 20
1   Ms letter dated April 1907, property of Mrs Hardie
2   Ms letter dated 21 April, 1907 property of Mrs Hardie
3 and 4   Ms letters, Greatham
5   *Dublin Review*, 1907
6 – 12   Ms letters, Greatham
13   Ms diary, Greatham
14 – 19   Ms letters, Greatham
20   Ms letter property of Mrs Hardie
21 and 22   Ms letters, Greatham
23 and 24   Ms letters at University of Texas
25 – 27 inclusive   Ms letters, Greatham
28   *Morning Post*, 16 December, 1909
29 – 32   Ms letters, Greatham
33   *Gilbert Keith Chesterton* by Maisie Ward (Sheed & Ward, 1944)
34 – 36 inclusive   Ms letters, Greatham
37   *Autobiography* by G. K. Chesterton
38   V.M. *Memoir*
39   Ms letter, Greatham
40   Ms of poem, dated Christmas, 1911, in Boston College Library

Chapter 21
1   Ms letter, property of Mrs Hardie

2 – 5 inclusive   Ms letters, Greatham
6   Information from Mrs Hardie
7   Information from Mrs Hardie
8 – 10 inclusive   Ms letters, Greatham
11   'Wares of Autolycus' in *P.M.G.* 'Lent is come with Love to Town'
12   'Wares of Autolycus' in *P.M.G.*
13   'Wares of Autolycus' in *P.M.G.* 'The Breath of July' July, 1899
14   'Wares of Autolycus' in *P.M.G.* 'Feast and Festa'
15   *Daily Chronicle* paragraph, 1911
16 – 19   Ms letters, Greatham
20   Letter from A.M. in *The Times* (date unknown)
21   Information from Mrs Hawkins
22   Review of Patmore's Poems in *The Tablet*, 13 August, 1887
23 – 27 inclusive   Ms letters, Greatham
28   *The Challenge* by Phyllis Bottome
29 – 45 inclusive   Ms letters, Greatham
46   *Times Literary Supplement*, 29 May, 1913
47 – 52 inclusive   Ms letters, Greatham
53   *The Times*, 6 June, 1913

Chapter 22
 1   V.M. *Memoir*
 2   Ms letter, Greatham
 3   Ms letter dated 25 March (1913?), property of Mrs Hardie
 4 – 13 inclusive   Ms letters, Greatham
14   *Times Literary Supplement*, July, 1914
15, 16   Ms letters, Greatham
17   Dixon Scott in *Liverpool Courier*
18 – 30 inclusive   Ms letters, Greatham
31   V.M. *Memoir*
32 – 36 inclusive   Ms letters, Greatham
37   Royal Society of Literature, The Academic Committee. *Address of Reception to Mrs Alice Meynell by Henry Newbolt* (Humphrey Milford, O.U.P. 1915)
38   Ibid
39   Ms letter, Greatham

Chapter 23
 1   Ms letters, Greatham
 2   Ms letter, property Mrs Hardie
 3   V.M. *Memoir*
 4 – 6 inclusive   Ms letters, Greatham
 7   Ms letter, property of Dr Mary Fisher
 8 – 10 inclusive   Ms letters, Greatham
11   *My Lives* by Francis Meynell
12   *The Mount of Vision* by Adeline Cashmore with introduction by A.M. (Chapman & Hall, 1910)
13 – 19 inclusive   Ms letters, Greatham

20 Ms letter, property of Mrs Hardie
21 – 24 inclusive Ms letters, Greatham
25 *The Sphere*, 8 December, 1917
26 *Land and Water*, 11 October, 1917
27 Ms letter, Greatham
28 Ms letter, property of Dr Mary Fisher
29 Ms letter, Greatham
30 *My Lives* by Francis Meynell
31, 32 Ms letters, Greatham
33 *My Lives* by Francis Meynell
34 – 41 inclusive Ms letters, Greatham
42 Ms letter to Madeline Lucas, property of Mrs Hardie
43 – 49 inclusive Ms letters, Greatham
50 V.M. *Memoir*

Chapter 24
1 – 5 inclusive Ms letters, Greatham
6 *My Lives* by Francis Meynell
7, 8 Ms letters, Greatham
9 – 11 inclusive Ms letters at Cambridge University Library
12 – 23 inclusive Ms letters and notebook, Greatham
24 Article, 'My Faith and My Work' in *Woman* 12 August, 1896
25 Ms letter Greatham
26 – 29 inclusive V.M. *Memoir*
30 Ms letter, Greatham
31 *Daily News*, 26 February, 1923. Sylvia Lynd on A.M.
32 *London Mercury* (date unknown)
33 V.M. *Memoir*
34 – 41 inclusive Ms letters, Greatham
42 V.M. *Memoir*
43 From a review of *Other Poems* by Mrs Le Bailly, *Daily Mail*, 16
    December 1903
44 – 46 inclusive Ms letters, Greatham

INDEX